WORKING TIME
AND
EMPLOYMENT

WORKING TIME
AND
EMPLOYMENT

Robert A. Hart

University of Stirling

Boston
ALLEN & UNWIN

London   Sydney   Wellington

Allen & Unwin, Inc.,
8 Winchester Place, Winchester, Mass. 01890, USA

the U.S. company of

Unwin Hyman Ltd
PO Box 18, Park Lane, Hemel Hempstead, Herts HP2 4TE, UK
40 Museum Street, London WC1A 1LU, UK
37/39 Queen Elizabeth Street, London SE1 2QB, UK

Allen & Unwin (Australia) Ltd,
8 Napier Street, North Sydney, NSW 2060, Australia

Allen & Unwin (New Zealand) Ltd in association with the Port
Nicholson Press Ltd,
60 Cambridge Terrace Wellington, New Zealand

First published in 1987

Library of Congress Cataloging-in-Publication Data

Hart, Robert A.
    Working time and employment.
Bibliography: p.
Includes index.
1. Hours of labor. 2. Labor supply. I. Title.
HD5106.H298   1987   331.25′72   86–28815
ISBN 0–04–331109–1 (alk. paper)

British Library Cataloguing in Publication Data

Hart, Robert A.
    Working time and employment.
1. Labor supply. 2. Hours of labor
I. Title
331.12′5   HD5707
ISBN 0–04–331109–1

Typeset in 10 on 12 point Palatino by Columns of Reading
and printed in Great Britain by
Billings and Sons Ltd, London and Worcester

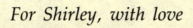

For Shirley, with love

Foreword

An attempt is made in this book to provide a systematic and integrated analysis of both theoretical and empirical aspects of the relationships between working time and employment. The work embraces the topics of workweek reductions, part-time employment, temporary layoffs, short-time working, labour subsidies, social security funding, mandatory and early retirement and collective bargaining.

A brief outline of chapter contents is given here while a more detailed résumé can be found in Chapter 1.

After a general introduction in Chapter 1, Chapter 2 provides a comparative international description – for a number of major OECD countries – of the working time variables that are of key interest in later developments. Chapters 3 and 4 set out those features of the labour market framework and the economic analysis that play the predominant roles in the overall text. Various empirical and analytical details in Chapters 2–4 are referred to quite frequently in the discussion of specific topics in the remaining chapters.

The effects of workweek reductions on employment, unemployment, hours of work and other variables comprise the subject matter of Chapters 5 and 6. The first of these chapters presents a thorough theoretical appraisal of the main modelling approaches in this area while, in Chapter 6, empirical evidence is reviewed. Both demand- and supply-side aspects of part-time employment (workers and hours of work) are considered in Chapter 7 with a particular focus on the issues highlighted in Chapter 5.

There is a change in emphasis in Chapter 8 which discusses hours of work, layoffs and implicit contracts. Research in this field has dominated United States academic interest on working time while the study of the implications of workweek reductions has had a more European and Australasian orientation. The subject of short-time working is also included in this chapter.

Chapter 9 deals with efforts to stimulate more jobs and shorter average hours by direct government intervention. The main policy instruments analysed are marginal and general employment subsidies as well as payroll taxes and tax ceilings.

The relationship between retirement (mandatory and early) and employment is the subject of Chapter 10. While the work here involves different time perspectives and analytical approaches, an attempt is made to link the essential points to the developments in earlier chapters.

The foregoing range of topics are re-examined in the light of collective bargaining considerations in Chapter 11. Finally, in Chapter 12, an overview is undertaken of those areas which appear most, and least, likely to stimulate employment through changes in working time.

Contents

Foreword	page	ix
Acknowledgements		xv
List of Tables		xvii
List of Figures		xix

1	***Background and Aims***	**1**

2	***Working Time and Employment in an International Perspective***	**11**
	2.1 Introduction	11
	2.2 Hours and Employment	13
	2.2(a) Long-run Trends	13
	2.2(b) Short-term Fluctuations	19
	2.3 Part-time Working, Short-time Schedules and Temporary Layoffs	24
	2.3(a) Part-time Employment	25
	2.3(b) Short-time Working and Temporary Layoffs	28
	2.4 Working Lifetime	33
	2.5 Concluding Comments	39

3	***A Labour Market Framework***	**41**
	3.1 Introduction	41
	3.2 A Simple Labour Market Schematic	42
	3.3 Variable Labour Utilization	47
	3.4 Other Relevant Issues	52

4	***Some Economic Concepts and Relationships***	**59**
	4.1 Introduction	59
	4.2 An Introductory Overview	62
	4.3 Paid-for and Effective Working Hours	66

4.4   Labour Demand   70
4.5   Hours Changes and Labour Productivity   78
4.6   The Capital Stock and Capacity Utilization   81
4.7   The Interrelation of Factor Inputs   85
4.8   Supply-side Considerations   88

5 *Employment Effects of Workweek Reductions:
   Theoretical Issues*   91

5.1   Introduction   91
5.2   The Effects of Standard Hours and Labour
        Cost Changes in Conventional Labour
        Demand Models with Given Wages   93
5.2(a) Cost Minimization with Endogenous
        Overtime   94
5.2(b) Other Results from Cost Minimization
        and Profit Maximization   97
5.3   Variations on the Conventional Model
        Theme   102
5.3(a) The Separation of Standard and Overtime
        Hours in the Production Function   102
5.3(b) An Alternative Specification of the Overtime
        Premium Schedule   106
5.4   Capital and Capacity Utilization   108
5.5   Wage Setting by Firms   111
5.6   Wage Setting by Unions   117
5.7   Some Wider Considerations   122
5.8   Summary   126
Appendix to Chapter 5   128

6 *Employment Effects of Workweek Reductions:
   Empirical Evidence*   131

6.1   Introduction   131
6.2   Labour Demand Studies   132
6.2(a) A Model of FRG Manufacturing
        Industries, 1969–81   133
6.2(b) Related Research   139
6.3   Micro Evidence   143
6.4   The Productivity of Hours   147
6.4(a) Production and Labour Demand Functions   147
6.4(b) Production Functions Incorporating Separate
        Measures of Standard and Overtime Hours   151
6.5   More on Labour Hoarding   153
6.6   Macroeconometric Models   154
6.7   Concluding Comments   159
Data Appendix   161

7   *Part-time Employment: The Demand and Supply of Workers and Hours*   164

   7.1   Introduction   164
   7.2   The Demand-side   165
   7.3   The Supply-side   176
   7.4   Assessment   181

8   *Hours, Layoffs and Implicit Contracts*   185

   8.1   Introduction   185
   8.2   Implicit Contract Models and
        Unemployment Subsidies   187
   8.3   Problems and Extensions   193
   8.4   Short-time Working   203
   8.5   Concluding Remarks   207

9   *Labour Subsidies and Social Security Funding*   209

   9.1   Introduction   209
   9.2   Marginal Employment Subsidies and
        Workweek Reductions   211
   9.3   Payroll Taxes and Ceilings   220
   9.3(a) Comparative Statics   220
   9.3(b) Empirical Outcomes from an
        Extended Model Structure   225
   9.4   Policy Conclusions   228

10 *Retirement and Employment*   231

   10.1   Introduction   231
   10.2   Mandatory Retirement   232
   10.2(a) Productivity of Older Workers   233
   10.2(b) Social Security   234
   10.2(c) Lifetime Wage and Productivity Profile   237
   10.3   Early Retirement   238
   10.3(a) Full-time Early Retirement   238
   10.3(b) Partial Early Retirement   240
   10.4   Assessment   246

11 *Collective Bargaining Constraints*   248

   11.1   Introduction   248

CONTENTS

11.2   Trade Union Attitudes   250
11.3   Employers' Attitudes   258
11.4   The Role of Government   262
11.5   Where Is There Most Mutual Agreement?   266

12   *More Jobs through Shorter Hours?*   268

Bibliography   277
Index   287

Acknowledgements

Work on this book was virtually completed while I was working at the Science Center Berlin. I am grateful to this institution for providing an excellent research environment as well as the required back-up facilities.

I owe a debt of gratitude to several persons who either directly or indirectly helped me in the task of preparation. First and foremost, I would like to acknowledge the influence of Felix FitzRoy who not only co-authored the work reported in Sections 7.2 and 8.3 but also stimulated a number of broad ideas on how to approach the general subject. Also, I benefited greatly from working with Seiichi Kawasaki and Peter McGregor. Joint work with Seiichi is discussed in Section 9.3 and work with Peter is mentioned in various places in Chapters 5 and 6. Further, I would like to thank Oliver Clarke of OECD who stimulated my initial serious interest in collective bargaining and international aspects of working time.

Rudolf Frees provided very competent research assistance with Chapters 2 and 6. Harris Schlesinger gave some very helpful comments on core parts of the text. Alan Harrison read parts of the text and raised a number of useful points. In various respects, Hiro Odagiri, Günther Schmid and Nick Wilson made helpful contributions.

Of course, none of the above are responsible for the errors and misconceptions that have remained despite their good counselling.

Finally, I would like to thank Ilona Köhler who typed repeated drafts of the entire text. Her professional and good-natured approach to the work, despite intense work pressure at times, is much appreciated. At several particularly severe 'crisis points' Linda v. Chamier-Cieminski kindly provided additional help.

University of Stirling
April 1986

List of Tables

Table		Page
2.1	Fluctuations in Average Hours per Worker, Number of Employees and Total Hours: USA, UK, France, FRG and Japan, 1970–83	16
2.2	Standard Deviations of Four-Quarter Percentage Rates of Change in Manufacturing Hours and Employment in USA, UK and Japan, 1963–80	18
2.3	Women's Percentage Share in Part-time Employment: France, FRG, Japan, Sweden, UK, USA, 1973–83	26
2.4	Labour Force Participation Rates: FRG, France, Japan, UK, USA, 1970–83	29
2.5	Full-time and Part-time Employment, Average Percentage Annual Growth Rates: France, FRG, Japan, Sweden, UK, USA, 1973–83	30
2.6	Estimates of Employment and Unemployment Effects of Short-time Working Scheme: FRG, 1974–84	31
2.7	Activity Rates of 55–64 and 65 and over Age-groups: FRG, UK, USA, Japan, 1960–80	37
2.8	Statutory Non-wage Labour Costs as Percentage of Total Labour Costs: FRG, UK, USA, Japan, 1975–81	38
6.1	Pooled GLS Results to Equations (6.6) and (6.7): FRG Manufacturing Industries, 1969–81	138
6.2	Coefficient Estimates of h_s for 52 Enterprises in UK Metalworking Industry, 1980	146
6.3	Estimates of Hours and Employment Elasticities from Cobb–Douglas Production Functions	149
A6.1	Source and Description of Variables of Regressions in Table 6.1: FRG Manufacturing	

	Industries, 1966–81	161
A6.2	List of Industries for Regressions in Table 6.1	163
7.1	Responses of Equilibrium Labour Inputs to Changes in Factor Prices and Standard Hours	169
9.1	Simulated Effects of Payroll Tax Changes on Factor Demand: FRG Manufacturing Industry, 1981	227

List of Figures

Figure		Page
2.1	Numbers of Workers in Manufacturing Industry: FRG, France, GB, Japan, and USA 1950–83	14
2.2	Average Annual Hours per Worker in Manufacturing Industry: FRG, France, GB, Japan and USA, 1950–83	15
2.3	Short-run Reactions of Workers, Hours and Capital Stock to a Unit Pulse in Sales	21
2.4	Hours of Work and Employment in the GB Metal Manufacturing Industry, 1963–80	23
2.5	Part-time Employment as a Percentage of Total Employment: FRG, Japan, UK and USA, 1973–83	27
2.6	Population 65 and over as a Percentage of Total Labour Force: FRG, Japan, UK and USA, 1960–2000	34
2.7	Population 55 and over as a Percentage of Total Population: FRG, Japan, UK and USA, 1950–2000	36
3.1	Holt Labour Market Schematic	44
3.2	Extended Labour Market Schematic	48
4.1	Relationships of $g(h)$, $g'(h)$ and $g(h)/h$ to h	73
5.1	Reactions of Equilibrium Workers and Hours to a Change in Standard Hours in a Firm Employing Equilibrium Overtime Hours	98
5.2	Reactions in Equilibrium Workers and Hours to a Change in Standard Hours in a Firm Employing Standard Hours	99
5.3	Wage and Employment Reactions to Hours Changes	121
7.1	Lower Wage Ceilings and Labour Cost Functions	174

9.1   Equilibrium Workers and Hours Reactions to
      Changes in Marginal Employment Subsidies   213
9.2   Equilibrium Workers and Hours Reactions to
      Joint Changes in Marginal Employment
      Subsidies and Standard Hours   214
9.3   Wage Distribution and Ceiling Limit   221
9.4   Wage Distributions and Ceiling Changes   223
9.5   Equilibrium Workers and Hours Reactions to
      Ceiling Changes   223
10.1 Job Splitting with $H_s > H_c$ 242
10.2 Job Splitting with $H_s < H_c$ 244

CHAPTER ONE

Background and Aims

Although the economic analysis of working time and employment has a long history, it is only in relatively recent times that the subject has gained strongly in importance and has developed systematically on a broad front. The core of the modern work is microeconomic in emphasis and concerns the relationship between employment and hours of work. Several of the key theoretical developments have taken place in the fields of quasi-fixed cost theory and implicit contract theory. Foremost policy interest has been focused on the subject of the employment effects of reduced average working hours of existing employees. In Europe and Australasia, this has taken the form of studying the chances of creating new jobs through reductions in the length of the workweek or working year of existing employees. In the United States, by contrast, hours–employment trade-offs have featured most prominently in work related to temporary layoff unemployment. Other working time topics that involve closely associated economic issues include the subjects of part-time employment, retirement and labour subsidies.

This book attempts to present the central theoretical, empirical and policy issues within a reasonably simple and integrated framework. The emphasis is on comparative static microeconomic analysis of the labour market. The principal intention is to convey, within analytical and subject-area limits (see below), the importance of the topic of working time to general labour market analysis.

As in many instances in economics, the new develop-

1

ments in this area have not proceeded independently of actual economic experience. A number of short- and long-run factors have combined to stimulate research activity. Perhaps the most obvious short-term influence has been the impact of the OPEC supply shocks in the middle and late 1970s. Not only did most industrial countries experience by far the highest postwar unemployment rates in the wake of oil shocks but it was also becoming increasingly apparent that the bulk of the unemployment was accounted for by persons experiencing relatively long spells out of work. In many countries, especially in Europe, the possibility of legislated structural changes in working time patterns emerged prominently on the menu of alternatives for tackling the unemployment problem.

Prolonged recession and serious unemployment did not in themselves necessarily presage a particular concentration on working time as a policy issue. The late 1970s also marked, coincidentally or otherwise, a growth in conservative economic orthodoxy by governments in several major economies. Preoccupations with money growth rates, high interest rate policies and balanced budgets superseded earlier demand management strategies that involved expansionary fiscal and monetary interventions. Since stagflation was also a feature of this period, special attention was confined to job creation strategies that appeared to minimize anticipated inflationary repercussions. At least in some political and academic circles, a *redistribution* of what was believed to be a fixed amount of work among a greater number of persons emerged as an attractive alternative. It was considered by many, however, that the relative success of this approach might well hinge on the wage implications of such 'worksharing'. Added to this, a widespread view emerged that the sluggish downward movement in working hours of those with jobs as well as a continued prevalence of overtime working in certain sectors were socially unjustifiable features alongside unemployment rates in excess of 10 per cent.

Interestingly there has been a marked United States/European dichotomy of interest in working time during the 1970s and up to the present time. In the early 1970s in the

USA, the 'new view' of unemployment began to dominate research interest in working time. This concentrated attention on 'voluntary' spells of unemployment of relatively short duration. The uppermost empirical fact that motivated much of this work is the prevelance in the USA of temporary layoffs, a high proportion of which involve subsequent return to the previous job. An important question arose in this work as to why layoffs rather than worksharing were a preferred form of strategy by both employers and workers. The work is dominated by implicit contract theory and this has provided many useful insights – irrespective of the main policy interest – into the general subject of working time and employment. Despite a number of strong empirical challenges to the 'new view', the general implicit contract approach retains a strong influence on the study of working time relationships.

Therefore, partly as a result of the preoccupation with the problem of short-spell unemployment, US economists have not been particularly concerned with the subject of systematic legislated reductions in working hours and the effects on related economic variables. Differences between the USA and elsewhere in the experience of and approach towards hours, employment, layoffs and other labour market variables will be brought out from time to time throughout the text.

Of the longer-term influences that have helped to promote increased interest in working time and employment, two stand out prominently.

The first involves a major growth since the mid-1950s in female participation in the labour market. This in turn has brought to the forefront a new dimension in the relationship between working time and employment. A significant labour market expansion in the demand for and supply of part-time workers and hours has accompanied the growth of female participation. Female workers comprise an extremely high proportion of the total part-time job slots. In several economies the growth of such jobs in recent times has outstripped that of full-time employment growth and part-time work is now established as a quantitatively significant part of total employment.

3

The second influence stems from changes in the demographic composition of the population. In most OECD countries, the postwar baby boom, which extended (roughly) to the mid-1960s, gave way to a significant long-term drop in the birth rate that has lasted up to the present time. Economic problems associated with the resulting large forecasted growth in the size of the retired population cohort relative to the economically active population – beginning in the early part of the next century – are already being urgently assessed by several governments. In particular, anticipations of large increases in the costs to firms and workers of funding pension provision have helped to stimulate considerable interest in the subject of the optimum age of retirement and its relationship with employment and labour utilization.

As with worksharing, it should be made clear that there exists no international uniformity of interest in either part-time employment or retirement. In the case of the former topic, Sweden, at one end of the spectrum, has one-quarter of its total workforce in part-time employment while in countries like Italy and Ireland, at the other end, such employment is relatively unimportant. As for retirement, the above demographic pressures will be experienced earliest and most acutely in Japan and measures are already under way to raise the average age of mandatory retirement. In Europe, on the other hand, the fact that unemployment is a far more serious problem than in Japan has led to a somewhat different direction of emphasis in retirement policy. Much recent European interest has been shown towards encouraging early retirement as a means of providing better job opportunities for the unemployed. This is a somewhat shorter-term focus, however, and it is quite likely that the problems currently facing Japan will also come to the forefront in Europe at a later stage.

The design of the present text is quite broad in the sense that it tries to represent the theoretical work underpinning the most important working time topics in European countries, the United States and elsewhere. Further, an attempt is made to provide a high degree of methodological

4

continuity throughout the text. The structure of the book is as follows.

The scene is set in Chapter 2 by giving, in reasonably succinct form, a comparative international description of the working time variables that feature most prominently in the later chapters. Descriptive statistics are provided for a number of major OECD countries on hours and employment – both long-run trends and short-term fluctuations – part-time working, short-time working, temporary layoffs and demographic trends. One function of the chapter is to introduce the reader to facts and figures that will be referred to in later chapters.

As stated earlier, the book concentrates on the labour market aspects of working time and employment. It is deemed to be necessary, therefore, to develop the labour market framework quite carefully. This is attempted in Chapters 3 and 4 which discuss in some detail a number of relationships that are of fundamental importance to later theoretical and empirical analysis. Chapter 3 is fairly descriptive and attempts, primarily, to bring out the important distinction between the extensive and intensive margins in decisions to change the composition of employment. It also provides an introduction to most of the labour market topics that are examined at later stages. The labour market variables discussed in Chapter 3 are then reappraised in Chapter 4 within a more analytical structure that provides some essential modelling groundwork. In particular, the chapter deals with the distinction between paid-for and effective working hours, the demand for workers and hours, the relationship between hours changes and labour productivity, the interrelated roles of the stock and utilization of capital as well as several supply-side considerations.

The first major topic of the book is then dealt with in considerable detail in Chapters 5 and 6. These chapters are devoted to theoretical and empirical aspects of the employment effects of reductions in standard hours. By 'standard' is meant those working hours per week or per year that are determined exogenously – at government level or by broad national-level collective bargaining agreement – as far as the individual firm is concerned. Other commonly used words that mean more or less the same thing are 'normal' and 'scheduled' working hours and these are interchangeably adopted from time to time. (Unfortunately, there is no *standard* expression for such hours among countries but no confusion should arise with respect to the meaning intended.)

Chapter 5 considers three main types of microeconomic models delineated principally by assumptions concerning the role of wages. These are labour demand models with predetermined wages, efficiency wage models (where the firm sets the wage) and union bargaining models. While some of the studies embrace the effects on unemployment of changes in standard hours, and these are examined where appropriate, the main interest is in the effects on employment. The theory is not restricted to the question of hours changes, however. Also important are the implications for employment and hours of work of changes in relative factor prices as well as the scale effects of changes in working time. The chapter also differentiates between the direct effects on employment of changes in both working time and relative factor prices as well as the indirect effects resulting from the labour productivity impacts of hours changes. Finally, some of the simpler models are discussed within a wider economic perspective; thus, for example, the influences on employment of hours changes via inflation and the balance of payments reactions are considered.

Empirical evidence relating to the theory of Chapter 5 is reviewed in Chapter 6. A large part of that chapter deals with research into the estimated effect on employment and total (or overtime) hours of a change in standard hours. Two main aspects of this work are considered. The first derives essentially from partial equilibrium labour demand specifications although the work here is further subdivided into models that have incorporated aggregate data (industry- or national-level) and those that are tested using plant- or firm-level data. It is shown that the latter provide results that are more consistent with the theory. The second type of modelling approach involves simulation exercises carried out on large-scale macroeconometric models and a review is undertaken of the findings from a wide variety of European studies. The other topic featured in the chapter concerns the labour productivity effects of hours changes, and work is examined, from a variety of countries, that has looked into this question by way of production and labour demand function estimation.

We have already commented on the growing importance of part-time employment within the general subject area and evidence to this effect is given in Chapter 2. An economic analysis of the demand for and supply of part-time workers and hours is presented in Chapter 7. Most of the existing research on part-time employment has been dominated by studies of the supply of female hours and female participation rates with the demand-side remaining relatively unexplored. Some attempt is made here to achieve a better balance. Moreover, the overall discussion relates very closely to the developments in earlier chapters since an evaluation is made of the effects of changes both in standard hours and relative factor prices on part-time (in relation to full-time) workers and hours.

As also mentioned above, the main developments by US economists in the area of working time and employment have taken place with respect to the analysis of temporary layoff unemployment. Earlier research on hours, layoffs and implicit contracts is reviewed in Chapter 8 and some detailed attention is given to limitations with and recent extensions to this work. Also in this chapter, the subject of short-time working is introduced; in certain respects this constitutes the intensive margin equivalent to temporary layoffs on the extensive margin.

The subject matter of Chapter 8 serves as useful background to the developments in Chapter 9. These concern the effects on working time and employment of changes in marginal and general labour subsidies as well as in employers' payroll tax contributions. The work relates to the temporary layoff literature in the sense that, given less than perfect experience rating, such layoffs are effectively subsidized since firms do not pay the actuarial value of their own layoffs. The implications of changing this form of subsidy involve similar considerations to those of changing marginal and general labour subsidies as a policy means of attempting to stimulate more worksharing.

While the relationship between retirement and employment involves an altogether different time dimension, it nevertheless relates quite closely to a number of concepts and issues of concern in the above outlined chapters. Chapter 10 attempts to capitalize on this by utilizing earlier developments as far as possible in a review of relevant research on retirement. It considers both mandatory retirement and voluntary early retirement. The latter topic is divided into a discussion of full-time and partial early retirement schemes that directly involve new job creation for the unemployed.

Many articles and books on working time integrate at the outset the interactive role of collective bargaining. The actions of trade unions, employers and governments often impose *a priori* restrictions on the degree to which given working time changes can take place – as well as on related changes in labour wage compensation – and these may well affect the scope and orientation of given analyses. A different line is purposely adopted in the present book since, for the most part, the presentation in Chapters 2–10 is devoted to attempting to understand economic relationships among working time, employment and related variables without overlaying a myriad of complications arising from collective bargaining considerations. The view is taken that this approach provides the best means of understanding fundamental economic relationships and, perhaps, makes it subsequently easier to appreciate the implications of the limits to action introduced by collective bargaining agents. Therefore, a discussion of the constraints imposed by collective bargaining on working time and employment outcomes is held back until Chapter 11.

Perhaps no publication on working time and employment is complete without offering a number of policy views on the wisdom and effectiveness of certain working time changes as a means of stimulating new jobs. To a rather limited extent, we allow ourselves the luxury of such speculation in Chapter 12. Little attempt is made, however, to indulge in detailed policy prescription.

The book attempts to give a more systematic and comprehensive coverage of the subject area than appears in most other related sources. Inevitably, however, a number of limitations have been imposed on the text in order to ensure greater integration of the material and to avoid unwieldiness. Also, certain areas of policy interest and methodological approaches are concentrated on at the expense of others. Accordingly, the following points are worth noting.

(1) As indicated by the book title, prime attention is given to working time and its relationship with *employment* rather than *unemployment*. In several important respects, it is the latter variable that has preoccupied writers and commentators in the working time policy debate but the emphasis here is defended for the following reason. While a few important economic analyses have attempted to tackle the somewhat more severe problems associated with assessing unemployment implications of working time changes – and these are reviewed (particularly) in Chapters 5 and 8 – it is work on the employment effects that has made most headway. The unemployment rate is a complex variable – involving demand, supply and participation decisions of firms and households – and in many instances model solutions hang on particularly bold simplifying assumptions. Any loss that is incurred through the approach here would seem to be more than offset by the greater breadth of coverage and the higher degree of uniformity permitted by the narrower orientation. Besides, in the policy domain, questions concerning increases in employment are usually closely related to those of reducing the rate of unemployment.

(2) *Both* demand and supply aspects of given problems are dealt with at all stages. However, the book does give more emphasis to the demand-side of the labour market than in many comparable sources and this is deliberately intended. Policy interest in questions of working time occurs most acutely during periods of economic recession. Given widely observed downward rigidities in factor prices at such times, it is highly likely that significant groups of individuals are effectively *demand constrained* in their choice of working hours. In support of this contention, one of the largest and most important studies of labour supply in the UK (see Brown *et al.*, 1984), undertaken for the UK Treasury,

concluded that a very high proportion of its sample of workers (about 80 per cent) would not have been allowed to work additional hours in their main job if they had so desired. It is the belief of the author that the great preponderance of supply-side studies on working time issues is out of all proportion to the role played by supply decisions. To repeat, the supply-side is by no means ignored in what follows but neither is it given the weight that can be found in many related sources. (An example of the pure supply approach we seek to avoid, that relates to the discussion in Chapter 5, is provided by Bronfenbrenner and Mossin, 1966.)

(3) For the large part, the economic theory covered here consists of comparative static analysis. Dynamic aspects of modelling are not dealt with in any depth. Perhaps one serious omission concerns those optimal control approaches (see Nickell, 1978, 1984) that attempt to explain the cyclical turning points of employment and hours given firms' expectations of cyclical variations in demand. For readers interested in such work, the whole area is very capably reviewed and extended in a recent book by Santamäki-Vuori (1986).

(4) Finally, the reader may be irritated by being unable to find mention of her or his favourite working time issue. No consideration is given to flexible working time arrangements, staggered work years, special work leave, school leaving and youth training and several other areas of concern in the general debate. For given groups of individuals in the labour market, these and other considerations are of great significance. They are often not, on the aggregate, likely to have much potential impact on the level of employment and this is the main criterion for their omission.

It might be mentioned as a final point that the book is, at least, 'reader friendly' in another direction. Thus, it contains *no* footnotes and while this may have reduced the efficiency of the writing style in places, it is hoped that the elimination of DFI (Disruptive Footnote Irritation) will provide ample compensation.

CHAPTER TWO

Working Time and Employment in an International Perspective

2.1 Introduction

In the vast majority of OECD member countries, working time and its relationship with employment is an important policy issue. The countries differ, however, over the particular emphasis given to one aspect of working time or another. In Europe and Australasia, there has been a strong recent collective bargaining interest in the relationship between cuts in the length of the standard workweek and employment. As we shall see (especially in Chapter 5) this has generated, after a rather long adjustment lag, a considerable growth in serious economic research work designed to analyse the employment, capital and other wider effects of cuts in standard hours. In Japan, by contrast, considerably greater stress has been laid on the importance of the expected length of the working lifetime and its relation to employment and other wider economic issues. Attention has focused particularly on the mandatory age of retirement. Up to the year 2000, Japan has a larger projected growth rate of the economically inactive elderly population relative to the active workforce than any of its main trading competitor countries. Accordingly, the Japanese government and employers are seriously worried about the economic implications of far higher levels of social security funding. Interest in working time in the United States embraces yet another set of issues; indeed, both the

11

length of the standard workweek and the age of retirement are given relatively little policy weight. None the less the relationship between cuts in working hours and the level of employment has been well researched in the USA although the concentration has been on overtime, not standard, hours reductions. Unlike many countries, minimum US overtime premium rates are quite stringently controlled by government regulation and economists have been interested in finding out the consequences for hours and employment of increases in the minimum rates. Further, a disproportionate amount of attention has been given in the USA to temporary layoffs and their relationship to employment, unemployment and hours of work.

Among the European countries, other divisions of emphasis emerge. In Sweden, the FRG and the UK, for example, the relationship between part-time employment and total employment/unemployment is an important issue largely because of the highly significant growth of part-time female employment in these countries since the Second World War. As another example, the FRG devotes rather more attention to short-time working than do most other European countries and, in fact, it finances short-time directly through its unemployment insurance system.

The central intention of this book is to discuss theoretical links, and associated empirical evidence, between various types of working time changes and employment. Most attention is given to the relationship between changes in weekly hours, and particularly standard hours, and employment since not only does this issue receive the largest amount of aggregate interest but also because cuts in the standard workweek provide the most quantitatively significant of all the potential working time changes. Other topics, such as part-time employment, the length of working life, short-time schedules and temporary layoffs, are also featured prominently.

In order to set the scene, this chapter is designed to provide a fairly broad international picture of the most important working time and employment variables. Attention is concentrated on hours of work, full-time and part-time employment, short-time working and retirement.

2.2 Hours and Employment

2.2(a) Long-run Trends

In his comments on two research papers dealing with the US labour market, Heckman (1984) argues that a deficiency of the work concerns the fact that it concentrates too much attention on labour market fluctuations at the intensive margin – that is, on average hours per employee. With reference to findings by Coleman (1984), Heckman shows that it is the variation in the stock of employment rather than in its utilization rate that accounts for most of the variation in total hours. If this pattern of employment – hours variation is observed for other countries then, at least in an immediate sense, this would serve to limit interest in the hours dimension of fluctuations in labour services. It may also go some way towards explaining why, unlike in the papers discussed by Heckman, an overwhelming proportion of labour market and related research deals with labour either in terms solely of the stock of employees or as total hours without differentiating between stock and utilization components. Heckman's US observation does not hold universally, however.

Figures 2.1 and 2.2 show, respectively, the long-term employment and hours trends during the period 1950–83 for five important OECD economies. In a number of dimensions, the contrast between the USA on the one hand and France, Japan, West Germany and the UK on the other is quite stark. As far as the stock of employees is concerned, the USA displays large cyclical fluctuations around its trend while the other four countries exhibit a much smoother employment path. As for average annual hours per worker, the USA has experienced remarkable stability over the entire period, in contrast to the patterns elsewhere. For example, Japanese average hours grew significantly up to the beginning of the 1960s followed by a long decline until the middle 1970s, from which point some systematic growth has recurred. The other three countries have shown persistent and significant declines in average hours, especially after the

13

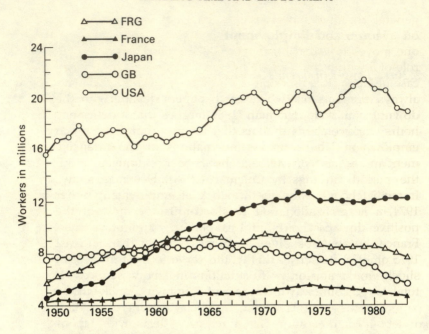

Figure 2.1 Numbers of workers in manufacturing industry: FRG, France, GB, Japan and USA, 1950–83.

Source: US Department of Labor, Bureau of Labor Statistics, Washington DC, June 1985.

early 1960s. Other features do not divide nicely into a USA/elsewhere dichotomy. For example, France, the FRG and the UK exhibit a relatively stagnant employment path over the entire period in contrast to both the USA, with a modest trend growth, and Japan, with relatively high trend growth.

The method employed by Coleman (1984), to divide the deviation from trend in total hours (Nh) into its workers (N) and average hours per worker (h) components, is employed for the five countries shown in Figures 2.1 and 2.2. The results, for the period 1970–83, are given in Table 2.1. The general finding by Coleman for the USA holds here. Thus, the percentage deviations from the Nh-trend in a typical year are dominated by the N- rather than the h-deviation. In general, for all countries except Japan, the N-deviations are, on average, somewhat larger than their h-equivalents. As one moves from left to right across the table, however, the role of h within the total Nh fluctuation increases and, in the case of Japan, it is *the* dominant influence. Although it is not always the case, the beginning of a significant cyclical downturn in economic activity is marked by a shortfall in hours below the trend path that precedes a fall in employment. The best example is the reaction of employment and hours to the OPEC oil supply shock during 1973/4; the period is indicated by a dashed line in Table 2.1. Immediately following the shock, all countries display, in 1974, a negative deviation of hours from the trend and a positive deviation in employment. With the exception of France, employment then drops below the trend in either 1975 or 1976. In Japan and the UK, the hours reaction to the shock would appear to account for the largest part of the total Nh adjustment. In the FRG and the USA, on the other

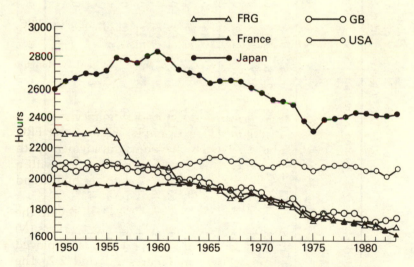

Figure 2.2 Average annual hours per worker in manufacturing industry: FRG, France, GB, Japan and USA, 1950–83.

Source: US Department of Labor, Bureau of Labor Statistics, Washington DC, June 1985.

Table 2.1

Fluctuations in Average Hours per Worker, Number of Employees and Total Hours: USA, UK, France, FRG and Japan, 1970–83 (deviation from trend in percentage points)

Year	United States			United Kingdom			France			Federal Republic of Germany			Japan		
	N	h	Nh	N	h	Nh	N	h	Nh	N	h	Nh	N	h	Nh
1970	0.22	-1.06	-0.84	-2.06	1.70	-0.36	-5.96	0.47	-5.49	-0.07	1.55	1.48	-1.89	3.13	1.23
1971	-3.92	-0.73	-4.64	-2.88	-0.08	-2.96	-3.41	0.69	-2.72	0.76	0.41	1.17	-0.24	1.73	1.49
1972	-1.39	0.91	-0.48	-3.73	-0.56	-4.29	-1.09	0.72	-0.37	0.14	0.10	0.24	-0.37	1.55	1.18
1973	3.55	1.24	4.79	-0.42	1.96	1.54	2.19	0.08	2.26	2.14	0.16	2.30	3.58	1.08	4.67
1974	2.96	-0.13	2.84	2.79	-1.05	1.74	4.46	-0.21	4.26	1.02	-1.16	-0.13	3.93	-3.15	0.78
1975	-6.17	-1.21	-7.38	0.41	-2.26	-1.85	2.56	-2.28	0.28	-2.96	-2.83	-5.79	-1.27	-5.15	-6.78
1976	-2.77	0.14	-2.63	-0.21	-1.27	-1.48	2.50	-0.92	1.58	-3.49	0.91	-2.59	-0.81	-2.05	-2.86
1977	0.71	0.77	1.48	3.04	0.12	3.17	2.92	-0.75	2.17	2.04	0.25	1.79	0.95	-1.45	-2.39
1978	4.63	1.11	5.74	5.20	0.40	5.61	2.22	-0.48	1.74	-0.38	-0.32	-0.71	-1.99	-0.55	-2.54
1979	7.00	0.74	7.74	7.34	0.99	8.34	1.40	0.38	1.78	1.56	0.10	1.67	-2.02	0.84	-1.19
1980	3.29	-0.34	2.95	5.56	-0.87	4.69	0.86	1.65	2.51	3.51	-0.09	3.43	-0.75	1.04	0.28
1981	2.61	-0.21	2.41	-2.71	-1.42	-4.13	-1.85	2.01	0.16	2.46	-0.49	1.97	0.70	0.74	1.44
1982	-4.53	-1.81	-6.35	-5.14	0.51	-4.63	-2.68	-0.11	-2.79	0.09	-0.08	0.02	0.76	0.85	1.61
1983	-6.20	0.57	-5.63	-7.18	1.81	-5.37	-4.12	-1.25	-5.37	-2.76	1.49	-1.27	1.32	1.74	3.06

Note: All estimates derived from the logarithmic values of N, h and Nh regressed on a constant and a linear trend.
Source: United States Department of Labor, Bureau of Labor Statistics, Washington DC.

hand, the subsequent downward adjustment in the employment stock is proportionately greater than the hours adjustment. Another feature of Table 2.1 is that, in certain countries, there exist relatively long time periods when the deviation in hours is opposite in sign to that of employees. This is particularly noticeable in France for the periods 1970–2 and 1974–8, in the FRG during 1980–2 and in Japan for 1970–2. There is no intention of investigating the historical reasons for this phenomenon; it would simply appear to add considerable weight to the need to study separately the reactions of workers and average hours per worker to economic events.

Some corroborating evidence for several of the findings in Table 2.1 is provided by Gordon (1982) in a study of the different wage and employment experience in the USA on the one hand and Japan and the UK on the other (see also Gordon, 1983). His findings with respect to workers and average weekly hours are summarized in Table 2.2 for the period 1963 to 1980. The relative volatility of workers and hours fluctuations are measured by standard deviations of 4-quarter percentage rates of change. For the entire period, the picture that emerges is in reasonable accord with our foregoing findings. In the USA the variations in N and h are, respectively, significantly higher and lower than in the other two countries. Note further that when the two components of labour services are added, in row 3, then the USA shows a higher variation than does either of the other countries and particularly so as compared with Japan. Gordon also emphasizes the importance of the OPEC supply shock by showing separate estimates of the standard deviations for the period preceding 1973. These figures are also shown in Table 2.2. It is noticeable that, while the relative differences between the USA and the other two countries with respect to N and h still hold, the absolute magnitude of the difference is significantly reduced.

Inevitably, the reasons advanced to explain the contrasting experience among the countries are highly complex and have economic, sociological and psychological explanations as well as long-run historical roots. One economic argument put forward with respect to the Japanese reliance on hours

Table 2.2
Standard Deviations of Four-Quarter Percentage Rates of Change
of Manufacturing Hours and Employment in USA, UK and Japan,
1963–80

Variables	1963(1)–1980(3)			1962(1)–1972(4)		
	USA	UK	Japan	USA	UK	Japan
N	4.05	2.18	2.03	3.39	1.95	2.15
h	1.09	1.74	1.98	1.06	1.37	1.17
$N+h$	4.78	3.22	1.09	4.06	2.70	0.91

Source: Gordon, 1982, p. 19.

fluctuations is that relatively high specific human capital investments in Japan, particularly in large firms, have made employers more wary of incurring investment losses due to permanent quits and/or layoffs in the face of unexpected downturns in product demand. Since both sides in collective bargaining agreements can be expected to share the periodic rents arising from specific investments (Hashimoto, 1979) then it seems sensible to emphasize hours fluctuations as a buffer against cyclical changes in demand rather than the potentially more costly strategy of changing the stock of workers. Hashimoto and Raisian (1985) produce evidence consistent with the human capital hypothesis. They show that Japanese male workers have longer job-tenure than their US counterparts: they estimate, for example, that by the time a typical male worker reaches the age of 65 in each country, he would have had approximately 5 jobs in Japan and 11 jobs in the USA. Also, the growth rate in earnings profiles associated with tenure are steeper in Japan than in the USA. Despite these differences, long job-tenure is a prevalent feature of US jobs (see also Hall, 1982), and, at best, human capital approaches offer only partial explanations of the observed hours/employment patterns. It is highly doubtful, for example, that they would account for a significant part of the divergent UK/US observations.

Japan and, to a lesser extent, the FRG and the UK have somewhat more flexibility in their wage payment systems that perhaps permit speedier reactions to unforeseen shocks in the system. In particular, the twice-yearly bonus system in Japan, to some extent a profit sharing device, would appear to play an important role in avoiding conflict. In the FRG and UK, the annual wage round provides the dominant compensation structure. In contrast, the US system has evolved the method of three-year contracts that may lead to larger deviations between actual and expected wage compensation when large shocks occur and, therefore, to more variable employment reactions.

Another feature of the US economy is that the large number of immigrants may have provided a degree of volatility in the job market that is not matched to the same extent in the UK and not apparent at all in Japan.

Irrespective of these and other explanations of the differences, the main conclusion arising from this summary of long-term trends is that, in several major OECD economies, variations in hours of work would appear to provide an important adjustment mode to fluctuations in economic activity. Further, there is significant evidence that it would be highly misleading to treat such adjustment as if it were adequately represented by movements in the stock of employment since both the timing and magnitude of change in the two component parts of total hours can diverge radically.

2.2(b)   Short-term Fluctuations

While the long-term cycles and trends in employment and hours of work are clearly of interest, especially in so far as they reveal substantial international differences, most economic analyses of these variables have centred on their short-run characteristics. In particular, the most important insights into the short-run adjustments of employment and hours have been obtained from factor demand analyses.

The seminal work of Nadiri and Rosen (1969, 1973) has given rise to a substantial literature that has investigated the own- and cross-adjustment responses of employment, hours and other input factors to changes in product demand. A comprehensive review of the relatively early studies can be found in Hamermesh (1976) while more recent contributions include Topel (1982), Chang (1983) and Rossana (1983, 1985). The general, although by no means universal, findings in these studies is that the demand for input factors reacts to changes in output after a lag although the adjustment in hours involves a considerably shorter lag than the adjustments of stocks of employment and capital. Nadiri and Rosen (1973) design an interrelated factor demand model which is tested on US manufacturing industrial data. Their factor inputs include production workers (N), average hours per production worker (h), the capital stock (K) as well as capacity utilization and stocks and utilization rates of non-production workers. Their estimating equations consist of regressing each input factor component on its own lagged value and the lagged values of other inputs as well as on sales (Sa), a time trend and relative factor prices. (A somewhat more technical discussion of this type of model is presented in Chapter 4.) From their estimates, they are able to derive distributed lag responses of each factor to a unit pulse in the sales variable. While they observe quite wide industrial responses, a stylized illustration of the typical reactions of three of the factor inputs to a unit pulse in sales (dx/dSa where $x = N$, h and K) is presented in Figure 2.3.

The response of workers to the change in the sales is gradual, achieving its long-run steady state value, typically, within five or six quarters in the Nadiri and Rosen study. Over this period, therefore, the level of employment is systematically different from its long-run value. Average hours per worker acts as a buffer to this short fall or excess of employment by overshooting its equilibrium value through a relatively large initial response and then slowly converging to long-run equilibrium. The capital stock reacts in yet another fashion. For obvious adjustment cost reasons, there is a delay before maximum response is achieved and then this is followed by a gradual tendency to long-run equilibrium resulting in a typical inverted U-shaped curve. Topel (1982) presents a more sophisticated version of this model by dividing changes in product demand into anticipated and unanticipated components. Also, he considers the interactive role of inventories within the short-run employment and hours responses. In general, his findings with respect to N and h are not dissimilar from those portrayed in Figure 2.3.

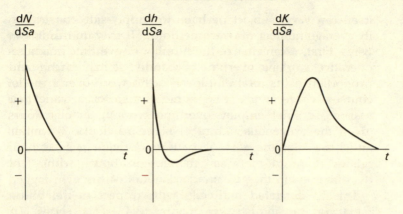

Figure 2.3 Short-run reactions of workers, hours and capital stock to a unit pulse in sales.

These sorts of employment–hours responses are predicted in theoretical approaches to dynamic labour demand that model the implications of the quasi-fixed costs (such as hiring, training and deferred fringe benefits) associated with changing the employment stock (for example, Nickell, 1978). Quasi-fixed labour costs also play an important role in some of the developments of the later chapters.

The response pattern of hours of work to changes in product demand illustrated in Figure 2.3 has been found in a large number of empirical studies in several OECD countries. It would be misleading to believe, however, that this type of measurement provides a complete picture of short-term reactions in labour utilization. Overlooking such features as part-time employment and shiftworking for the moment, there are a number of different ways in which average hours per operative may be adjusted to a product demand or a relative factor price shock. The first is largely exogenous to the firm and involves standard hours. In most countries, a high proportion of hours worked are determined at a national collective bargaining level of negotiation and this sets a standard for weekly working hours. It may be, for example, that a fall in aggregate demand may stimulate policy action to cut standard hours in order to 'preserve' jobs. Over and above standard hours, the firm

21

itself can vary, subject perhaps to supply-side constraints, its average number of overtime hours. It may do this in two ways. First, it can change the number of overtime hours per operative working overtime. Secondly, it may change the proportion of its total employees who work overtime. (Of course, we recognize that some firms, for a variety of reasons, do not employ overtime working at all.) Now, given the exogenous nature of standard hours, we might anticipate that the sort of pattern derived in Figure 2.3 relates more to marginal changes in hours within the overtime region than to standard hours of work.

This is illustrated indirectly with respect to the British metalworking industry in Figure 2.4. This shows, in quadrants (a), (b) and (c), respectively, the movements in standard hours, average overtime hours and the proportion of workers working overtime for quarterly periods from 1963–83 in quadrant (a) and 1963–80 elsewhere. Quadrant (a) reveals a step function between 1964 and 1968 when two major reductions in standard hours occurred, followed by a plateau until the end of 1981 and then, again, a further downward step. As would be expected, the graphs of overtime per worker and proportion of workers working overtime exhibit strong cyclical variations and they have very similar patterns. Employment is also plotted in Figure 2.4, in quadrant (d), and it displays significantly different behaviour from the hours graphs. After 1965, the industry has experienced fairly persistent falls in employment over the period, relieved only by occasional short-lived and relatively minor upturns.

Note that the 1964/5 standard hours cuts in quadrant (a) take place at a time of a gently rising trend in overtime working in (b) and (c) and fairly stagnant/marginally falling employment in (d). These phenomena are in line with the experience of total UK manufacturing industry at this time and an economic appraisal can be found in Hart (1983). While, of course, it is dangerous to draw conclusions on the basis of one, aggregate-level industry, the outcomes are, at least, consistent with the predictions of certain economic models that will be reviewed in Chapter 5. Further, empirical work with respect to the UK metalworking industry is reported in Section 6.3.

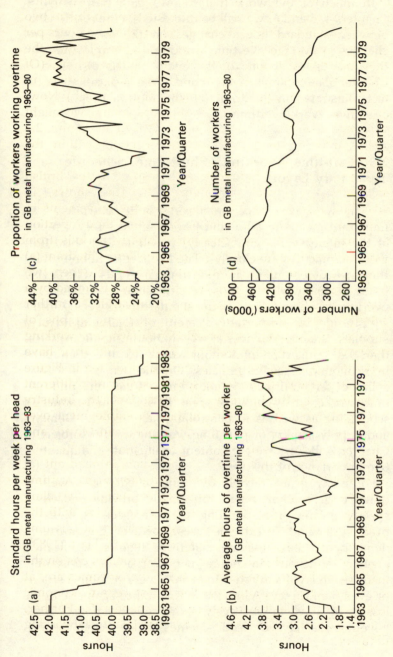

Figure 2.4 Hours of work and employment in the GB metal manufacturing industry, 1963–80.

Source: Department of Employment, *Employment Gazette*, London, various numbers.

In much of the work that follows, and particularly in Chapters 4, 5 and 6, we will be interested in the relationship between standard hours changes on the one hand and changes in average overtime working and employment on the other. Also, in one of the micro models discussed in Chapter 5, attention is given to one of the implications of the fact, illustrated in quadrant (c), that only a proportion of operatives work overtime.

2.3 Part-time Working, Short-time Schedules and Temporary Layoffs

So far, we have concentrated on hours of work as an important means of adjusting labour services requirements at the intensive margin. Clearly, part-time and short-time working practices are closely related concepts. In one sense, they provide potentially more extreme methods of achieving hours flexibility beyond those of either marginal changes in overtime working or cuts in the standard workweek. On the supply-side, an important element of total employment supplies its labour services at weekly hours significantly less than the standard 35- or 40-hour workweek. It is dominated by economically active females. On the demand-side, the ability of certain firms to employ a mix of part-time and full-time workers may provide great flexibility in production scheduling as well as in controlling labour costs. Demand and supply aspects of part-time working are the subject of Chapter 7. Below, we are content to illustrate the quantitative importance of this topic.

For many firms, flexible overtime schedules as well as other special working time arrangements provide a relatively speedy means of responding to unforeseen changes in product demand. In extreme cases, however, downturns in demand may be so severe that firms require significantly greater reductions in hours per worker or substantial increases in layoffs in order to avoid severe economic strains or even bankruptcy. As a form of insurance against chronic losses of jobs in relatively extreme conditions, some governments have devised schemes that effectively subsi-

24

dize firms that require large-scale cut-backs in their oper-
ations. Workers in such firms are compensated, in part, for
their loss of earnings (usually in comparison to standard
weekly earnings), as a result of being required to work
short-time schedules. A closely related form of subsidy,
particularly prevalent in the USA, takes the form of state
compensation for loss of earnings of temporarily laid-off
workers who are subsequently re-employed by the firm
when conditions improve. The essential difference between
the subsidies is that, in the former case, unutilized hours are
spread across the entire workforce in the form of worksharing while, in the latter case, a certain group of workers
take the full amount of the slack by taking 'implicitly agreed'
periods of full leisure. A review of work in these two areas is
undertaken in Chapter 8 and, again, the discussion here is
aimed at summarizing briefly the quantitative significance of
these two forms of working time.

2.3(a) Part-time Employment

Part-time employment is, overwhelmingly, a feature of the
female part of the labour market. This is illustrated in Table
2.3 which shows women's percentage share in part-time
employment for six OECD countries between 1973 and 1983.
In 1983, women account for well over 80 per cent of total
part-time employment in four of the countries while, in
Japan and the USA the figure is 70 per cent. With the
exception of Sweden and the UK, which experienced some
slight falling off in the female share over the entire period,
there has been a tendency for this percentage to increase
somewhat between 1973 and 1983. Figure 2.5 shows, for
four of the countries in Table 2.3, part-time employment as a
percentage of total employment. In 1983 the *combined* male
and female percentage varies between 10.5 per cent in Japan
and 19.1 per cent in the UK. When divided into male and
female percentages of respective male and female totals,
however, a highly contrasting picture emerges. In 1983, the
male percentage varies between 1.7 per cent in the FRG and 7.6
per cent in the USA. In sharp contrast, the female
percentage in the same year varies between 21.1 per cent in

Table 2.3
Women's Percentage Share in Part-time Employment:
France, FRG, Japan, Sweden, UK, USA, 1973–83

	1973	1979	1983
France	77.9	82.0	84.6
FRG	89.0	91.6	91.9
Japan	60.9	64.5	70.7
Sweden	88.0	85.2	84.6
UK	90.9	92.8	89.6
USA	68.4	69.8	70.3

Source: OECD, Employment Outlook, Paris, September 1985.

Japan and 42.4 per cent in the UK. There is no general trend in these percentages between 1973 and 1983: some countries display a gradual upward trend whereas, in others, there is some downturn in the later years.

While the ratio of part-time to total employment has remained fairly static since the mid-1970s, another statistic indicates the growing importance of female employment. In several countries the total labour force participation rate has been declining throughout the 1970s and into the 1980s. When broken down into a male–female dichotomy, however, the common picture is one of a decline in male participation rates offset partially by an increase in female participation rates. There are exceptions to these trends but our selected group of countries, shown in Table 2.4, are reasonably representative. In the FRG, for example, total labour force participation between 1970 and 1983 fell steadily from 69.5 to 64.8 per cent. However, while the male rate fell from 92.5 to 80.2 per cent over this period, the female rate actually rose from 48.1 to 49.6 per cent. A similar sort of picture holds also for Japan and the UK. Some countries, not shown in Table 2.4, display even more marked divergences in the male–female patterns. For example between 1970 and 1983 the Swedish total participation rate *increased* from 74.3 to 81.3 per cent. This consisted, however, of a *fall* in male participation (89.2 to 85.9 per cent) and a substantial *rise* in female participation (59.4 to 76.6 per cent).

The economic analysis of part-time employment is domin-

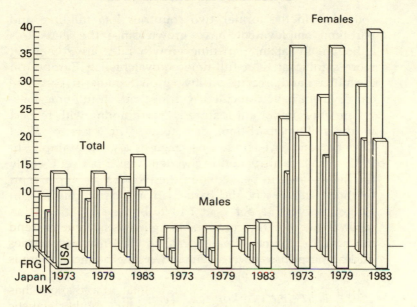

Figure 2.5 Part-time employment as a percentage of total employment: FRG, Japan, UK and USA, 1973–83.
Source: OECD, *Employment Outlook*, September 1985.

ated by the supply-side literature. The vast richness of this work is well summarized in Killingsworth (1983). For the sorts of quantitative reasons highlighted in Figure 2.5 and Table 2.3, the work is dominated by attempts to explain both the supply of total part-time hours and female labour force participation rates. In Chapter 7, emphasis is also given to the demand-side of the problem since this is an extremely important, though neglected, area for consideration. One aspect of our analysis is that it is important to distinguish between full-time and part-time jobs as well as the various gradations of time worked below full-time hours. Within this particular context it is interesting to note that in several OECD countries, particularly in Europe, the growth of part-time employment contrasts with a general decline in full-time employment. Growth rates are shown for the periods between 1973–5 and 1981–3 in Table 2.5. The experience of the USA and Japan contrasts significantly with the European countries. In the former two countries *both* full-time and part-time employment have grown since the mid-1970s although, in Japan, part-time growth rates are somewhat more significant than full-time equivalents. In Europe, on the other hand, recent positive growth rates in part-time employment have coincided with declines in full-time jobs.

One other important feature is worth noting with respect to the full-time/part-time dichotomy. The cases of West Germany and Sweden can be taken as a good example. In 1981, female participation in Sweden was 75 per cent, easily the highest in Europe, while in the FRG it was 50 per cent. Of those females who did participate in the two countries in 1981, however, 54 per cent had full-time jobs in Sweden while in the FRG the comparable figure was 74 per cent. In other words, the participation rate by itself may give a very misleading picture of *total* female working hours.

2.3(b) Short-time Working and Temporary Layoffs

It will suffice to report relatively briefly on short-time working practices and on temporary layoffs.

In several European countries short-time working is effectively subsidized by the government in those individual firm cases where it can be shown that adverse economic conditions require a substantial reduction in the working time of existing employees in order for the firm to remain viable. (Specific details on regulations concerning the most important countries can be found in Hart, 1984c.) The firm is subsidized because part of its standard wage bill is reimbursed without rating the firm's own short-time working experience. A similar type of subsidy occurs in the case of temporary layoffs discussed below.

The FRG has perhaps the best developed scheme together with the largest potential subsidies. If a given firm satisfies certain stringent requirements as to economic necessity, a wage subsidy may be granted to its employees for lost working hours below standard hours; the subsidy usually lasts for no longer than six months, and it amounts to 68 per cent of the net wage lost due to the hours reductions. The Institut für Arbeitsmarkt- und Berufsforschung (IAB) has

Table 2.4

Labour Force Participation Rates: FRG, France, Japan, UK, USA, 1970–83

	Total				Male				Female			
	1970	1975	1979	1983	1970	1975	1979	1983	1970	1975	1979	1983
FRG	69.5	67.9	66.8	64.8	92.5	87.0	84.5	80.2	48.1	49.6	49.6	49.6
France	67.7	67.9	68.5	66.4	87.0	84.3	82.8	78.4	48.3	51.2	54.1	54.3
Japan	72.0	70.4	71.8	73.0	89.4	89.7	89.2	89.1	55.4	51.7	54.7	57.2
UK	72.4	73.5	74.2	72.8	94.1	92.1	90.5	87.9	50.7	55.1	57.9	57.8
USA	66.8	68.7	71.8	72.8	87.1	85.4	85.7	84.7	48.9	53.2	58.9	68.1

Source: OECD, *Employment Outlook*, Paris, September 1985

Table 2.5

Full-time and Part-time Employment, Average Percentage Annual Growth Rates: France, FRG, Japan, Sweden, UK, USA, 1973–83

	1973–5		1975–9		1979–81		1981–83		Employment (thousands) 1983	
	Full-time	Part-time	Full-time	Part-time	Full-time	Part-time	Full-time	Part-time	Full-time	Part-time
France	0.6	8.3	0.4	0.4	−0.2	0.3	−1.2	7.2	19299	2062
FRG	−2.5	3.2	0.4	0.9	1.2	4.2	−1.5	1.4	22671	3276
Japan	−0.7	12.5	1.7	0.9	1.9	3.9	1.8	4.7	36650	4330
Sweden	1.7	5.1	−0.9	6.9	−0.1	2.6	−0.2	0.4	3151	1073
UK	−0.9	3.1	1.0	−0.1	−2.6	2.5	−1.9	3.0	18901	4537
USA	−0.1	1.3	3.9	3.6	0.1	0.5	0.6	0.4	73624	12417

Source: OECD, *Employment Outlook*, Paris, September 1985

Table 2.6

Estimates of Employment and Unemployment Effects of Short-time Working Scheme: FRG, 1974–84

	1974	1975	1976	1977	1978	1979	1980	1981	1982	1983	1984
Total beneficiaries of scheme (thousands)	292	773	277	231	250	88	137	347	606	690	384
Estimated numbers unemployed in absence of scheme											
(a) in thousands	48	147	63	36	33	19	30	72	141	155	92
(b) as % of total beneficiaries	16	19	23	16	17	22	22	21	23	22	24
Estimated numbers unemployed and 'hidden' unemployed in absence of scheme											
(a) in thousands	73	223	96	55	50	29	46	108	202	222	132
(b) as % of total beneficiaries	25	29	35	24	26	33	34	31	33	32	34

Source: *Mitteilungen aus der Arbeitsmarkt- und Berufsforschung*, Nos 1/79 and 4/84

attempted to calculate the employment saving effect of the short-time working scheme. The estimates from 1974 until 1984 are shown in Table 2.6 The total beneficiaries from this scheme are broken down into two groups of people. The first is an estimate of those who would have registered as unemployed if the subsidy had not been available. The second is an estimate of those who would have been registered as unemployed *as well as* those who would have joined the 'hidden' unemployed (*stille Reserve*). The year 1975 and the years 1982–3 are easily the most quantitatively significant. In order to put the figures into some better perspective we take 1975 as an example. Leaving aside the 'hidden' unemployment category, the estimated numbers unemployed in the absence of the scheme are in the region of 147,000. This represents an 'unemployment saving effect' due to the subsidy in that year that is equivalent to a 0.7 percentage point increase in the rate of unemployment. Most other years involve significantly lower numbers and it would appear that the overall quantitative impact of this scheme is not substantial. (For example, the average saving effects for the periods 1975–9 and 1980–4 were equivalent to 0.3 and 0.5 per cent increases in the rate of unemployment, respectively.) None the less, considerable policy interest is given to the subject of short-time working.

In the USA, it is temporary layoffs rather than short-time working that provide the more important example of this sort of working time reduction. By contrast, temporary layoffs are relatively unimportant in Europe. Feldstein (1975) and Lilien (1980) show that, on average, about two-thirds of all layoffs in American manufacturing industry are temporary in the sense that the laid-off workers are re-hired by their original employer. Topel (1982) shows that of all employer-initiated layoffs in manufacturing, temporary layoffs account for just under one-half. Specific industrial breakdowns are also provided by Topel. The realization of the seeming importance of this phenomenon in the 1970s led to an influential literature, dominated by implicit contract theory, that emphasized the short-run, voluntary nature of unemployment. More recently, it has been discovered that the importance of temporary layoffs within total unemployment has been greatly exaggerated by several of the earlier studies and there has been a movement back towards trying to understand the nature of permanent layoffs and longer-term unemployment. These measurement issues, together with a comparison of short-time and temporary layoff unemployment, are left to Chapter 8 for discussion.

2.4 Working Lifetime

The foregoing topics have dealt with working time arrangements that can usefully be described within relatively short intervals of time, say a working week or year. In a longer-term perspective, the length of working lifetime introduces further issues of relevant interest. Of these, the predominant subjects concern the age of retirement and activity rates of the older age-groups. Only this aspect of working lifetime is discussed in this book although it is acknowledged that, at the other end of the age spectrum, topics such as length of schooling and general youth training programmes are of some quantitative interest and have received much recent attention in some countries.

At a later stage (see Chapter 10), we will discuss two aspects of retirement in relation to employment; these are once-for-all changes in the mandatory age of retirement as well as more flexible retirement arrangements, such as early and 'partial' retirement. By the latter is meant, for example, the possibility that an older worker undertakes part-time employment, sharing her/his job with a younger recruit taken from the ranks of the unemployed. Some mention of early and partial retirement experience in several countries is given below. Also we highlight broad international statistics concerning relative sizes of retirement cohorts, activity rates of older persons, and some associated trends in related social security contributions.

Figure 2.6 shows the population aged 65 and over as percentage of the total labour force in the FRG, UK, USA and Japan, both historically from 1960 to 1980 as well as a projection to year 2000. (For a study of ten nations,

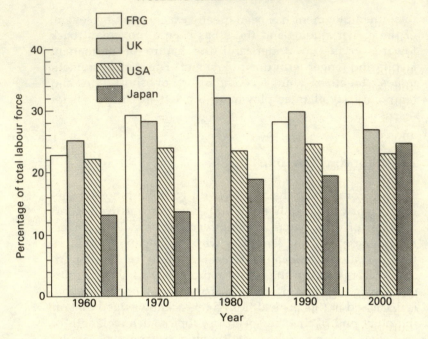

Figure 2.6 Population 65 and over as percentage of total labour force: FRG, Japan, UK and USA, 1960–2000.

Source: International Labour Office, *Labour Force Projections 1975–2000*, Geneva, 1980.

including the four shown here, see Zeitzer, 1983, who gives details of the number of persons in the labour force under age 65 for each person aged 65 and over between 1950 and 2000.) In 1960–80 the growth of these percentages has been most marked in the FRG and UK and, in 1980, the values stood at over 30 per cent in both economies compared to around 20 per cent in the USA and Japan. The United States displays the greatest stability in the percentages over the entire period, past and forecast. Indeed, the USA is one of only two OECD countries (the other being Canada) that has shown a decline, albeit quite small, in the population 65 years and over as percentage of the total labour force from the mid-1960s until the present time. Japan is the only country to show a persistent (actual and forecast) rise in the percentage from 1960 to the year 2000; while it started at a very low base in 1960, by the end of the period it is forecast to be a larger percentage than in the USA and to lie not far behind the UK. Forecasts beyond the year 2000 reveal that the trend in Japan will continue and that, in fact, it will outstrip its main OECD competitor countries.

The type of predicted trends given in Figure 2.6 are even more hazardous to make than the usual demographic forecasts since the size of the labour force is a particularly difficult variable to ascertain. Labour force size is subject to influences from *both* natural demographic factors and also regulation by exogenous policy decision. For example, governments can exert some control over the age at which the average person enters and leaves the labour force (see Chapter 10). In the case of Japan, the problem is particularly acute since the mandatory retirement age is typically somewhere between 55 and 57 years but there is a strong expectation that this will be significantly increased in future years towards levels approaching those of the USA and European countries. For this reason alone, the projected changes in the size of the older population relative to the labour force in Japan might be expected to be less than those relative to the *total* population. This is confirmed in Figure 2.7 which shows the number of persons 55 and over as a percentage of the total population between the years 1950 and 2000. After 1980, the projected Japanese growth in these percentages are greater than their equivalents in Figure 2.6 and, by the year 2000, the Japanese percentage is greater than those of the UK and the USA.

Despite the fact that the mandatory age of retirement in Japan is significantly lower than in other OECD countries (55-7 years of age compared to, typically, 60-5 years of age), it would be misleading to conclude that this difference constitutes a sizeable gap in the proportion of Japanese economically inactive population within the older cohorts compared to the other countries. In the Japanese economy, a high proportion of retirees return to the labour market, often at significantly reduced rates of compensation, and continue to work. Participation rates of Japanese males between the ages of 55 and 64 are well over 80 per cent: this is

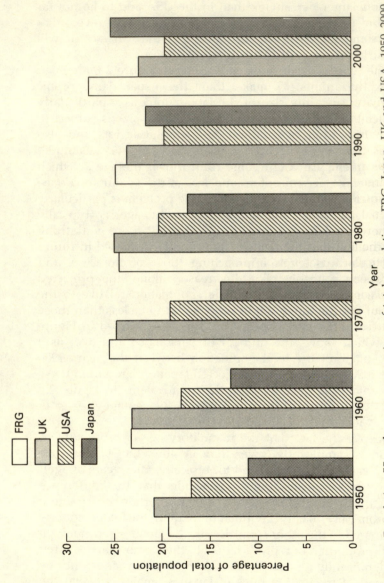

Figure 2.7 Population 55 and over as percentage of total population: FRG, Japan, UK and USA, 1950–2000.
Source: International Labour Office, *Labour Force Projections 1975–2000*, Geneva, 1980.

considerably higher than in most other OECD countries. (For international comparative statistics of participation rates among the older age-groups, see Casey, 1984a.)

On a somewhat narrower basis, the activity rates of persons aged between 60 and 64 and over 65 in the FRG, UK, USA and Japan are shown in Table 2.7 for the period 1960–80. All countries have shown some decline – especially the FRG – although, particularly for the latter age-group, the activity rates in Japan are considerably higher than in the other three countries.

A major reason for the relatively low participation and activity rates of the older age-groups in Europe has been a substantial growth in persons choosing to take early retirement. This has been encouraged in many European countries by early retirement schemes that offer full or partial pension rights at ages less than the normal mandatory retirement age (see Casey, 1984a, for a wide description of the European schemes). In several of these countries – particularly Belgium, France and the UK – such financial inducements to retire early are conditional on the firm replacing each retiree by an unemployed worker. (For a broad analysis and discussion see Drèze, 1985, while for detailed FRG and UK assessments see Franz, 1984, and

Table 2.7

Activity Rates of 55–64 and 65 and over Age-groups:
FRG, UK, USA, Japan 1960–80

Age-group/Country	1960	1965	1970	1975	1980
55–64					
FRG	50.5	50.0	48.7	48.1	44.7
UK	57.9	61.3	64.0	64.0	–
USA	60.2	60.5	60.9	60.9	55.5
Japan	64.7	66.7	68.1	67.5	64.4
65 and over					
FRG	14.2	11.8	9.7	9.2	4.6
UK	13.4	12.3	11.4	11.0	–
USA	20.3	18.2	16.2	15.2	12.6
Japan	35.6	35.3	34.9	32.3	28.7

Source: ILO, *Yearbook of Labour Statistics*, Geneva, various issues.

Metcalf, 1985, respectively.) Such initiatives to create new jobs appear to have been quantitatively quite successful, involving relatively modest exchequer costs. On the other hand, attempts to encourage partial early retirement whereby an older worker shares a job with an unemployed person on a part-time basis have proved to be largely unsuccessful (see Drèze, 1985, and Metcalf, 1985).

Table 2.8
Statutory Non-wage Labour Costs as Percentage of Total Labour Costs: FRG, UK, USA, Japan, 1975–81

	1975	1978	1981	1975–81 (% change)
FRG	17.6	18.4	18.5	5.1
UK	7.2	9.3	9.7	34.7
USA	7.5	8.1	8.1	8.0
Japan	6.1	6.8	7.5	23.0

Source: Statistisches Bundesamt, Fachserie 16, Reihe 4.1, 'Arbeitnehmerverdienste im Ausland'.

Whether due to adverse demographic factors affecting the older age-groups or increased retirement subsidies or a combination of both, governments throughout the OECD have been increasingly concerned about the economic consequences of increases in pension financing. One of the recent trends has been to investigate the possibilities of switching from a pay-as-you-go pension contribution structure to more privately based funded systems. Table 2.8 shows, for the same four countries, the proportion of statutory non-wage labour costs as a proportion of total labour costs for the period 1975–81. These costs (see Hart, 1984a) are dominated by pension and health contributions. As can be seen, such statutory contributions are far higher in the FRG than in the other countries although the growth rates in the contributions, from admittedly much lower bases, are most significant in the UK and Japan. The major fear in Japan is that the growth of such non-wage labour costs as a percentage of total labour costs will, if anything, accelerate as the economy moves into the next century with,

potentially, serious problems for relative Japanese international labour costs. Interesting examinations of these
trends can be found in Shimada (1980) and Hiraishi (1980).

Social security and other economic aspects of mandatory
and early retirement are discussed in Chapter 10.

2.5   Concluding Comments

At the beginning of this chapter, it is pointed out that
countries differ considerably over their policy emphasis on
given working time topics. In Section 2.2 it is shown that the
USA has experienced more employment variation and less
hours variation than some other major OECD countries.
Perhaps associated with these trends, US economists have
tended to show more interest in changes in the stock of
employment – for example, through temporary layoff unemployment – than in changes in worker utilization. In
Europe, on the other hand, large reductions have taken
place in the length of the standard workweek since the
Second World War and European economists have shown
far more interest in studying the related employment
repercussions and in forecasting what might happen if
future workweek cuts are undertaken. The variability of
Japanese working hours appears to be the greatest of all;
however, this would appear to have more to do with hours
acting endogenously as a buffer to changes in aggregate
demand rather than with exogenous changes in the standard workweek. For instance, after the middle 1970s (see
Figure 2.2) there has been a tendency for average hours to
rise somewhat in Japan. Elsewhere, in Sections 2.3 and 2.4,
we have noted substantial international differences in part-
time working practices and in the age structure of the older
working population. Again, given wide divergences of
experience, it is not difficult to understand why countries
lay a greater or lesser emphasis on these working time
topics.

Despite international differences in experience and policy
orientation, a large part of the remainder of the book will
concentrate on working time and employment without

reference to the interest of individual economies. The somewhat greater attention given to economic theory in this text than in most other related books enables us in many places to avoid being side-tracked – and perhaps bogged down – by international facts and figures. One major advantage of this approach is that the common economic methodology can be applied to different types of working time problem and therefore related to the particular interests of particular economies. This chapter helps to provide some factual 'backdrop' to these developments. It should be added, however, that a substantial amount of empirical work is also presented and here individual country studies are obviously important.

CHAPTER THREE

A Labour Market Framework

3.1 Introduction

The economic analysis of the relationships between working time and employment is rendered less than meaningful if care is not taken at the outset to design a suitable labour market framework. To give a crude example: suppose that the labour market is described in such a way that no allowance is made for deviations from standard time working or for variations in the effective use of standard hours. While, as illustrated in Section 3.2, this sort of simplicity provides a useful analytical starting point, it is obviously inadequate as the basis for undertaking a realistic appraisal of the employment repercussions of, say, a reduction in the length of the standard workweek. Indeed, it would not be surprising if the resulting employment changes under these artificial conditions were viewed as being relatively attractive from a policy standpoint. A failure to recognize that the loss in standard hours might be partially accommodated by more effective use of existing hours or more overtime working would clearly entail potentially serious consequences for the accuracy of predicted outcomes concerning changes in employment and relative labour costs. Moreover, any initial errors in forecasting immediate labour market implications would be compounded in more broadly based analyses of related macroeconomic considerations such as the implications for wage and price inflation, exchange rates and tax revenues.

If a reasonably full evaluation of the labour market

41

responses to this type of shock to the system is precluded at the outset, then this necessarily involves a false appraisal of the *ex post* relative prices of factor inputs. As an example, a cut in the standard workweek alters the marginal cost of increasing overtime working relative to hiring additional workers. It also alters the marginal costs of both the hours and worker components of total labour input relative to the stock of capital. Such changes produce potential substitutions among inputs and these need to be assessed before a full evaluation of net employment repercussions can be undertaken. Further, it is necessary to recognize that scale effects may also accompany relative factor price changes.

In this chapter and the next an attempt is made to represent the main features of the relationships involved when trying to model the labour market effects of changes in working time. Later chapters will then draw quite heavily on this framework. The present chapter concentrates on a somewhat descriptive representation of the main issues involved while the following chapter focuses more precisely on some key technical relationships. As a means of simplifying the discussion, special attention is given to the labour market effects of standard hours reductions. In later chapters, a much wider range of working time topics are dealt with.

3.2   A Simple Labour Market Schematic

Irrespective of the above stated intentions, it is worth concentrating initially on a fairly crude labour market structure. It is assumed in this section that, for those persons in employment, there is no deviation from standard time working. In particular, suppose that each member of the economically active population is either in employment and working an effective 'full-time' 40-hour workweek or out of employment and working zero hours per week. By 'effective' we mean that there is no slack time, labour hoarding or other gaps between paid-for and effective working hours and, moreover, the firm considers that both the intensity and organization of working hours are at optimum levels. We do not exclude, however, the fact that certain hours during the standard workweek may not be utilized for direct production. Such hours may include set-up time as well as periods devoted to specific training and maintenance work. There is a single-shift system and there is no possibility of changing the flow of labour services through an alteration in existing worktime patterns.

In this situation, it does not matter essentially whether labour services are defined in terms of numbers of workers or manhours. Given the hours and utilization assumptions, we might just as well deal in terms of persons or 40-hour equivalents. With an eye to future developments, however, we will proceed in terms of manhours. A useful illustration of the workings of a labour market under these conditions is that portrayed in the sort of schematic proposed by Holt (1970). This is shown in Figure 3.1.

Suppose that the market is in equilibrium with respect to manhours; that is, the demand for and supply of manhours are equal. Now, consider that there is an exogenous cut in standard hours, from 40 to 35 per week, and that the reduction is *not accompanied* by a change in the demand for goods and services. In this case, the cut in the workweek renders the aggregate desired level of manhours to be in excess of those currently employed. This would be reflected by an increase in the demand for available manhours (vacancies) relative to the supply of available manhours (unemployment). Worker–job match would be improved resulting in a fall in the stock of unemployment and a rise in the stock of employment. There may well be a partial movement back towards initial stock levels, however. Better job opportunities, represented by a rise in the duration of vacancies relative to unemployment, are likely to induce an increase in quits. In turn, this would tend to retrigger the process since the probability of worker–job matches would again rise as the quits create increases both in the duration of vacancies and in the stock of unemployment. Further, the general tightening of the labour market due to the initial excess demand shock, the lengthening in the duration of vacancies and the increase in quit rates, would induce employers to reduce layoffs. More quits will follow as the

43

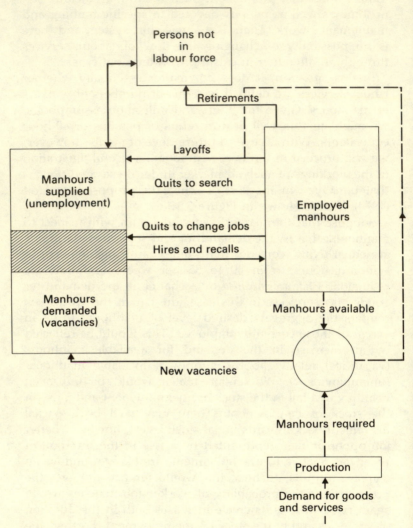

Figure 3.1 Holt labour market schematic.

reduction in layoffs leads to an increase in the stock of employed workers and a reduction in the stock of unemployed workers – also reducing new hires – and this again increases the duration of vacancies relative to unemployment. The overall tendency is for the system to display negative feedback producing the net result of a fall in the percentage rate of unemployment.

Alternatively, within a working time context, the above process might have been stimulated by an exogenous increase in the number of persons not in the labour force. For example, a reduction in the mandatory age of retirement would reduce the existing number of employed manhours and, again for a given demand, create an excess of desired total employed manhours with similar resulting implications for the stock of employment and unemployment.

A cut in the standard workweek can be treated as an exogenous event to the typical firm since it can reasonably be imagined to result from government or national collective bargaining decision-making. The policy goal may well be one of attempting to reduce the stock of unemployment. Beyond such initiatives, the government may also attempt to influence the speed at which the adjustment process takes place so that, for instance, it may reap larger short-term political recognition of its actions. As an example, it may attempt to reduce the potential hiring costs to firms by initiating training programmes that are geared to improve worker–job match and thereby to reduce initial quasi-fixed cost barriers. It might also attempt directly to reduce the cost of new hires by subsidizing firms' wage and non-wage costs with respect to net additions to their workforce. On the quit side, it may endeavour to reduce the transaction costs of search and job switch. For example, it could seek to improve the portability of pension and other private fringe benefits or it could provide mobility and other relocation grants. In other words, government policy may be directed both towards changing the stock levels of employment and unemployment as well as the rate of flow between one level and another.

In the absence of other considerations, the way in which this scenario has been set up appears to lead firmly to the conclusion that a cut in the standard workweek (or a decrease in the age of retirement) would lead to a reduction in the stock of unemployment and an increase in the stock of employment. These outcomes hinge primarily on the treatment of hours and on an assumed inelastic product demand given hours and stock changes. (A more technical illustration of this type of example is given in Section 5.2(b).) Even within this restricted labour market framework, however, an unequivocal view as to outcomes is unwarranted. Nothing so far has been inferred, for example, about the interrelated role of the capital stock and its rate of utilization. We will leave discussion of this and other matters until Section 3.4 (and elsewhere) and concentrate here and in the next section on perhaps the most critical simplification contained in the schematic in Figure 3.1.

One of the most significant shortcomings in the analysis so far has been to express manhours in terms of effective standard (40-hour) units. This is obviously unsatisfactory since many firms are in a position to vary utilization rates of labour. Although other possibilities exist, there are two important ways in which they may do this. The first involves variations in hours per worker around the standard-norm. Depending on prevailing economic conditions, firms may employ overtime or short-time working schedules. They might also fill 'full-time' job slots by two or more persons – through employing part-time workers. The second concerns variations in the average intensity of work effort during paid-for working hours. For a number of reasons, which we discuss in some detail in the next chapter, there is likely to be at any given time a gap between paid-for and effective working hours and, moreover, this gap may be expected to vary counter-cyclically.

Accordingly, before widening the discussion to embrace many of the issues that will concern us throughout this book, it is first essential to amend our description of the labour market by allowing for variations in the rate of labour utilization.

46

3.3 Variable Labour Utilization

Up until now, it has not only been assumed that all workers are employed for a workweek of standard length but also that each and every per-worker hour is worked to the same level of effectiveness or intensity. Both types of assumption must necessarily be relaxed in a realistic representation of the workings of the labour market. While we might reasonably define a standard workweek as being constant over all workers and firms, *actual* weekly working hours within a given firm may display positive or negative deviations from the standard. At given times, the firm may employ average total hours that are in excess of standard hours while, in more depressed economic conditions, it may adopt short-time working schedules. Further, there are likely to exist gaps between measured or paid-for hours of work and effective working hours that are also dependent on the prevailing economic climate. A more technical discussion of such issues is left to later chapters; here, the definition of the labour market is extended in order to take account of these possibilities. This is attempted with reference to the schematic shown in Figure 3.2.

It is recognized in Figure 3.2 that the firm can react to a position of excess labour demand through two distinct labour market channels. The first, the *external* market, relates to the stocks of vacancies and unemployment as in Figure 3.1. The second, the *internal* market, recognizes the distinction between the demand for and the potential supply of manhours among existing employees within the firms themselves. In this latter respect, supply in excess of demand might consist of paid-for hoarded manhours or a willingness to work more overtime per period at the given marginal premium rate or an underutilization of standard hours due to enforced short-time working. In order to avoid extreme complexity, Figure 3.2 continues to ignore such features as part-time working and shiftworking.

Suppose that, as before, there is an exogenous cut in the standard workweek that renders total desired manhours in the labour market to be greater than utilized manhours.

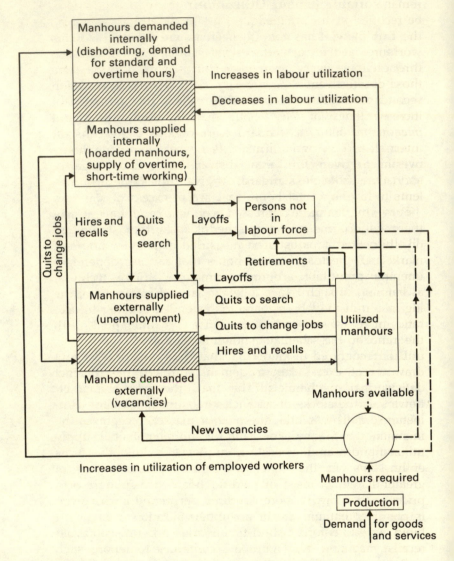

Figure 3.2 Extended labour market schematic.

Again, we assume that the demand for goods and services remains unchanged. The deficiency in manhours may now be rectified by a combination of each market's reactions. In the first place, firms may seek to change the size of their workforce at the *extensive margin*; in other words, they act through the external market with similar repercussions to those described in relation to Figure 3.1. There now exists a second option, however. Firms may be in a position to increase the utilization of the existing workforce at the *intensive margin*; this would involve operating through the internal market in order to dishoard labour, increase overtime working at given premium rates and reducing short-time schedules. These are the internal market equivalents to hires and recalls on the external market.

Providing that both labour market channels are activated, there will be an initial fall in the stock of available manhours on the external and internal markets. On the external market, the increase in the stock of vacancies relative to unemployment will mark the beginning of the same process as before, characterized by negative feedback and culminating in a reduction of the unemployment/employment stock ratio. Increased demand on the internal market will reduce the ratio of excess unused manhours (at given prices) to utilized manhours. Notice that the firm would not only draw directly on the internal market to help restore the deficiency of manhours but also that there would be direct flows between the external and internal markets. For instance, quits would be expected to take the form of losses in manhours that, on the average, are comprised of both utilized and non-utilized elements. Stated somewhat differently, some workers who quit would have been offering a greater supply of manhours than those demanded at given prices in their previous employment. As another example, it is possible that not all the manhours offered by a newly hired worker would be utilized, in which case hires (and recalls) may flow both to productive utilized manhours as well as to non-utilized manhours.

The critical issue becomes one of ascertaining the relative degree to which the labour market response to the cut in hours takes place at the extensive relative to the intensive margin. The paramount consideration in answering this question is the relative price of changing the size of the workforce compared to changing the utilization of existing workers. While a reasonably precise discussion of the role of relative factor prices is left to later chapters (see, especially, Section 4.4), it is worthwhile at this point giving some flavour of what is involved.

To simplify matters, suppose that there is no labour hoarding or short-time working on the labour market. Firms have the possibility, however, of extending overtime working. We consider two ways of achieving this, both of which are relevant to subsequent developments. First, firms may be able to extend overtime working at *existing* premium rates. In this case, the internal market would be characterized by a stock of manhours which represents a positive gap between the level of overtime hours workers are willing to work at existing premium rates and those that are currently demanded. This is in the spirit of the assumptions lying behind Figure 3.2. In the second case, firms attempt to create such a gap by offering increased premium rates at the margin.

Consider that, in initial equilibrium, there exists an excess supply of manhours at given premium rates. In order to increase manhours through internal market channels firms must pay for additional hours at the given rate. It is important to note, however, that they will also be required to pay a 'premium' in order to obtain external market manhours. The premium here is represented by the quasi-fixed costs associated with search, hiring and training workers as well as possibly certain types of fringe benefit payments. A market in equilibrium would be characterized as one where the ratio of marginal costs at the extensive and intensive margins is equal to the respective ratio of marginal products (see Section 4.4 for precise details). Suppose that the market is in this sort of equilibrium when standard hours are reduced. Assuming that the ratio of the market's marginal products remains unaffected by the cut, what can we say about the marginal cost ratio? Since we are assuming that there is an excess supply of overtime hours at existing premium rates then there is *no* rise in marginal cost at the intensive margin. This is not the case on the external market, however. Here, hours have to be purchased in full-time worker 'batches'. The cost of each existing batch would rise as a direct result of the standard hours cut since now a smaller proportion of it can be purchased at the cheaper standard rate: at the extensive margin, marginal costs rise directly with the fall in standard hours. The net outcome is, perhaps, somewhat surprising. In order to minimize costs, firms have an inducement to substitute more overtime working for fewer workers given a reduction in standard hours.

If we now assume that, in order to obtain more internal manhours, firms face a rising premium overtime schedule then the foregoing clear-cut results are not obtained. Naturally, much depends on the shape of the overtime schedule and, therefore, on the relative rise in marginal cost at each margin. Again, in the following two chapters we will consider the consequences of using an overtime schedule where premiums are a positive function of hours.

If firms display a general tendency to substitute overtime hours for workers given a cut in standard hours then governments, with a primary interest in reducing the stock of unemployment, might consider offsetting policy initiatives. They might, for example, instigate increases in premium rates of overtime pay by legislating for minimum rates that are, on the average, above existing norms. Alternatively, they might endeavour to subsidize wage and non-wage labour costs for additional hires in order to improve the relative marginal cost at the extensive margin. This latter sort of intervention is considered in some detail in Chapter 9.

Other more dynamic and short-term reasons might explain the differential use of the external and internal labour market. If we assume that, for a variety of reasons, firms are keen to meet existing orders at the same rate as before a cut in the standard workweek, then they might be relatively attracted towards a greater short-run recourse to internal market responses since this may offer a speedier adjustment alternative. Dishoarding manhours or extending overtime working might well be achieved more promptly than searching for and training new employees to given work requirements. In the longer term, of course, firms would gradually be able to adjust their mix of workers and hours per worker in line with the relative factor prices. This is illustrated in the stylized examples in Figure 2.3. For this sort of reason, it becomes important to attempt to disentangle dynamic adjustment associated with short-term relative transactions costs from the long-run comparative static outcomes associated with changes in standard hours and relative factor prices. Several of the following developments will be undertaken with this sort of distinction in mind.

3.4 Other Relevant Issues

A number of other considerations are introduced in this section that not only serve to elaborate on the picture portrayed in Figure 3.2 but also involve additional labour market features that are not captured in the schematics. While these new issues represent some of the main areas of interest in this book, they are not intended to cover exhaustively the topics to be dealt with at later stages.

A convenient simplifying assumption in the previous two sections is that changes in working time leave the aggregate demand for manhours unaltered. It is perhaps unreasonable to suppose that changes in labour costs due to alterations in working time do not lead to scale impacts on factor demand. Even if we assume that the firm is a price-taker in the product market, the demand for the product of the industry may well be a function of industry price. Since reductions in standard hours typically apply to *all* firms, then industry price is affected and scale responses become potentially important. In later chapters we consider the consequences of hours reductions given the assumptions of both exogenously given demand and demand that is functionally related to product price. In general, it is the case that there are less favourable consequences for employment given exogenous hours reductions under the latter assumption.

So far no mention has been made of the effect of

workweek reductions on the productivity of working hours. As will be seen in later chapters, this is a somewhat thorny subject area since the employment impact of productivity changes is open to considerable theoretical and empirical ambiguity. Two simple and contrasting examples suffice to illustrate the difficulties in this area. In the first place, suppose that the existing standard workweek is of relatively long duration. A significant reduction in standard working hours may help to improve workers' weekly work rates and performance due to a reduction in fatigue and boredom. For a *given* product demand, and making no assumptions concerning changes in wage compensation, the resulting productivity increase means effectively that less labour is needed to produce the same output. In this event, the productivity impact might be to reduce employment demand at the extensive margin. This result will be modified, however, if the firm has a relatively high product elasticity of demand and it is able to pass on the productivity gains in the form of lower unit selling prices. As a counter-example, suppose that the length of the existing workweek is not sufficient to involve problems of fatigue and boredom. Moreover, suppose that a significant part of the firm's effective manhours are devoted to machine set-up time. From this position, a fall in standard hours may produce a reduction in labour productivity since proportionally less time is devoted to direct production activity. The fall in manhours would be associated with a proportionately greater fall in output per period of time and, *ceteris paribus*, the firm may need to recruit more employees at the extensive margin. Again, however, this outcome would be modified under the assumption of relatively high product demand elasticity since the implicit higher unit costs due to the productivity decline may produce negative scale impacts.

Another potential shortcoming in the discussion relating to Figures 3.1 and 3.2 is that, while acknowledging that the firm might react to a tighter labour market by reducing layoffs, it is implicitly assumed that the firm acts passively regarding job losses due to an increase in quits. The existence of quasi-fixed labour costs, especially those related to specific training, may well require modifications to this treatment of quits and wage compensation. Assume that the quit rate is a negative function of a firm's own wage relative to the average of its labour market competitors as well as to job opportunities on the labour market. The firm may *set the wage* in order to maintain the quit rate at a level concomitant with minimizing losses in specific investments. Suppose, again, that standard weekly hours are reduced. Fewer standard hours would make quits relatively more expensive since, *ceteris paribus*, there is now a shorter time over which to amortize training and other fixed labour investments. Further, the hours reduction would not only involve a rise in the cost per quit but also, possibly, in the quit rate itself due to more job opportunities created by an excess demand for manhours (that is, given the scenarios in Figures 3.1 and 3.2). In order to stem the increased cost per quit, and a possible rise in the quit rate, the firm may seek to increase its wage rate. Given a competitive market and a *general* reduction in the standard hours, other firms may also be expected to act in similar fashion and so the ratio of the firm's wage rate to the average of its competitors may remain reasonably constant with no significant reduction in quits. The level of wages, however, has risen and, allowing for negative scale effects on employment (and/or capital–labour substitution – see below) the firm's demand for manhours at the extensive margin may fall. Indeed, we might imagine that the only way for the firm to reduce quits in this situation would be through a fall in the probability of a worker finding a job or, in other words, for the stock of unemployment to rise relative to its rate before the cut in standard hours. This type of wage setting by firms, and the resulting labour market consequences, closely relate to the efficiency wage literature and a review of relevant work is undertaken in Section 5.5.

The ability of firms to react to exogenous changes in working time, as well as the form of the reaction itself, are often constrained by supply-side influences. By far the greatest interest in this direction has been centred on the behaviour of unionized firms given working time changes. Unions may act in a number of ways that serve to alter or modify outcomes that would arise from pure demand-side considerations. At the extreme, employment outcomes to working time changes may largely be determined on the supply-side in cases where unions effectively set wages. In Section 5.6, we discuss workweek reductions within models that are 'driven' on the assumption of wage setting by a monopolistic union.

It should be added that, in general, models are analysed in the more theoretical chapters *without* imposing assumptions concerning possible union-led wage reactions to hours reductions. The intention is to derive labour market results in the absence of (what are often) *ad hoc* inferences over wage responses. The subject is broached elsewhere in the text, however, especially in Chapter 11 where collective bargaining issues are considered.

Unions may also influence employment outcomes in other ways. For example, they may institute a seniority-based compensation system whereby downturns in the demand for labour are not met by worksharing – through reduced average hours for all workers – but rather by selective layoffs (temporary or permanent) among less senior workers. This aspect of the subject is discussed in Chapter 8. Also in Chapter 8, and in a more general context, the supply-side is integrated into the overall analysis through an implicit contract formulation whereby firms provide some degree of wage and employment insurance against fluctuations in wage income.

In line with Section 3.2, several of the models in later chapters proceed 'as if' paid-for hours are the same as effective hours. In reality, however, the relationships among employment, wages and working time are intimately tied up with the topic of labour hoarding. At various stages throughout the book, therefore, complications introduced by a possible gap between paid-for and effective working hours due to labour hoarding are discussed. Generally, we concentrate on labour hoarding within a human capital framework. Firms with significant levels of specific investment may retain manhours even though the marginal productivity of hours is insufficient to cover the periodic rent. This has an interesting implication for policies directed towards *reducing* labour costs as a means of expanding employment during relatively depressed economic conditions. If a significant number of firms are not recovering their expected periodic rents, then wage reductions due to targeted labour subsidies or general incomes policies may provide little incentive for new employment. For a proportion of the firms, a reduction in labour costs may not succeed in restoring the equilibrium marginal condition let alone provide conditions that are conducive to an expansion of the workforce.

While Figures 3.1 and 3.2 help to illustrate some important aspects of the labour market, it is clearly unacceptable to treat the problem as if the firm only employed one variable factor of production. It also employs capital and, at any given time, the stock of capital and its rate of utilization can be treated equivalently to the size of the workforce and average hours worked per worker, respectively. Also, in a much shorter-run context, the firm may be able to meet changes in product demand and relative factor prices through varying its levels of inventory holding and lengths of delivery lags. One obvious implication of introducing capital into the framework is that a cut in the standard workweek may raise the price of labour relative to capital, thereby inducing capital–labour substitution. This in turn may serve to modify the potential employment gain (or exacerbate the employment reduction) that arises purely with respect to the labour market. We should note that – *ignoring the complications introduced by overtime working* – reduced standard hours may serve to raise the price of capital. Fixed interest and depreciation charges on capital would be expected to rise since falls in labour utilization due to lower hours will mean a reduction in the utilization of the capital stock. In a similar vein, the price of labour is increased in so far as the cost of per-period specific investments is raised due to a lower utilization of the labour stock. In the event of a relative worsening of the price of labour, governments may attempt to intervene in order to increase the price of capital services by reducing government subsidies to capital user costs. Some discussion of this possibility is presented in Section 9.3.

In order to offset relative increases in the labour and capital costs following a workweek reduction, the firm may attempt to increase utilization rates of the two factors by increasing effective manhours per period. In terms of the schematic in Figure 3.2, it may have recourse to dishoarding labour, employing higher levels of overtime or reducing the amount of short-time working. Two further strategies may also be available for the increase of labour utilization. These are an increase in the number of shifts per period of time and a more careful tailoring of available manhours to required manhours through an increase in part-time employment.

In the case of shiftworking, one possible scenario may proceed as follows. A given firm undergoes a statutory reduction in the length of the workweek and experiences a relative rise in labour costs, perhaps exacerbated by a union insistence on partial or full wage compensation for the loss of wage earnings. Supply constraints may prevent it from employing significant levels of overtime working (see the discussion in Chapter 11) and, for simplicity, we assume that there is little labour hoarding. While the capital stock may be assumed to be fixed in the short run, the hours reduction will produce a rise in the cost of capital due to an increase in depreciation and interest charges. The firm may seek to persuade its workforce that in order to offset increased factor costs it should introduce (or extend) a shiftworking system thereby allowing capital equipment per period to be operated more intensively. One long-run disadvantage of this strategy as far as employment is concerned is that the shift system may improve the return on capital relative to labour thereby reducing longer-term employment prospects. The shift system itself, however, may induce some new employment potential. For example, indivisibilities within the firm may require that a net increase in the workforce takes place in order adequately to man each shift. Further, due to greater unsocial hours and fatigue introduced by more shifts, the average length of shift may need to be significantly shorter than the original one-shift (or fewer-shift) system and, again, more workers may be required to produce a given output. Some mention of the

57

role of shiftworking within theoretical and empirical models is made at various stages throughout the book.

A more direct stimulus to employment may be for two or more persons to share existing jobs *within* a given shift. The economic feasibility of increasing employment through the creation of part-time jobs begs a series of complicated questions. In Chapter 7 we examine some of the more important of these from both demand- and supply-side perspectives. For example, we investigate problems associated with the fixed costs to the firm *and* to households given an increase in part-time employment. Also, the implications of reducing the standard workweek on the relative demand for full-time and part-time employment is examined. Finally, part-time working in relation to social security contributions is discussed both within the standard theory of the firm (in Chapter 7) and in relation to early retirement and job splitting (in Chapter 10).

As mentioned at the outset, this chapter has been designed primarily to introduce some of the more important labour market concepts and related issues necessarily involved in a discussion of changes in working time. Other considerations outside the immediate labour market – for example, related to inflation and balance-of-payments issues – are also relevant to a full understanding of the economic implications of working time changes. These and other topics are also discussed in later chapters.

CHAPTER FOUR

Some Economic Concepts and Relationships

4.1 Introduction

The assessment of the employment impact of changes in working time depends critically on the realistic formulation of certain key economic concepts and relationships. This chapter highlights some of the most important of these. The discussion is of particular relevance to the analysis of the effects of changes in weekly working hours in the following three chapters. Many of the details, however, are pertinent to a wider set of issues and so the development in this chapter will also prove useful throughout the remaining text.

Perhaps the central difficulty that confronts investigations of employment–hours relationships is the fact that working hours cover only one aspect of the firm's total of factor inputs and an accurate assessment of their individual role involves 'taking out' the influence of the other factors from the complete model. As we have emphasized in the preceding chapter, labour services are a function of combinations of numbers of workers (a stock variable) and hours per worker (a flow or utilization variable). A parallel definition pertains to capital services; namely the capital stock and its flow equivalent, the rate of capacity utilization. The firm may be able to produce any given final output by a large number of different combinations of these four different components of factor inputs. Indeed, within a short-run context, the firm often has a fifth, albeit temporary, means of satisfying final demand in that it can alter the rate at which it depletes its inventory holdings. Unravelling the unique role of working hours from these considerations involves a number of conceptual problems, not the least of which involves the likelihood that the factors themselves are interrelated with different component parts acting as complements to or substitutes for one another.

A fundamental reason for the need to distinguish clearly between the stock and flow dimensions of each input factor is that their respective factor prices are not the same. The user cost of capital is measured as a per-period proportion of the capital stock. Ignoring for the moment taxes and subsidies, user costs consist of an investment goods price deflator multiplied by the sum of the opportunity cost of capital and its rate of depreciation. The first two items represent fixed costs in that they are incurred irrespective of the utilization rate of capital. The depreciation rate, on the other hand, is dependent on capacity utilization as well as time. As for labour services, while variable labour costs (wages, bonuses and certain non-wages) apply to both workers and hours per worker, there are well-known quasi-fixed costs (for example, training, hiring and set-up costs) that relate only to the worker stock component.

The picture is even more complicated when it is considered that there exists no uniform price for working hours themselves. In the first place, the price varies with respect to the per-period (for example, daily or weekly) length of working hours. Typically, there is a standard hourly rate for a given job that applies to a fixed number of standard or normal hours. Both the rates for and lengths of these hours are often negotiated collectively at industry level and are also likely to be influenced by statutory legislation. Certainly, they may often be regarded as being exogenously determined *vis-à-vis* an individual firm. For many workers, hours worked beyond the agreed standard are paid at a premium rate. This involves some increment above the standard rate that is positively, though perhaps non-monotonically, related to time. The average number of such hours worked per period of time, in contrast to standard hours, is usually endogenously determined within the firm itself. Outside constraints may play some part, however. For instance, there may exist legislatively imposed maximum limits to per-period overtime working. Rates of overtime compensation may also partially reflect exogenous influences. In some countries, for example, minimum premium rates are set by legislation. Further, the rates are often influenced by widely based collective agreements, such as between trade unions and employers' associations at the national level.

Beyond these considerations, non-standard rates usually apply to a range of other eventualities. These include additional payments for shiftworking, piece-rate working, adverse working conditions and working in lieu of holidays. With the exception of shiftworking, minimal attention is paid in this book to these types of compensation and their related working time topics.

Before investigating these issues in more depth, another basic conceptual problem must be faced. This relates to the distinction between *measured hours*, as recorded in published data sources, and *hours effectively worked*. The former usually refers to the total number of hours per period of time for which the employer incurs direct labour compensation. Often, they are referred to in the literature as paid-for hours. For a number of quite diverse reasons, measured hours are invariably greater than effective working hours. Certain paid-for hours are unproductive; here we would include payments for sickness, agreed work stoppages and other 'slack' times. Other paid-for hours are productive only in an *indirect* sense. For example, set-up time, while clearly essential to productive activity, does not itself involve working hours that *directly* enhance physical output or services. In the economic relationships discussed in this and later chapters, it is effective hours that are of most relevance to the analysis. Accordingly, the implications of the gap between measured and effective hours constitutes, of necessity, an important consideration.

So as to set the general scene, some of the main economic problems of concern are briefly discussed within the context of a simple illustrative example in Section 4.2. The distinction between measured and effective working hours is the subject of Section 4.3. Theoretical and empirical approaches to modelling the employment effects of hours reductions have been dominated by labour demand models that differentiate between adjustments at the extensive and intensive margins and their respective adjustment costs. Some important comparative static features of these models are illustrated in Section 4.4 within a simple structure in which the stock of capital is held fixed. Emphasis is given to labour demand by a cost-minimizing firm. With an eye on later development, a number of variations to modelling are also mentioned; those include profit maximization as an optimizing rule, the relevance of efficiency wage theory as well as alternative specifications of hours and wage functions. Possible relationships between labour productivity and reductions in working hours are discussed in Section 4.5. The demand framework is modified in Section 4.6 to allow for the introduction of both the stock of capital and its rate of utilization. As a natural sequence, Section 4.7 deals with problems of short-run factor adjustment as well as the interaction among stock and flow components of factor inputs. Attention is given to supply-side issues at various stages throughout the book. Examples include hours reductions within union bargaining models, the supply of part-time hours and workers and working time within efficient contract models. A brief outline of related considerations is given in Section 4.7.

It should be re-emphasized that, while a few simple results are derived here, the main intention of the chapter is to introduce and set out clearly a number of key economic relationships. These are then analysed in much more theoretical and empirical depth in later chapters.

4.2 An Introductory Overview

Let us first give a flavour of the sort of issues that will be embraced in this and several later chapters by means of a simple example.

Imagine a non-unionized firm producing widgets that employs a production workforce of 100 workers who each are paid for *and* effectively work a standard 40-hour week. We assume that there is no slack time, apart from agreed-upon stoppages. Suppose that in the recent past the firm has been faced with a given, stable demand for its product and that it does not anticipate that this demand will change in the short-term future. Its labour and capital are geared to producing *x* amount of widgets per week. Now, let us imagine there is a shock to this state of the world. This could take several forms, including a change in working time, but it is assumed that it is represented by an unanticipated increase in the demand for widgets. Suppose further that the firm does not know for how long this increase will be sustained but, just in case it turns into a long-term contractual arrangement, the firm considers that it is a prime objective to fulfil the extra demand. What would be the likely short-run predictions concerning the effects of this shock on the firm's employment of factor inputs?

The firm may well be faced with a number of potential means of reacting to the demand increase. In broad terms, it can extend its manhours employed beyond its existing 4,000 hours per week and/or invest in new capital stock. Other possibilities include running down its inventory of widgets below the present level and increasing the utilization of its plant and equipment by better work organization. While these latter two strategies may be important in general terms, we discount them as far as the present scenario is concerned. For two general reasons, we might expect that, in the early phase of the upturn in demand, the firm would be more likely to emphasize a manhour rather than a capital stock reaction. In the first place, the transaction costs of purchasing new equipment and installing it in such a way as to complement its existing factor endowments and work organization may be such that a longer adjustment lag, relative to that of labour, is required. A second reason may involve the firm's reticence over additional new investment net of depreciation. Since it is unsure of the length of the demand increase, it may decide that the risk of investment losses in new fixed plant and equipment are initially higher than comparable financial risks involved in extending manhours.

63

So let us suppose that the firm's first reaction is to increase its demand for manhours in order to meet the extra product demand. In line with the discussion in Section 3.3, it now has two obvious further options; it can increase its workforce beyond 100 workers and/or increase its hours by requiring all or part of its labour force to work overtime. Clearly, the main question that now arises is by what degree it will increase workers as opposed to average hours per worker. Both strategies involve extra costs. Overtime may only be purchased at wage rates in excess of those paid for standard working hours. In employing new workers, the firm must advertise new vacancies, select the best candidates and then train new recruits to perform equivalently to established workers. These per-worker costs are often referred to as the initial quasi-fixed costs of employment. The anticipated length of the demand increase would be expected to play an important part in the firm's assessment of the relative costs of these two strategies. In general, the greater the firm's uncertainty about the length of the new demand position the more heavily is it likely to discount against the costs of its initial investments in new employment and the more favourably it would be expected to regard the costs of employing premium hours. In the absence of serious collective bargaining constraints, the firm is likely to perceive less cost related to reversing, wholly or partially, its hours increases compared to increases in employment. The latter may not only involve the sunk-costs of the initial hiring investments but also statutorily imposed and/or contractually agreed redundancy payments.

Given that the firm is likely to want to minimize both hours and worker cost increases subject to the constraint that it wishes to produce the extra widgets, then it may reasonably employ the following decision rule. It will employ that combination of more workers and more hours per worker up to the point where the marginal cost of the new employment is equal to the marginal cost of extra working hours after discounting over the expected period of the demand increase.

While this optimizing rule might appear to be a relatively simple strategy for the firm to follow, it could well be faced

64

with another problem in the short run that prevents the attainment of the optimum workers–hours combination. If it is not possible for the firm to meet the extra demand in the immediate term by, say, changes in inventories or work organization, then it may be obliged to increase hours *more than* the optimum amount in the short run and employ workers at less than optimum levels. This follows simply because the process of hiring and training labour requires a longer period of adjustment, in likelihood, than obtaining agreements to work more overtime. In the very short run, therefore, average hours may tend to overshoot their optimum level while the workforce would be constrained to be less than its optimum amount. We have already mentioned empirical investigation along these lines in relation to Figure 2.3.

If the firm perceives the demand increase to be permanent, then other strategies to fulfil the extra production would be deemed to be feasible. It could extend its plant and machinery, improve the vintage of its capital stock and alter its work organization in order to achieve greater efficiency. It may be the case, therefore, that it would cut back its manhours below short-run levels after sufficient time has elapsed to permit the employment of these other measures. In the longer term, therefore, the manhour–capital dichotomy may play a similar adjustment role to the hours–worker dichotomy in the short run. A shortfall in actual compared to optimum capital stock, perhaps due to early caution in judging the permanence of the demand increase, may be compensated for by a greater initial use of manhours than that dictated by longer-term considerations.

The firm is likely, in other words, to view its various input factors as playing a highly interactive role along the path towards achieving its longer-term desired combination of factors.

At the outset, we made the critical assumption that, apart from agreed-upon stoppages, all weekly hours are effectively worked. What if we were to relax the assumption and admit the possibility that some part of each worker's 40 weekly hours is unproductive? This would naturally put a new complexion on the above story. Clearly, the firm may be able to meet the extra demand, either completely or in part, by requiring *existing* workers to work effectively up to the 40-hour standard. In the extreme case of all the extra demand being met by the take-up of slack time, there may be no effect whatsoever on other input factors, especially in the shorter term. Moreover, if such slack time does normally occur, then an analyst who used the firm's paid-for hours of work as a measure of effective hours would obtain very misleading information as to the repercussions of changes in working time. The fact that there is, at any given time, likely to be a gap between paid-for and effective working hours is the subject of the following section.

4.3 Paid-for and Effective Working Hours

There are four main categories of explanation for expecting a positive gap between paid-for and effective working hours.

(i) *Payments for days not worked*
Most employers compensate labour for a certain fraction of the working year despite the fact that no labour services are forthcoming. Obvious examples include payments for vacations, public holidays and sickness leave. For the typical firm, a large proportion of such payments for days not worked result from statutory requirement although many firms also make extra compensation either through collective bargaining agreements or unilateral decision. While statistical series often exclude the periods to which these payments relate, within total paid-for hours, it is usually the case that other information is available with which to separate out such hours.

(ii) *Agreed daily stoppages*
There are periods of time in which no work is carried out but are regarded nevertheless as part of the standard working day. Examples of regular daily occurrences of such stoppages include rest time, tea-breaks, travel-to-work time, get-ready time and cleaning-up time. Other stoppages are of a less systematic nature and include attendances at union

meetings and special works conferences. At a micro level, it is a reasonably simple exercise to calculate how much potential productive time is lost due to these reasons. Usually, however, such information is somewhat more difficult to obtain from official statistics at an industrial level of aggregation.

(iii) *Technical constraints*
While certain working time is 'effective' in the sense that it is essential to the attainment of final output, it is none the less productive only in an indirect sense. For example, in many production processes, time has to be allocated to setting up machines for a given production run as well as to machine maintenance. Continuity of operation is clearly dependent on both activities. In many firms, particularly smaller ones, both set-up and maintenance work may well be carried out by production workers themselves; that is, by those workers who also operate the machines in order to produce final output. As shown below (see Section 4.4), it is important to distinguish between the two activities since to treat them 'as if' they were strictly compatible may produce seriously misleading estimates of the returns to hours worked. Often, even at the micro level, it is quite difficult to obtain precise estimates of the amount of time that is devoted to set-up and maintenance, especially in the case where such work is performed by production workers. In larger firms, the problem is often minimized because separate details are usually available on the numbers of the 'non-production' workers who are largely responsible for carrying out these sorts of tasks.

(iv) *Labour hoarding*
The most difficult category of non-productive working time, from an analytical viewpoint, relates to the commonly referred to phenomenon of 'labour hoarding'. Under this concept, cyclical downturns in production demand are marked by a wider than average gap between paid-for and effective manhours as firms hold underutilized reserves of labour. Fay and Medoff (1985) have provided recent direct survey evidence on the basis of 168 US manufacturing

establishments that suggests that, during the trough quarter of its most recent downturn, the typical plant hoarded 4 per cent of its blue-collar paid-for hours.

Hoarding is commonly explained via a human capital approach. It has already been mentioned that hiring new recruits involves quasi-fixed costs. A large element of these costs involves specific investments by firms in the human capital endowment of their workforce. In its selection and training process the firm will attempt to develop the sort of worker skills that are most easily adapted to its organizational structure, capital endowment and work practices. Returns to specific investment can be measured by the increment to a worker's marginal product over and above that which would have been realized in the absence of careful screening and specific training. A part of a worker's specific human capital will be acquired through an on-the-job learning process whereby he/she gradually gains knowledge of the working methods and applications most suited to the firm's requirements. The firm will wish, at least, to recover its share of the initial investment and other subsequent training expenditures and its ability to do so partly depends on workers remaining within the firm for a time sufficiently long to allow the discounted per-period returns to the investments to equal their initial and ongoing costs. In deciding on the level of specific investments, the firm will need to take a view not only of the quality and skill potential of the labour involved but also on the market prospects for its particular products. If it thinks that the demand outlook is relatively stable then it may be expected to undertake relatively higher specific investments for a given homogeneous group of workers than when there is more demand uncertainty. In any situation, however, once the investments are made they represent irreversible or sunk costs.

Suppose a given firm finds that its particular demand expectations are unfulfilled. In particular, assume there is an unanticipated fall in product demand that is regarded as being only temporary in nature. In the face of the fixed costs of employment, it may not be advisable in all circumstances to reduce the workforce proportionately to the drop in production (with the aim of leaving effective hours worked per employee at a constant level). It may judge that by paying workers for hours in excess of those effectively worked, or in other words, not laying off workers by the amount dictated by classical marginal productivity theory, it will achieve higher returns in the longer term. Optimization would take place at the point where the discounted costs of writing off specific investments are equal to the drop in returns during the anticipated length of the shortfall in product demand. A similar explanation of labour hoarding arises from the fact that many firms, when anticipating laying off workers, have to face directly associated transactions costs. These include redundancy payments that are statutorily imposed or that have been agreed to in contractual commitments. On the basis of the same sort of discounted estimates, the firm might deem it to be worthwhile to avoid a part of such costs and, instead, to reduce the degree of utilization of existing workers.

Other short-run alternatives to hoarding unutilized hours during a recessionary period may be available to the firm. For example, it might increase its inventory stocks above normal levels or satisfy its order backlogs at a faster than planned rate. Optimum combinations of reserves of unutilized hours and excesses of inventory holdings would be expected to depend on the implicit relative cost of a given degree of adoption of each strategy. Somewhat partial approaches towards understanding labour hoarding along these lines can be found in Miller (1971) and Greer and Rhoades (1977). Closely related work involves integrating inventory adjustment lags into the analysis of the demand for workers and hours (see Nadiri and Rosen, 1973; Topel, 1982; Rossana, 1983, 1985).

It is worth noting that, in practice, it may be difficult to distinguish clearly between manhours devoted to maintenance and related work, mentioned under (iii), and hoarded manhours. Some of the special maintenance jobs, such as large machine overhauls, may be postponed until cyclical downturns in activity at which times a proportion of manhours are switched from direct production activity in order to perform them. Of course, unlike pure hoarding, a direct productive return to such activity could be observed, in theory, after a lag. In their study, Fay and Medoff (1985) calculate that the percentage of blue-collar paid-for hours devoted to 'worthwhile other work' during trough periods was as much again as their estimate for hoarding.

At later stages (see, especially, Sections 4.5 and 6.4) we discuss the employment implications of changes in hourly productivity induced by workweek reductions. It is in this area that the existence of labour hoarding can cause acute empirical problems. Suppose that, during a given interval of time, a firm employs a significant unutilized percentage of its potential manhours as hoarded labour. If we attempted to measure its elasticity of output with respect to paid-for hours, then this would give extremely misleading results as to the returns to working hours. Returning to the example of the previous section, the firm may be able to produce significantly more widgets per unit of time through virtually *no change* in measured hours since the extra production may be found through dishoarding labour. In this case, a large increase in output will be associated with a relatively small change in hours worked thereby producing a high measured output–hours elasticity. This elasticity would be very different from its theoretically 'correct' equivalent, the output elasticity with respect to effective working hours. The latter measure is observed when the firm is 'on' its production function.

4.4 Labour Demand

A very useful starting point in building a framework in which to analyse factor demand in general is to illustrate some of the essential concepts within the confines of a comparative static model that concentrates on the labour input. Accordingly, we ignore here problems connected with the capital stock, inventory holdings, supply constraints and other issues.

At the outset, two basic modelling choices are available depending on assumptions about the firm's optimizing behaviour. In the *cost minimization* approach, sales are treated as exogenous and can be viewed as being constrained by aggregate demand. Examples of work adopting this assumption include Rosen (1968), Ehrenberg (1971), Bell (1982) and Hart (1984a, 1984b). In the *profit maximization* approach, the firm chooses the quantity it sells on the basis of product price and input costs. Raisian (1978) and FitzRoy and Hart (1985) provide examples of work in this direction. The two approaches have been dubbed, respectively, the 'Keynesian' and 'classical' regimes by Calmfors and Hoel (1985) who undertake a fairly comprehensive theoretical analysis. In several important respects the models overlap and, to avoid duplicating results, we develop a cost minimizing model in this and the next chapter. Where differences in results do occur, these are reported in Section 5.2(b). Also, at later stages, more complicated models – with respect to part-time employment in Chapter 7 and implicit contracts in Chapter 8 – will be analysed within a profit maximizing framework for mathematical convenience.

Consider a competitive firm whose flow of labour services is derived from combinations of the stock of workers (N) and the rate at which these workers are utilized. Conveniently, and without great loss of accuracy, we may represent the utilization, or flow, dimension of the labour input in terms of average working hours (h). These hours need not be strictly 'effective' in the sense that they are purged of all elements that account for the gap between paid-for and effective hours. Normally, however, they would not be expected to include payments for days not worked. At this stage, we also exclude the possibility of labour hoarding. Average working hours may include such items as set-up costs and tea-breaks, however, and this has a significant bearing, as shown below, on the specification of the labour services function.

It is essential, as a minimum requirement, to separate explicitly the labour input into its stock and flow dimensions. The cost to the firm of employing an extra worker compared to that of equivalently extending the per-period working hours of existing workers are *not* the same. As we shall see, this has implications for worker–hours substitution both with respect to changes in the cyclical demand for the

71

firm's final output (examined in later sections) as well as for changes in relative factor prices.

Variable labour costs are directly related to average hours worked per period of time. In general, they are comprised of several items of direct remuneration, including basic as well as premium wage rates, certain types of bonus payments and special non-wage labour costs. Here, we assume that there are only two types of variable labour cost. The first cost is direct wages, $w(h)$ defined as the total wage-cost per worker per period for h hours of work. Given information costs associated with attempts to allocate labour efficiently on the basis of complex contractual arrangements, it is assumed that, as a second-best solution, the wage is predetermined (see, for example, Hall and Lazear, 1984). The second cost is a payroll tax, $P \geq 1$ that varies directly with $w(h)$. Specific functional forms of $w(h)$ are given later.

Per-worker labour costs, on the other hand, pertain only to the absolute number of persons employed. Again, although there are a large number of examples, we identify only two categories of fixed costs. The first costs are the employer's per-period share of specific labour investments, defined as

$$Z = (q+r)z \tag{4.1}$$

where z are once-over hiring and training costs, q is the quit rate and r is a discount rate that reflects the opportunity cost of capital. The second costs, T, are those per-period payroll tax contributions that depend only on numbers of workers and that do not vary with average hours. No essential results are lost, here or at later stages, through omitting other types of fixed and variable labour costs. A full cost description can be found in Hart (1984a).

Per-period total labour costs C_L are therefore given by

$$C_L = (Pw(h) + Z + T)N \tag{4.2}$$

Output Q is related to labour services L through the production function $Q = f(L)$ with $f'(L) > 0$, $f''(L) < 0$. Earlier, it was stated that labour services are functionally related to workers and average hours. In general form, we may represent this by the expression

$$L = F(h,N) \quad F_h, F_N > 0 \qquad (4.3)$$

Following Ehrenberg (1971), a class of labour services function belonging to (4.3) is chosen that is multiplicatively separable in h and N. Specifically, this may be written

$$L = g(h)N^{1-\alpha} \qquad (4.4)$$

where $g(0)=0$, $g'(h) > 0$, $g''(h) < 0$ and $0 \leq \alpha < 1$. These restrictions imply that as h increases, L increases at a diminishing rate and also that employment and labour services are positively related.

Following the discussion by de Regt (1984) (see also Chapman, 1909; Barzel, 1973; Feldstein, 1976) it may be appropriate to specify $g(h)$ somewhat more elaborately. It may be the case that $g''(h) > 0$ for small values of h; for example, following initial set-up activity, marginal produc-

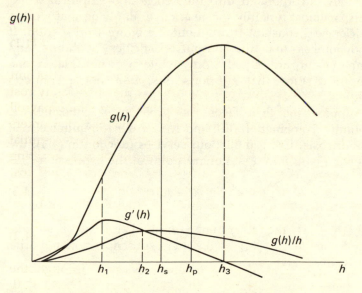

Figure 4.1 Relationships of $g(h)$, $g'(h)$ and $g(h)/h$ to h.

73

tivity first rises. As fatigue (or, perhaps, boredom) takes effect, then $g''(h) < 0$ for larger values of h. This is illustrated in Figure 4.1 where marginal product rises up to the point h_1 and then declines between h_1 and h_3 after which point it falls back to zero. Average product, $g(h)/h$, reaches a peak at h_2. The restrictions on (4.4) can alternatively be regarded as implying that the firm is operating within the range h_1 to h_3. Given the specific forms of $g(h)$ that are adopted later, $g''(h) < 0$ is required as a necessary optimizing condition although it will also be shown that the empirical findings are mixed.

An intuitively appealing property of (4.4) is that equilibrium hours are scale-independent. Letting $\bar{h}$ and $\bar{N}$ represent optimum levels of h and N, then it follows that

$$\frac{\partial \bar{N}}{\partial L} > 0 \text{ and } \frac{\partial \bar{h}}{\partial L} = 0.$$

It is quite common to find a simpler form of (4.4), namely $L = hN$, incorporated into theoretical and empirical work. This is almost certainly too restrictive, implying that worker efficiency is constant throughout the entire work period. It also implies that the output elasticities of hours and employment are equal and, while we note later one empirical study that supports this, it is not a common finding.

Suppose the firm faces the problem of choosing the optimum combination of h and N in order to minimize total labour costs. Using the labour services function in (4.4), the problem is to find a stationary point of the expression

$$J = C_L + \lambda(L - g(h)N^{1-\alpha}) \tag{4.5}$$

where λ is the Lagrangian multiplier. The first-order conditions $J_h = J_N = J_\lambda = 0$, where subscripts denote partial derivatives, give

$$Pw'(h)N - \lambda g'(h)N^{1-\alpha} = 0 \tag{4.6a}$$

$$Pw(h) + Z + T - \lambda(1-\alpha)g(h)N^{-\alpha} = 0 \qquad (4.6b)$$

$$L - g(h)N^{1-\alpha} = 0 \qquad (4.6c)$$

Dividing (4.6a) by (4.6b) gives

$$\frac{w'(h)}{g'(h)} = \frac{w(h) + \tau}{(1-\alpha)g(h)} \qquad (4.7)$$

where $\tau = (Z+T)/P$. As noted above, hours in (4.7) are independent of L. Following Raisian (1978), the equilibrium expression (4.7) can be interpreted as follows. The firm minimizes costs at the point where the marginal cost of labour at the intensive margin ($w'(h)/g'(h)$, that is, where L is varied by varying h holding N constant) is equal to the marginal cost of labour at the extensive margin ($\{w(h)+\tau\}/\{(1-\alpha)g(h)\}$, that is, where variations in L are obtained by varying N and holding h constant). Expression (4.7) is simply an equivalent way of writing the more familiar condition that an optimum is achieved by equating the ratios of marginal cost to marginal product for hours and workers, respectively: that is

$$\frac{w'(h)N}{w(h) + \tau} = \frac{g'(h)N}{(1-\alpha)g(h)}$$

It will be useful for later purposes to write equation (4.7) alternatively as

$$(1-\alpha)Gw'(h) = w(h) + \tau \qquad (4.8)$$

where $G = g(h)/g'(h)$.

For later developments, a number of explicit expressions of $w(h)$ and $g(h)$ are postulated. Two forms of the wage function $w(h)$ are considered. In the first, we assume a piecewise linear schedule in which the premium rate for overtime working is paid at some constant proportion $a > 1$ of the standard rate w_s; this may be written:

$$w(h) = \begin{cases} w_s h_s + a w_s (h - h_s) \text{ for } h > h_s \\ w_s h \qquad\qquad\qquad \text{ for } h \leq h_s \end{cases} \qquad (4.9)$$

The second formulation follows Santamäki (1983) and generalizes the overtime pay assumption of (4.9) by postulating a premium wage function for per-period hours in excess of standard hours. This takes the form

$$w(h) = \begin{cases} w_s h_s + \psi(h,h_s) w_s (h - h_s) \text{ for } h > h_s \\ w_s h \qquad\qquad\qquad\quad \text{ for } h \leq h_s \end{cases} \qquad (4.10)$$

where $\psi(h,h_s) > 1$ and $h > h_s$, $\psi_h > 0$, $\psi h_s < 0$. Thus, the premium wage function is assumed to be positively related to total hours and negatively related to standard hours.

It should be noted at this point that it is not intended to confine attention entirely to predetermined wage schedules. For example, an alternative modelling approach arises from the efficiency wage literature (see Stiglitz, 1984). The central hypothesis here is that productivity of workers is a function of the wage rate. In the present context, productivity is tied up with specific investments, z in (4.1). Also through (4.1), the return to these investments is determined in part by the quit rate, q: a higher quit rate, *ceteris paribus*, would lower the per-period return. It might seem reasonable to expect that the quit rate is negatively related to the firm's wage relative to those of other firms. In order to safeguard productivity levels, it may be in the firm's interest to offset higher potential quits by raising its wage. Similarly, the firm may raise its wage if, for a given quit rate, the expected cost per quit were to rise.

It is in the latter context that the influence of hours reductions on wage rates and employment is introduced. Ignoring possible overtime reactions, an exogenous reduction in per-period hours will reduce the amortization period of once-over specific investments thereby effectively increasing the discount rate r in (4.1). Essentially, quits become more expensive and the firm may try to counteract

76

this by raising its wage relative to other firms in an attempt to reduce the quit rate. In turn, such induced wage changes may influence employment through changes in relative factor prices. A more formal discussion of this topic is presented in Section 5.5.

As far as explicit expressions for $g(h)$ in (4.4) are concerned, the first simple expression, following FitzRoy and Hart (1985), recognizes a minimal set-up time, s, per worker and takes the form

$$g(h) = (h-s)^{\varepsilon}, \quad \varepsilon < 1. \tag{4.11}$$

For $h > s$, we may postulate, in line with Figure 4.1, that there are initially increasing and ultimately decreasing returns. Note, however, that in (4.11) attention is restricted to the latter possibility, thereby conforming with $g'(h) > 0$, $g''(h) < 0$ in (4.4). As stated earlier, the assumption of decreasing returns is required in order to satisfy a necessary condition for optimization (see Section 5.2) although, in the next section and elsewhere, implications of increasing returns are also discussed in relation to empirical findings.

Two further expressions for $g(h)$ concern special forms of the function

$$g(h) = g\{h_s, (h-h_s)\}$$

in which an explicit distinction is made between standard and overtime hours.

Ignoring set-up costs, the first of these takes the form

$$g(h) = \begin{cases} \{h_s + k(h-h_s)\}^{\beta} & h > h_s \\ h^{\beta} & h \leq h_s \end{cases} \tag{4.12}$$

where $0 < k \leq 1$ and $\beta < 1$.

Suppose that $k = 1$ in (4.12). Then, $g(h) = h^{\beta} \ \forall h_s$, and the function simply allows us to plot two points on the $g(h)$ and $g'(h)$ functions in Figure 4.1; two such points are shown at $h = h_s$ and $h = h_p$. Obviously, the greater the gap $(h-h_s)$

then the lower the marginal return of an overtime compared to a standard hour. For $0 < k < 1$, the picture is more complicated because this would produce a kink in the $g(h)$ function at h_s and a corresponding discontinuity in the $g'(h)$ function.

But why accommodate the possibility $0 < k < 1$? There are two possible reasons. First, suppose that only a proportion of the firm's workforce work overtime. (This is at least consistent with the industry-level data shown in Figure 2.4c.) Following Santamäki (1984), if we now define $(h-h_s)$ in (4.12) as average overtime hours of *those workers who are willing to work overtime* then k may be regarded as the proportion of such workers within the total labour force. Secondly, overtime hours may contain significant amounts of economic activity that does not *directly* enhance production. Maintenance work and set-up work (for example, setting up machines for the next day's production run) provide two possibilities. More discussion along these lines is given in Section 5.3(a).

As an alternative to (4.12), we have

$$
g(h) = \begin{cases} h_s^{\gamma_1} (h/h_s)^{\gamma_2} & h > h_s \\ h^\gamma & h \le h_s \end{cases} \qquad (4.13)
$$

Expression (4.13) can be related to (4.12) under the assumptions that $k = 1$ and that standard and overtime hours are homogeneous, by setting $\gamma_1 = \gamma_2 = \gamma = \beta$.

Combinations of $w(h)$ and $g(h)$ expressions, represented by (4.9)–(4.13), can be entered into the cost minimizing problem in (4.8) and the various effects of changes in hours on employment analysed. The form of the solutions and their implications for worksharing are discussed in the next chapter.

4.5 Hours Changes and Labour Productivity

A reduction in working hours may induce changes in the firm's labour productivity which itself may have implications for employment. Unfortunately, the direction of this latter response is by no means certain. There exist quite strong arguments that lend support to the possibilities of either rises *or* falls in labour productivity following a cut in working hours. Any uncertainty is reinforced, as we shall see in Chapter 6, by empirical evidence that is correspondingly less than clear-cut. For this reason, no attempt is made to integrate the productivity effects into the type of labour demand equations outlined in the previous section. Rather, the topic is treated separately at various stages in the text although it is recognized that it may serve to modify certain important results.

It is most suitable to investigate questions related to the productivity impacts of hours reductions within relatively broadly based models that, among other features, treat the firm's (or the industry's) product demand as a function of its price. A good example of such work is provided by Brunstad and Holm (1984). In their comparative static framework, employment responses to reductions in hours (treated as a strictly exogenous variable) are dependent on possible productivity changes after simultaneously taking into account the elasticity of substitution between labour and capital, the product elasticity of demand and the product elasticity of capital.

In order to introduce the topic in the simplest possible manner, consider the labour services function in (4.4) in which $g(h)$ is defined by (4.11); thus, we have

$$L = (h-s)^{\epsilon}N^{1-\alpha} \tag{4.14}$$

where ϵ is the product elasticity of hours $(= \{\partial L/\partial\ (h-s)\cdot(h-s)/L\})$.

Suppose that empirical estimates of (4.14) are obtained for a cross-section of firms in an industry. There is no overtime or part-time working and all firms employ a single-shift system. The hours variable in (4.14) is defined in terms of standard weekly hours and the average value for all firms is 40 hours. Estimates of parameters in (4.14) are not constrained to satisfy *a priori* theoretical conditions concerning ϵ and $(1-\alpha)$.

Consider three estimates of ε

(1) $\hat{\varepsilon} = 0.6$;   (2) $\hat{\varepsilon} = 1.0$;   (3) $\hat{\varepsilon} = 1.4$

Now suppose weekly hours are reduced from an average of 40 to an average of 35, that is by *12.5* per cent. The percentage loss in weekly output in the industry corresponding to each value above is

(1) 7.5;   (2) 12.5;   (3) 17.5

These values represent falls in output that are, respectively, proportionately less than, equal to and greater than the percentage cut in the workweek. This can be expressed equivalently in terms of labour productivity or output per working hour. For a 1 percentage reduction in working hours, productivity changes by $(1-\hat{\varepsilon})$ per cent. Thus, for a 12.5 per cent cut in the standard workweek, the respective percentage labour productivity changes are

(1) 5.0;   (2) 0;   (3) −5.0

On the assumptions that the industry's product demand is a function of its price and that there are no compensating increases in the wage rate and negligible relative price and capital substitution effects, what are the possible employment effects of these changes? Under case (1), the productivity effect is tantamount to the demand curve for labour shifting outward but since the same work load can now be performed by fewer workers, employment will only expand if there is a product demand increase. A positive employment effect would depend essentially on the industry's ability to pass on unit-price decreases to its customers combined with a relatively high price elasticity of demand for its product. Under case (2) there is no labour productivity effect. Under case (3), there is a decrease in labour productivity. The demand for labour would now decrease, *ceteris paribus*. If, however, the industry's product demand is relatively price-inelastic, and re-emphasizing the assumption of no factor input substitution effects, employment could increase.

As indicated in relation to Figure 4.1, it is not possible to anticipate, *a priori*, likely values of ε. A value significantly below unity may indicate a relatively long standard workweek with firms, typically, operating towards the right of $g(h)$ function in Figure 4.1. Values in excess of unity may indicate a workweek short enough that the increasing returns arguments connected with the left of the $g(h)$ function predominate in most firms. Empirical evidence from extended versions of the production function in (4.14) is reviewed in Section 6.4(a).

A further complication in this area of interest arises with $g(h)$ specifications such as in (4.12) and (4.13) where standard and overtime hours are separated. Here, it becomes important to establish the *relative productivity* effects of the two forms of hours before a final assessment can be undertaken. This topic is discussed in relation to empirical evidence in Section 6.4(b).

4.6 The Capital Stock and Capacity Utilization

Capital services are defined in terms of a capital stock (K) and the per-period flow of services per unit of the capital stock. This latter variable is somewhat more difficult to define than its equivalent expression within labour services. This is usually attempted, indirectly, in terms of capacity utilization, c_u. Imagine a firm that experiences marked cyclical fluctuations in its product demand. Suppose also that there is a reasonably constant trend growth in its capital stock. Given high transactions costs of changing the stock, we might imagine that the firm would meet demand towards the peak of the cycle not by net additions to the stock itself but rather by increases in the utilization of the stock. Similarly, cyclical trough periods are more likely to be associated with falls in the utilization of the capital stock rather than, say, accelerated rates of capital depreciation. In other words, for major anticipated deviations from trend, the firm, after allowing for non-work periods as well as maintenance and set-up time, may well plan a given amount of spare capacity into its 'normal' use of plant and machinery. At cyclical peaks, the machines are manned and run in such a way that they maximize their full output potential within the effective work time available.

Approximating excess capacity utilization at, say, industry level may now proceed along the following lines. Suppose we were to graph industrial output per manhour against time and connect cyclical peak points by trend lines that are taken to represent maximum potential output per manhour. The method of fitting such trend lines may take into consideration, or proxy, improvements in technological know-how. Then, the ratio of actual observations to the trend-through-peaks line can be taken to represent the degree of capacity utilization. In fact, allowing for a number of statistical and other refinements (see Klein and Preston, 1967), this sort of procedure is commonly adopted. Slightly more sophisticated methods involve simulations with the estimated parameters of production functions (see Evans, 1969, pp. 255–6). For our purposes, it suffices to declare that, in our future references to capacity utilization, we have these sorts of measures in mind.

Suppose that, during a given interval of time, the firm's actual output per manhour is below the maximum potential level and there is a rise in product demand. There are a number of ways in which the firm would be able to increase its utilization of existing capital in order to meet the new demand increment. Perhaps the most important of these involves extending machine running per period of time. Ignoring, for the moment, the possibility of introducing changes in shiftworking, it cannot do this independently of its utilization of labour. In order to run machines by one further hour per day, for example, it would need to require its existing employees to work longer hours, probably by offering overtime premium payments. Given that we have already firmly established distinct expressions for working hours within the definitions of labour services, it would now seem to be inappropriate when defining total factor inputs to include an additional measure of capacity utilization. It might be assumed that changes in hours effectively proxy changes in capacity utilization. The omission of capacity utilization for this reason would be erroneous, however. We have already detailed, in Section 4.3, the differences between measured or paid-for and effective working hours. Let us concentrate, for the moment, on one aspect of this difference; namely, labour hoarding. If, before the increase in product demand, the firm was hoarding labour then it may be able to meet a part or all of the increased demand for its product by requiring its workforce to work more intensively during *existing* paid-for hours. In this case, output would rise more than proportionately to (measured) hours and there is no guarantee that the change in the degree of capacity utilization and the change in average measured hours would necessarily be closely correlated. Therefore, in the absence of data on effective working hours, there is a strong argument for including *both* the stock and utilization components of capital alongside their equivalent labour input components within the total description of the firm's production process.

While the flow and stock dimensions of the labour input are both explicitly accounted for in the labour cost function (4.2), the flow dimension of capital services has a more implicit representation within the equivalent cost of capital expression. Suppose we have a measure of the capital stock in constant prices. How do we express the cost of capital service in terms of a per-period proportion of this stock? It is not sufficient merely to estimate the per-period price of capital goods, ϱ_k, since, as with once-over specific labour investments, the financial assets tied up in capital goods entail an opportunity cost. This may be represented by a suitable after-tax (market) rate of return, r_k. Also, the per-period cost is critically dependent on the amount of the physical capital stock that is used up through deterioration or obsolescence during a particular period. This latter cost may be accommodated by multiplying the cost of capital by a suitable discount rate d. As for fiscal considerations (see Hall and Jorgenson, 1967), let u be the marginal rate of corporation tax, k the investment tax credit and δ the discounted value of depreciation allowances against tax. Finally, let σ represent the expected rate of investment goods price. The user cost of capital, c, may then be written:

$$c = \frac{1-k-u\delta}{1-u}\varrho_k \, (r_k+d-\sigma) \qquad (4.15)$$

Helliwell (1976) provides a useful detailed discussion of the construction in (4.15) as well as several near alternatives.

Depreciation, d in expression (4.15) is clearly partly related to the degree of utilization of physical capital as well as to the expected time horizon of the capital's employment. In this way, capacity utilization is implicitly introduced into (4.15); that is,

$$d = d(c_u, t) \qquad (4.16)$$

Total capital costs to the firm may now be written

$$C_K = cK = \left[\frac{1-k-u\delta}{1-u}\varrho_k \, \{r_k+d(c_u,t)-\sigma\}\right] K \quad (4.17)$$

where K is the stock of capital.

Let Y_i $(i = 1, 2, 3, 4)$ denote, respectively, h, N, c_u and K. For simplicity, suppose that the production relation among these inputs is adequately represented by a Cobb–Douglas formulation,

$$Q = A \prod_{i=1}^{4} Y_i^{b_i}, \; b_i < 1 \qquad (4.18)$$

where Q is output and b_i is the output elasticity for the ith factor input.

The extended cost minimization problem may now be written

$$J = C_L + C_K + \lambda \{Q - A \prod_{i=1}^{4} Y_i^{b_i}\} \qquad (4.19)$$

A solution to this type of problem is discussed in Section 5.4 although the addition of capital and its rate of utilization features in several places throughout the text.

Recall that one of the main reasons for including capacity utilisation c_u is to pick up variations in intensity of use of the capital stock due to changes in labour hoarding and dishoarding. If effective hours are observable then, of course, this type of argument holds less validity. But even in this case, it may be possible for certain firms to vary capacity utilization other than through changes in per-period average hours worked. They may be in a position to change the number of shifts, S, per period of time as an alternative mode of adjustment on the intensive margin. This possibility has led several authors (see Brunstad and Holm, 1984; Calmfors and Hoel, 1985) to define capital services, K_s in terms of the capital stock measured in capital-hours and multiplied by the number of shifts per period. This may be written

$$K_s = hSK \qquad (4.20)$$

where h refers to effective working hours. We will report later (see Section 5.4) on the consequences of changing S when K_s in (4.20) is incorporated in the factor demand system.

4.7 The Interrelation of Factor Inputs

The model outlines so far are couched purely in comparative static terms. This is clearly unsatisfactory, especially in the light of earlier discussion, in Chapters 2 and 3, where it is emphasized that we would expect adjustment lags between actual and desired levels of factor inputs. In modelling terms it is obviously important to capture these adjustment impediments, otherwise, in empirical tests, there would be great uncertainty as to the degree to which given observed changes are due to the long-run influences of changes in relative factor prices and scale variables or to shorter-term reaction functions.

The standard way of dealing with this problem is to

distinguish between desired levels of factor inputs and the adjustment of actual values of factors to those levels. Retaining the four-factor input system of the previous section, let Y_{it} represent the actual level of factor i in period t where the is are ordered as before. Then, letting Y^*_{it} represent the desired level of the ith input at t and μ equal a finite speed of adjustment, we may portray the relationship between actual and desired values of each input by the well-known partial adjustment scheme

$$Y_{it}/Y_{it-1} = (Y^*_{it}/Y_{it-1})^{\mu_i}, \quad 0 \le \mu_i < 1. \tag{4.21}$$

The simple relationship in (4.21) represents the own-adjustment speed of the ith factor in period t. Following the discussion in Section 2.2(b), we might anticipate that the value of μ may be greater with respect to hours of work than to numbers of workers employed. In general, the latter variable may be expected to have higher levels of adjustment costs than those associated with changing labour utilization. A similar comparative cost structure probably also applies with respect to the stock and utilization components of capital.

The likelihood that μ_is vary across factors suggests that (4.21) will be an inadequate representation of factor adjustment. Suppose that the firm experiences an unanticipated increase in product demand that increases the desired size of its workforce. Due to labour market impediments with respect to search, hiring and training, it may well be prevented from reaching the desired employment level in the initial periods. In this event, it might well be in the firm's economic interest to make up for a short-term deficiency in employment by requiring its existing labour force to work longer hours, perhaps through more overtime working. The implications of this scenario are as follows. Not only does a potentially relatively small value of μ in the workers' equation provide a direct statistical reason for modelling own-adjustment, as represented by the relevant part of expression (4.21), but it may also have a significant bearing on short-run hours adjustment as well. For example, hours may adjust beyond their desired level in the short run in order to accommodate the shortfall between the actual and desired size of the workforce (see Figure 2.3). Capacity utilization may play a similar role *vis-à-vis* the capital stock. Moreover, we cannot rule out short-run relationships between manhours and capital services in the adjustment process.

Following Nadiri and Rosen (1973), it has become popular to model all possible interrelationships by means of a generalized partial adjustment system of the form

$$\Delta y_{it} = \sum_{j=1}^{4} \mu_{ij}(y^*_{jt} - y_{it-1}), \ i = 1, \ldots, 4 \qquad (4.22)$$

where μ_{ij}s are fixed own- and cross-adjustment coefficients and where small ys denote the logarithms of the factor inputs. Expression (4.22) allows for own-adjustment lags as well as for excess demands in any given factor either to increase or decrease the employment of each of the remaining factors via a complementary or substitution response. As we have noted earlier, research workers have extended the y_is in (4.22) in order to differentiate between production and non-production workers as well as to include the interaction of stocks of finished goods, materials, goods-in-progress and unfilled orders.

Since hours of work (y_1 in (4.22)) typically refer to paid-for hours then, in the absence of the inclusion of capacity utilization (y_3), a positive gap between paid-for and effective hours due to the cyclical influence of labour hoarding would provide misleading estimates of the 'true' returns to labour services. The returns would in fact be overestimated since output variations with respect to paid-for hours are greater than those with respect to effective hours. Including capacity utilization helps to correct for this bias. Recall that a typical measure of capacity utilization is the ratio of actual output per manhour to maximum-potential output per manhour. The implicit assumption concerning the latter variable is that, at the peaks of the business cycle and along interpolated trend lines, measured and effective hours of work coincide. A more direct method of modelling the gap between measured and effective labour services is provided by Fair (1985).

4.8 Supply-side Considerations

Attention so far has been focused solely on the demand-side of the story. Of course, the ability of firms to reallocate factor inputs in response to changes in working time as well as other economic stimuli may also be strongly influenced by supply-side constraints. In a standard neo-classical approach, an individual worker would endeavour to maximize utility, defined in terms of real wage income and leisure, subject to some income–expenditure constraint. Now, equilibrium in the labour market would be attained when, at a given level of utilization, the demand and supply of workers is equated. A worker's decision rule over whether to remain in or to quit the firm given, for example, an unanticipated change in demand is based on much the same criteria as that of the firm itself. In a human capital setting, workers have expected economic rents that represent their share of specific training. For a given demand shock, they will recalculate the expected rent relative to the opportunity cost of remaining in the firm and thereby establish an employment decision rule. As shown by Hashimoto (1975), it is possible that in certain situations workers may be willing to accept wage reductions in order to avoid a forced separation and to preserve a positive rent both to themselves and to the firm. Wage–employment strategies, given both sides' optimizing goals and within a framework similar to that introduced in Section 4.4, are discussed by Raisian (1978).

In certain circumstances it might be argued, at least in a short-run context, that a failure to model supply-side responses is not so important. There are likely to be high transaction costs in bargaining over marginal changes in working time or working conditions. For example, Hall and Lilien (1979) argue that efficient layoffs in response to short-term fluctuations can be generated by overtime and shift-work premiums that are renegotiated at relatively long intervals of time. Many of the results discussed in the following chapters are derived from the sort of myopic maximization implicit in the Hall and Lilien approach. We do not wish to ignore, however, important supply-side aspects of the working time literature.

As we will see, particularly in relation to the discussion on layoffs and worksharing in Chapter 8, an influential area of the implicit contract literature (for example, Feldstein, 1976) expressly distinguishes between workers and hours per worker. In this more general setting, workers' utility can be directly incorporated into the firm's optimizing behaviour. Assume that utility is represented by

$$V = U(wh) - D(h) \qquad (4.23)$$

where U', D', $D'' \geq 0$ but $U'' \leq 0$. Then, defining a suitable profits function π, the firm chooses an efficient contract by maximizing expected profit holding expected utility constant, or

$$\max E\pi \text{ subject to } EV = C_L. \qquad (4.24)$$

Setting up the problem in this way is particularly useful in analysing decisions to lay off workers or reduce average hours of existing workers given changes in employee benefits from and/or employer contributions to social welfare provision. The expectation of such changes will affect the utility and/or total labour cost functions in (4.24) with implications for factor allocation. These topics are discussed at some length in Chapters 8 and 9.

Special supply-side problems over changes in working time are likely to arise in strongly unionized firms. We also discuss later how the degree of unionization partially influences the strength of the outcomes under the implicit contract approach. Beyond this, some writers have studied working time reductions in models where the union is the driving force in wage setting. For example, Calmfors (1985) and Hoel (1984) consider the effects of a cut in working time given a utility maximizing monopoly union that sets the wage rate. Hours are treated as being exogenously given and the level of employment, given maximum union utility, is determined by the firm through a suitable factor demand relationship. This type of model is considered in Section 5.6.

Perhaps *the* dominant issue in the supply-side literature in relation to working time concerns the supply of female working hours as well as the decision of females over whether or not to participate in the labour market. As we have seen in Section 2.3(a), a very important aspect of female labour market activity concerns the issue of part-time employment. In Chapter 7 a model of the supply of part-time hours is discussed and results are compared to the outcomes of a demand-side model of part-time hours and workers.

CHAPTER FIVE

Employment Effects of Workweek Reductions: Theoretical Issues

5.1 Introduction

Although there exists an extensive literature on the effects of reductions in the length of the workweek on employment and other variables, it is only in relatively recent times that economists have attempted to construct well-defined analytical models based, at least to some limited extent, on micro foundations. The main purpose of this chapter is to review the most significant of these models within a framework that concentrates on comparative static relationships.

Focusing our attention on the treatment of wage determination, three broad classes of model can usefully be delineated. The first builds on the framework introduced in Section 4.4 and treats the wage as predetermined. In the second, the firm is viewed as a wage setter. Typically, in this sort of model, it is recognized that cuts in working time increase the costs of quits when there are significant specific investments. The firm attempts to control such costs to a level compatible with its overall optimizing behaviour. Accordingly, it adjusts its wage relative to that of its competitors in order to minimize the turnover costs associated with quits. In sharp contrast, the third class of model deals with the situation where a large monopoly union sets the wage. The firm is left to determine the optimal employment level commensurate with that wage and its other relative factor costs.

No given general approach to modelling can be regarded as adequately representing the experience of a 'typical' firm let alone the labour market behaviour of industrial and other macroeconomic aggregates of firms and enterprises. In some economies, such as the Scandinavian, there may exist relatively more cases that tend towards the union wage setting representation. Elsewhere, such as in the non-unionized/highly competitive sectors of OECD countries, firms may set wages partly with an eye to minimizing turnover costs. In between these extremes, firms may view predetermined wages as providing optimal second-best solutions in the face of uncertainty and moral hazard. The essential point is that no single model can realistically be expected to generalize all major possibilities and so the approach of discussing each class of model in turn and then comparing their analytical outcomes would appear to be the most rewarding.

Of course, there are other ways in which individual models may be sorted into distinguishable groups. Some researchers, for example, emphasize the important distinction between overtime hours, treated as an endogenous labour input, and 'standard' hours that are exogenously given to the firm. Other work, by contrast, while distinguishing between workers and hours, does not embrace an endogenous component of hours. Further, various models give more or less weight to the role of specific human capital investments. We shall deal fairly comprehensively with these, and other, aspects of modelling. Our division of the models into the above three classes has more to do with ease of presentation than with special emphasis on the importance of the wage compensation assumption.

Models with predetermined wages are discussed in Sections 5.2, 5.3 and 5.4. In Section 5.2 we examine some comparative static results from a 'conventional' version of the cost minimizing system set out in Section 4.4. Emphasis is given to the employment and total hours effects of changes in standard hours. The section is in two parts: in 5.2(a) the results are derived for a firm that employs equilibrium overtime and the outcomes are compared, in 5.2(b), with those for a firm working standard hours only.

Also in this latter subsection, equivalent results for a profit maximizing firm are reviewed. With an eye on future developments, the effects on the demand for workers and hours of changes in relative factor prices are examined in Section 5.2 as well as in the subsequent two sections. Retaining the same basic framework, the robustness of the key results derived in Section 5.2 is examined in Section 5.3 in the light of the somewhat more elaborate labour services and wage functions that are introduced in Section 4.4. This section is also in two parts: in 5.3(a) alternative labour services functions are discussed and 5.3(b) deals with a general form of the overtime premium schedule. Parallel to the developments of Chapter 4, the simple one-factor comparative static model is extended, in Section 5.4, by adding the capital stock and its rate of utilization. The latter measure may include the effects of shiftworking. An assumption of wage setting by the firm in Section 5.5 replaces that of a predetermined wage. Discussion is centred on the workings of an efficiency wage model. Section 5.6 deals with the third type of wage-behavioural assumption, the union wage setting model. The discussion is then broadened, in Section 5.7, beyond specific modelling of the labour market to consider outside macroeconomic influences. These largely concern considerations of inflation and international trade. An overview of the key results from the various modelling approaches is undertaken in Section 5.8 and some mathematical background to various derivations is presented in an appendix.

5.2 The Effects of Standard Hours and Labour Cost Changes in Conventional Labour Demand Models with Given Wages

We examine here some key comparative static results in a 'conventional' version of the cost minimization system set out in Section 4.4. It is so named because it represents the most commonly adopted structure of this type of demand model; earlier examples include Brechling (1965), Rosen (1968), Ehrenberg (1971), Bell (1982), Hart (1984b), Calmfors and Hoel (1985). Comparable results from the equivalent profit maximizing model are also reported. So as not to clutter the section with too much detail and repetition, major emphasis is given, in Section 5.2(a), to one aspect of the cost minimizing model. This establishes the general procedure and it suffices, in Section 5.2(b), to deal with other cost minimizing and profit maximizing outcomes somewhat more succinctly.

5.2(a) Cost Minimization with Endogenous Overtime

Consider a firm that employs positive average overtime hours in equilibrium; thus $\bar{h} > h_s$. Its capital stock is assumed to be fixed. The wage schedule is represented by the piecewise linear function in (4.9) which, given the overtime assumption, may be written

$$w(h) = w_s h_s + a w_s (h - h_s), \quad a \geq 1, \quad h > h_s.$$

The hours part of its labour services function in (4.4) is given by expression (4.11), that is

$$g(h) = (h - s)^\varepsilon, \quad \varepsilon < 1.$$

Substituting these two expressions into the first-order equilibrium equation (4.8) gives

$$(1-\alpha)(\bar{h}-s)a w_s = \varepsilon \{ w_s h_s + a w_s (\bar{h} - h_s) + \tau \}.$$

Rearranging gives the equilibrium hours equation

$$\bar{h} = \frac{\{ -h_s \varepsilon w_s (a-1) + \varepsilon \tau + (1-\alpha) s a w_s \}}{(1-\alpha-\varepsilon) a w_s}. \tag{5.1}$$

Given the labour services function $L = (h-s)^\varepsilon N^{1-\alpha}$, the second-order necessary condition required to achieve a minimum solution to the problem in (4.5) can be expressed (see appendix to this chapter for derivation):

94

$$\frac{(1-\alpha)Paw_sL^2}{N(h-s)}\,\{\varepsilon-(1-\alpha)\,\} < 0. \tag{5.2}$$

Empirical evidence on whether or not the condition $(1-\alpha) > \varepsilon$ is normally satisfied is reviewed in the next chapter. On the *assumption* that the condition holds then, from (5.1) we obtain

$$\frac{\partial \bar{h}}{\partial h_s} < 0. \tag{5.3}$$

The assumptions of positive marginal products, in (4.3), that is F_N, $F_h > 0$, combined with the Lagrangian constraint in (4.6c), namely $L-g(h)N^{1-\alpha} = 0$, combine to give

$$\frac{\partial \bar{N}}{\partial h_s} > 0. \tag{5.4}$$

The outcomes are unambiguous. A fall in standard hours, for example, will induce the firm to substitute more overtime hours per worker for fewer workers. Why should this be so? The firm's goal in this model is to minimize its total labour cost while meeting a *given* labour services requirement. The latter constraint means that a fall in standard hours requires a replacement increase in either the size of the workforce or per-period overtime working per employee or a combination of both. From (4.7), however, it is clear that the marginal labour cost on the extensive margin has risen relative to the intensive margin. The marginal cost of an additional worker has risen relative to an increase in overtime hours because a smaller fraction of $w(h)$ in (4.7) is compensated at the cheaper standard rate w_s. The results in (5.3) and (5.4) are also illustrated diagrammatically in the next subsection.

For a large number of reasons, we must exercise great caution over these results. In the first place, such hours–

workers substitution is conditional on the firm working overtime in equilibrium. Secondly, very simple, and not necessarily the most realistic, $g(h)$ and $w(h)$ specifications are adopted. Thirdly, no allowance is made for scale effects. Fourthly, it is assumed implicitly that there are no productivity offsets to standard hours changes. Fifthly, the interactive role of capital is ignored. Sixthly, there are no supply-side responses. These and other considerations are considered later in this and in following chapters.

Several other results are worth reporting at this stage, however. Just as a fall in standard hours increases marginal cost at the extensive relative to the intensive margin, an (exogenous) increase in the overtime premium (a) would be expected to work in the opposite direction. We note that, although a appears in the numerator of both sides of the equilibrium condition (4.7), a proportional change of a on each respective side (after substituting the piecewise schedule into $w(h)$) gives

$$\left| \frac{da}{a} \right| > \left| \frac{da}{a} \cdot \frac{w_s(h-h_s)}{w_s(h-h_s) + (w_s h_s + \tau)/a} \right|.$$

Thus, a rise in a increases marginal cost at the intensive margin more than proportionately to the extensive margin. By way of confirmation, we find that

$$\frac{\partial \bar{h}}{\partial a} = \frac{-w_s \varepsilon(h_s w_s + \tau)}{(1 - \alpha - \varepsilon)(a w_s)^2} < 0 \qquad (5.5)$$

with $\partial \bar{N}/\partial a > 0$, given (4.3) and (4.6c) as before. A rise in the wage premium leads the firm to substitute a larger workforce for a smaller labour utilization.

The standard wage w_s also appears on both sides of (4.7). As with the wage premium, however, a change in w_s produces a change in marginal cost at the intensive margin that is more than proportional to that at the extensive margin. Again with reference to the respective sides of equation (4.7), we have

$$\left| \frac{dw_s}{w_s} \right| > \left| \frac{dw_s}{w_s} \cdot \frac{ah+h_s(1-a)}{ah+h_s(1-a)+\tau/w_s} \right|.$$

In accord with the expected direction of labour force adjustment given this inequality, we find that

$$\frac{\partial \bar{h}}{\partial w_s} = \frac{-\alpha \varepsilon \tau}{(1-\alpha-\varepsilon)(aw_s)^2} < 0 \qquad (5.6)$$

with $\partial \bar{N}/\partial w_s > 0$. A rise in standard wages leads to workers–hours substitution.

The result in (5.6) is, perhaps, somewhat counter-intuitive. It is easier to understand when explained in a slightly different way. Falls in both w_s and a, *ceteris paribus*, increase the ratio of quasi-fixed labour costs to variable labour costs. The cost minimizing firm has an incentive, therefore, to reduce these per-worker costs per unit of labour input by a greater utilization of fewer workers. A more detailed discussion of the role of the ratio of quasi-fixed to variable labour costs within labour demand theory can be found in Ehrenberg (1971) and Hart (1984a).

It follows immediately from (5.1) that

$$\frac{\partial \bar{h}}{\partial \tau} > 0 \qquad (5.7)$$

and so $\partial \bar{N}/\partial \tau < 0$. Recalling that $\tau = (Z+T)/P$, we have the well-known result that a rise in the ratio of fixed to variable labour costs, following the logic discussed above, induces the firm to substitute more labour utilization for a smaller workforce. Finally, since set-up costs are simply another form of fixed labour cost, we find $\partial \bar{h}/s > 0$ and $\partial \bar{N}/\partial s < 0$, as expected.

5.2(b) Other Results from Cost Minimization and Profit Maximization

Most of the studies cited at the beginning of Section 5.2 have illustrated comparative static outcomes in the cost minimiz-

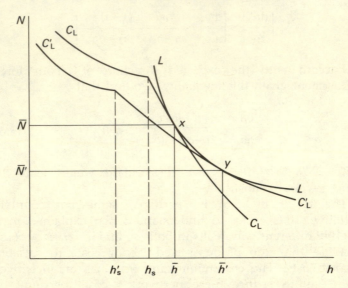

Figure 5.1 Reactions of equilibrium workers and hours to a change in standard hours in a firm employing equilibrium overtime hours.

ing model by means of a diagrammatical representation (but see, in particular, Brechling, 1965; Rosen, 1968; Calmfors and Hoel, 1985). This approach is adopted here, in Figures 5.1 and 5.2, both to illustrate further the important results in (5.3) and (5.4) as well as to consider new possibilities.

The isoquant locus with respect to the labour services function (4.4) is represented by the curve LL in Figures 5.1 and 5.2. Its slope is given by

$$\frac{\mathrm{d}N}{\mathrm{d}h} = -\frac{\partial L}{\partial h}\bigg/\frac{\partial L}{\partial N} = \frac{-\varepsilon N}{(1-\alpha)(h-s)} < 0. \qquad (5.8)$$

Differentiating (5.8) with respect to h gives $\mathrm{d}(\mathrm{d}N/\mathrm{d}h)/\mathrm{d}h > 0$ and so the locus is convex to the origin.

The isocost curve, $C_L C_L$ is kinked at h_s. For $h > h_s$, costs are $C_L = [P\{w_s h_s + a w_s(h-h_s)\}+Z+T]N$ and the slope of the isocost curve is given by

98

$$\frac{dN}{dh} = \frac{-aw_sN}{w_sh_s+aw_s(h-h_s)+\tau} < 0. \qquad (5.9)$$

For $h \leq h_s$, costs are $C_L = (Pw_sh+Z+T)N$ and the slope of the isocost curve is given by

$$\frac{dN}{dh} = \frac{-w_sN}{w_sh+\tau} < 0. \qquad (5.10)$$

Both segments of C_LC_L are convex to the origin since, for (5.9) and (5.10), $d(dN/dh)/dh > 0$.

In Figure 5.1, we reconsider the effect of a reduction in h_s when $\bar{h} > h_s$. Initially, the firm is in equilibrium at point x, the tangent of LL and C_LC_L, employing $\bar{N}$, $\bar{h}$ combination of manhours. (Note that both LL and C_LC_L are convex and the necessary condition to achieve a tangency point is given by (5.2).) Suppose that standard hours are reduced from h_s to

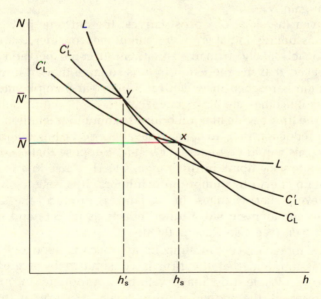

Figure 5.2 Reactions in equilibrium workers and hours to a change in standard hours in a firm employing standard hours.

h_s'; this produces the isocost curve $C_L'C_L'$. In the overtime region, the slope of the isocost 'flattens' which can be shown by differentiating (5.9) with respect to h_s to obtain

$$\partial\left(\frac{dN}{dh}\right)\Big/\partial h_s = \frac{aw_s{}^2N(1-a)}{\{w_sh_s+aw_s(h-h_s)+\tau\}^2} < 0.$$

The new equilibrium is at point y which represents a rise in equilibrium hours, $\bar{h}'-\bar{h}$, and a fall in employment, $\bar{N}-\bar{N}'$; this is in accord with previous results. Substitution effects between $\bar{h}$ and $\bar{N}$ for changes in a, w_s, τ and s can be illustrated in like manner.

Consider now a firm that is in initial equilibrium at the corner solution $\bar{h} = h_s$; this is shown in Figure 5.2 at point x, the kink of C_LC_L. Again, h_s is reduced to h_s'. On the assumption that the firm moves from one corner solution to another, employment must *increase* since the working time reduction is binding. This is shown in Figure 5.2 by a change in equilibrium from x to y, representing an employment gain $\bar{N}'-\bar{N}$.

Given the slope of isocost curves, the outcome in Figure 5.2, assuming initial $\bar{h} = h_s$, might be considered to be reasonably likely in many situations. It could be the case, however, that the reduction in h_s is so large that an interior solution is reached in which case $\bar{h} > h_s'$ and employment–hours outcomes are ambiguous.

If the firm begins in equilibrium at an interior solution $\bar{h} < h_s$, a reduction in h_s to h_s' may have *no* effect on equilibrium $\bar{h}$, $\bar{N}$; this would be the case if $\bar{h} < h_s'$. Suppose that the firm is free to vary hours in this range. Clearly a rise in a would have no effect on equilibrium manhours. It is easy to show, however, that changes in w_s and τ produce the *same* hours–employment substitution effects as in (5.6) and (5.7) for $\bar{h} > h_s$ (see also Rosen, 1968).

The foregoing cost minimizing approach is dependent on the assumption that the firm is constrained by aggregate demand. While this may well be appropriate in many instances at the individual firm level, it is clearly more difficult, for example, to justify output exogeneity at an industry- or economy-wide level of aggregation. In the equivalent profit maximizing model, the firm – or group of firms – can choose the quantities of output to be sold at prevailing costs and prices. It will suffice to report briefly on the main results for a profit maximizing firm. More technical detail can be found in FitzRoy and Hart (1985) and Calmfors and Hoel (1985).

Setting output price to unity by choice of units, the equivalent problem in this case can be expressed

$$\max_{h,N} \pi = F\{g(h)N^{1-\alpha}\} - C_L$$

where π is profit. An important point to note is that, for employment, there are *both* substitution *and* scale effects of changes in standard hours and factor prices. If $\bar{h} > h_s$, the negative employment response to a reduction in h_s in (5.4) still holds; indeed, the $\bar{h}$–N substitution effect is *reinforced* by a negative scale effect due to an increase in unit labour costs. Given that hours are scale-independent, $\partial \bar{h}/\partial h_s < 0$ in (5.3) also holds given the substitution effect. For the same reason, the hours' partial derivatives with respect to factor prices also hold. There is some ambiguity with respect to employment, however. For example, while an increase in the overtime premium a produces an $\bar{N}$–$\bar{h}$ substitution effect in the cost minimizing model, this is *offset* in the profit maximizing case by a negative scale effect.

One final point is worth noting with respect to profit maximization. If initial equilibrium is at a corner solution (such as point x in Figure 5.2), a reduction in h_s produces an ambiguous employment response. The possible positive employment effect comparable to the cost minimizing case (that is, through moving from one corner solution to another) is offset by a countervailing negative scale effect.

In general, therefore, the employment responses to a reduction in standard hours are *less* favourable under profit maximization compared to cost minimization while the hours responses are the same. These latter outcomes are conditional, as elsewhere, on the choice of labour services function.

101

5.3 Variations on the Conventional Model Theme

Before widening the analysis, it is first important to explore the sensitivity of the key results in (5.3) and (5.4) – that is, the changes in equilibrium factor inputs given an exogenous change in standard hours – to variations in the specifications of $g(h)$ and $w(h)$ in the cost minimizing problems set out in (4.5). We will also keep in mind the results concerning factor price changes in (5.5), (5.6) and (5.7).

There are two major types of model variation that should be considered. The first concerns the separation of standard and overtime hours within the labour services function itself. As we consider below, there are both theoretical and policy grounds for examining the productive performance of each of the two component parts of average hours. The second consideration concerns the shape of the premium hours schedule in the wages function. Typically, in the 'conventional' model, overtime is assumed to be paid at some simple constant multiple of the standard wage rate. It can be argued that, under certain circumstances, a continuous schedule is more appropriate and so we report on the implications of such a specification for our key results. It has also been implicit in the discussion so far that, when $h > h_s$, all employees work overtime hours. In reality, individuals may be free to choose whether or not they work overtime and it is clearly of interest to examine the effects of allowing variations in the proportion of employees working overtime. Fortunately, the implications of both types of modifications to the conventional model have been thoroughly investigated in two interesting papers by Santamäki (1983, 1984). In large part, therefore, it will suffice for our purposes to outline the main features of that author's findings.

5.3(a) The Separation of Standard and Overtime Hours in the Production Function

Hart and McGregor (1987) give three arguments to support production function specifications that allow explicitly for the separation of standard and overtime hours. The first is closely related to an argument typically advanced in support of the general form of labour services function in (4.3). This latter expression is designed partly with the view of accommodating differences in the degree of fixity between workers and hours; for example, the transactions costs of changing the stock of workers may be higher than those associated with varying the rate of labour utilization. Similarly, although with a greater emphasis on institutional constraints, the firm is not likely to be in a position to adjust standard hours as easily as overtime hours. Standard hours are often set by national-level collective bargaining agreements, or even by direct government legislation, and the short-run barriers to change, even beyond the individual firm level, can be quite formidable. In certain situations, firms may have the option of temporarily employing hours below the standard through the use of short-time working. As we have seen in Chapter 2, however, the typical constraints to be faced here, certainly compared to changing overtime schedules, are often quite considerable. In summary, since standard hours are relatively fixed in the short run while the firm has more scope to vary overtime schedules, it might not be surprising to find different product elasticities with respect to each of these components of total working hours.

In the second place, the nature of the firm's productive use of standard hours may differ from that of overtime hours. Standard hours are purchased at the cheapest per unit labour cost and they determine the length of the most important periods of continuous economic activity. Business trading hours, length of production runs and machine running times are all in an important way determined by this standard. In certain circumstances, the firm may attempt to maximize the productive efficiency of standard hours by gearing its overtime activity to play the supporting role of ensuring efficient standard time working. For example, overtime may be employed in the evening in order to set up machines and to organize work for the next day's production. In similar fashion, maintenance work may also be an overtime activity. Further, where absenteeism or sickness threaten normal time production, existing workers may be asked to fill the gaps by working rest days or other leisure periods in return for compensation at premium rates. Survey evidence for Ireland and the UK supports the notion that some overtime is used to facilitate efficient normal time working (University College, Galway, 1980). It should be emphasized that it is not the intention here necessarily to play down the traditional view of the demand for overtime, such as to meet rush orders. Rather, it is merely suggested that activity such as set-up time may not only lead to differences in product elasticities with respect to workers and hours but also with respect to overtime and standard time hours.

A third reason for separation concerns a more general, policy-oriented, argument. As we have already mentioned with respect to the working time debate in Chapter 1, a central issue for trade unions, employers' associations and governments concerns the relative economic effects of changes in standard hours as *opposed to* overtime hours. This interest not only involves differences in factor prices, but also focuses on the relative productivity of the two hours' components. One interest group may argue that, in many instances, overtime hours are largely unproductive and merely serve as part of the agreed-upon, or guaranteed, wage compensation structure. Another group might contend that overtime is an essential part of the production process – to accommodate rush orders or unforeseen production bottlenecks – and that their elimination may have serious implications for labour productivity. Estimates from production functions that incorporate average *total* hours are not directly helpful towards discriminating between the relative strengths of these positions. Accordingly, even in the absence of strong *a priori* theoretical motivation, it is worth separating standard and overtime hours in order to test for their separate contributions to productivity.

Two particular forms of hours' function that distinguish between standard and overtime hours are given in (4.12) and (4.13). Both are analysed in some detail in Santamäki (1984) within the context of a cost minimizing framework similar to that set out in Section 4.4. Here, a sketch is given of the main comparative static results using one of the functions and then Santamäki's findings for the other case are merely reported.

We retain the piecewise wage formulation in (4.9) but, for the case $\bar{h} > h_s$, now introduce the multiplicative version of $g(h)$ given by (4.13), that is

$$g(h) = h_s^{\gamma_1}(h/h_s)^{\gamma_2}.$$

Substituting these $w(h)$ and $g(h)$ expressions into (4.8) and reorganizing gives:

$$\bar{h} = \frac{\gamma_2(\tau-(a-1)w_s h_s)}{aw_s(1-\alpha-\gamma_2)}. \quad (5.11)$$

The second-order necessary condition for cost minimization given the labour services function $L = N^{1-\alpha}h_s^{\gamma_1}(h/h_s)^{\gamma_2}$ requires that $(1-\alpha) > \gamma_2$ (see appendix to this chapter). Assuming that this requirement is satisfied, it is clear from (5.11) that we obtain $\partial\bar{h}/\partial h_s < 0$ as in the conventional model.

The induced changes in $\bar{N}$ and $\bar{h}$ given a change in h_s under this formulation depend purely on the relative rises in their marginal costs. As shown by Santamäki (see also the appendix), the ratio of marginal products remains unaltered, or $d(L_h/L_N)/dh_s = 0$. Unlike the conventional model, the sign of $\partial\bar{N}/\partial h_s$ is ambiguous. Replacing h by its equilibrium value $\bar{h}$ in the labour services function, we obtain

$$\text{sign}\,\frac{\partial\bar{N}}{\partial h_s} = \text{sign}\left(\frac{\gamma_2-\gamma_1}{\gamma_1} - \eta_{\bar{h}h_s}\right) \quad (5.12)$$

where $\eta_{\bar{h}h_s}$ is the elasticity of equilibrium hours with respect to standard hours. A favourable employment outcome given a cut in h_s, or $\partial\bar{N}/\partial h_s < 0$, is obtained if $|\eta_{\bar{h}h_s}| < (\gamma_1-\gamma_2)/\gamma_2$. Empirical evidence on this is reviewed in the next chapter.

An alternative hours function that separates standard and overtime hours is given in (4.12) as

$$g(h) = \{h_s+k(h-h_s)\}^\beta, \quad 0 < k \le 1, \quad \beta < 1$$

where, as discussed in Section 4.4 the 'k' term is interpreted by Santamäki as the proportion of employees who choose to work overtime. (Thus, $h-h_s > 0$ occurs only for workers who are willing to work overtime.)

Again, this expression can be combined with the piecewise version of $w(h)$ in (4.9) and substituted into (4.8) to obtain an expression for equilibrium hours $\bar{h}$ and so on. With respect to the complete labour services function, the new second-order condition (see appendix) requires that $(1-\alpha) > \beta$. As shown by Santamäki (1984), three main results hold. First, given $0 < k < 1$ we obtain, as before, $\partial\bar{h}/\partial h_s < 0$. The reduction in h_s, with constant β and k, reduces average total working hours thereby increasing the marginal productivity of hours relative to the marginal productivity of workers. Second, despite the rise in equilibrium hours for a fall in standard hours, average total hours decrease. Third, it follows that the equilibrium workforce must increase, or $\partial\bar{N}/\partial h_s < 0$, in order to meet the given production requirement. Therefore, this particular formulation of $g(h)$ would appear to give unequivocally the result that standard hours reductions produce *positive* employment effects. Empirical estimation of this form of hours function is also reported on in the next chapter.

5.3(b) An Alternative Specification of the Overtime Premium Schedule

So far we have made the convenient assumption, represented by expression (4.9), that overtime is paid at some constant rate of the standard wage (that is, aw_s with $a > 1$). Not only is the assumption mathematically convenient but it may also be argued that it represents a reasonably accurate description of actual practice in many firms. Overtime is often scheduled at a given premium rate for working in excess of normal hours during weekdays, then at a somewhat higher rate for Saturday working, and finally, at the highest rate for Sunday and holiday working. Now, it may well be the case that, for a given firm, the fluctuation in product demand is such that, in the short run at any rate, overtime working beyond weekdays is not envisaged.

Indeed, the firm may expressly attempt to avoid weekend working since operating beyond the normal workweek may well involve significant extra fixed costs associated with extending set-up work as well as providing, for example, canteen facilities and security services.

On the other hand, it is easy to imagine two main types of situations in which a simple piecewise assumption concerning overtime payments is inadequate. In the first place, with large fluctuations in product demand, the firm's plans over future labour services requirements may well include the full potential range of overtime scheduling; that is, it faces all possible gradations of premium rates as weekly overtime hours are extended. Secondly, given the possibility of a range of premium rates, overtime working may be unevenly distributed among the firm's workforce. Some workers may work only weekdays, others weekdays and Saturdays, and so on. Of course, this argument becomes even more persuasive given an aggregation of individual firm-level data to, say, an industrial level of analysis. In both types of cases, the piecewise function in (4.9) ceases adequately to describe labour compensation at the intensive margin and the continuous function represented by (4.10) becomes a more apt representation.

It seems to be intuitively obvious that, in general, introducing a schedule whereby overtime pay increases with overtime hours will produce ambiguity over the direction of hours–worker substitution given a cut in standard hours. With the piecewise schedule in (4.9), a reduction in h_s produces $h-N$ substitution because the marginal cost of workers is increased while overtime can be purchased at an assumed constant marginal rate. In the new situation, the firm would experience a marginal cost increase if it tries to replace reduced manhours by *either* new workers *or* more overtime hours per worker. The direction of substitution would seem to depend on the relative 'steepness' of the cost increases at the extensive and intensive margins.

Such intuition is largely supported in work by Santamäki (1983) who has investigated the main comparative static outcomes of the conventional model when the piecewise function in (4.9) is replaced by its continuous counterpart in

(4.10). Combining the general form of the labour services function, $L = F(h,N)$ in (4.3), with (4.10), she finds that sign $(\partial \bar{h}/\partial h_s)$ no longer holds unambiguously as in (5.3). In fact, it is shown that $\partial \bar{h}/\partial h_s < 0$, as in (5.3), only holds in the special case of a rise in h_s increasing the premium wage function such that $\psi_{hh_s} \cdot (h - h_s) > \psi_h - \psi_{h_s}$. The partials $\partial \bar{h}/\partial w_s$ and $\partial \bar{h}/\partial \tau$, on the other hand, retain their unambiguous signs as in (5.6) and (5.7).

If assumptions are made concerning the specific form of the continuous overtime schedule, Santamäki goes on to show that the result, $\partial \bar{h}/\partial h_s > 0$ can hold unambiguously: this is the *opposite* of the conventional outcome in (5.3). One such schedule that produces this result is given by substituting the explicit function

$$\psi(h, h_s) = b(h/h_s), \quad b > 1$$

into (4.10).

5.4 Capital and Capacity Utilization

Capital input, like its labour equivalent, has both a stock and a utilization component. The latter is closely related to hours of work per period but, as indicated earlier, it may not be proxied adequately by measured hours if these deviate significantly from effective hours worked. We have seen that capacity utilization may be introduced through a depreciation term, as in (4.16), or more directly through a capital services function. If variation in the numbers of shifts worked is allowed for then, irrespective of hours of work, this kind of capacity utilization should be incorporated, as in (4.20). In this section, some consequences for the foregoing comparative static models of introducing the stock of capital and its rate of utilization are discussed.

We begin with the assumptions that measured hours are equal to effective hours and that there is a single-shift system. Also, for simplicity, fixed and variable payroll taxes, T and P respectively, are ignored. We assume that, in equilibrium, the firm employs overtime working and, retaining the spirit of the last subsection, we assume that rises in average hours continuously increase premium payments, or $a'(h) > 0$. Using a simple Cobb–Douglas production function, a modified version of (4.19) may be written

$$J(h,N,K,\lambda) = ZN+w_sh_sN+aw_s\ (h-h_s)N+cK$$
$$+\lambda(Q-Ah^{\beta_1}N^{\beta_2}K^{\beta_3}). \tag{5.13}$$

First-order conditions for cost minimization are $J_x = 0$, for $x = h,N,K,\lambda$, which yield respectively

$$aw_s(1+v)N-\lambda\beta_1(Q/h) = 0 \tag{5.14a}$$

$$Z+w_sh_s+aw_s(h-h_s)-\lambda\beta_2(Q/N) = 0 \tag{5.14b}$$

$$c-\lambda\beta_3(Q/K) = 0 \tag{5.14c}$$

$$Q-Ah^{\beta_1}N^{\beta_2}K^{\beta_3} = 0 \tag{5.14d}$$

where v is the premium wage rate elasticity with respect to hours or

$$v = (h/a)(da/dh) > 0.$$

Dividing (5.14b) by (5.14a) gives the equilibrium hours equation

$$\bar{h} = \left[\frac{Z}{aw_s}+h_s\left(\frac{w_s}{aw_s}-1\right)\right]\bigg/\left[\left(\frac{\beta_2}{\beta_1}\right)(1+v)-1\right] \tag{5.15}$$

and so assuming, as earlier, $\beta_2 > \beta_1$, and given $v > 0$ and $a > 1$, we again obtain $\partial\bar{h}/\partial h_s < 0$. Further, after somewhat tedious algebra (for a brief outline, see appendix) we obtain, as expected, $\partial\bar{N}/\partial h_s > 0$, and also $\partial\bar{K}/\partial h_s < 0$.

That the results in (5.3) and (5.4) are again obtained after the inclusion of K is not surprising. A fall in h_s now raises the price of N relative to *both* h and K and the addition of the second factor merely provides the firm with an alternative

109

means of substituting out of the stock of employment. As for the partials with respect to the other factor prices, the results are much in line with those of Nadiri and Rosen (1969) who analyse the full comparative static problem in (4.19), although without separating the two components of h. It will suffice to report these briefly. From (5.15), $\partial \bar{h}/\partial a < 0$, $\partial \bar{h}/\partial w_s < 0$ and $\partial \bar{h}/\partial Z > 0$ as in (5.5), (5.6) and (5.7), respectively. Also, equilibrium hours are independent of cross-price effects. As can be seen in the appendix, while $\partial \bar{N}/\partial Z < 0$ holds as expected, $\partial \bar{N}/\partial a$ and $\partial \bar{N}/\partial w_s$ cannot be signed: a rise in direct wages increases hours per worker relative workers *but also* raises the price of labour relative to capital thereby producing two conflicting substitution effects. Finally, as expected, $\partial \bar{N}/\partial c > 0$ and $\partial \bar{K}/\partial c < 0$: an increase in the user cost of capital produces worker–capital substitution.

Adding capacity utilization as a separate factor component of the Cobb–Douglas production function in (5.13) does not alter the main results obtained above. This variable is of more interest from an empirical viewpoint, and within a more dynamic structure, and so comment will be left until the next chapter. Of somewhat more interest for comparative static analysis is the incorporation of the capital services term, $K_s = h \cdot S \cdot K$ in (4.20), into the production function.

Calmfors and Hoel (1985) study the effect of changing the number of shifts per period, S, in both a cost minimizing and a profit maximizing model. The role of K_s within the latter type of model is also studied by Brunstad and Holm (1984). For example, in the cost minimizing case, Calmfors and Hoel incorporate a production function of the form

$$Q = Q \left[g(h), \, N, \, K_s \right]$$

in the problem in (5.10). For simplicity, they also set $h - h_s = 0$ and treat hours as an exogenous variable. To compensate workers for the inconvenience of working shifts, the wage is postulated to be an increasing function of the number of shifts.

Under this formulation, the number of shifts can be

regarded as playing a similar role to overtime in that it provides a factor utilization alternative to changing the stock of workers in the face of a working time reduction. It turns out that, as with the employment–overtime dichotomy, hours reductions are more likely to increase utilization (number of shifts) and reduce employment. One reason for this is that there is likely to be an improvement in the marginal productivity of shiftwork relative to that of employment. This result is not certain, however, and a more decisive finding is that an hours reduction improves the marginal factor cost of shifts relative to that of employment.

While this particular extension of the conventional model is an interesting direction to explore, it does not have the same potential impact as the equivalent one-shift model with endogenous overtime. In the first place, the results concerning relative marginal costs given hours reductions hinge on the fact that workers have associated fixed costs (Z) while the costs of changing the number of shifts are purely variable. This latter assumption is almost certainly false. Very large changes in working time, such as from a one- to a two-shift system, are likely to involve fixed costs associated with maintaining a satisfactory working environment. Canteen facilities, security provision and cleaning services, for example, may have to be provided at a cost which is independent of the specific length of the second shift. Secondly, unlike the case with overtime, it is not at all clear that significant numbers of firms are in a position (due to technical and labour supply constraints, see Chapter 11), to vary the number of shifts as a short- or medium-term response to hours and factor price changes.

5.5 Wage Setting by Firms

Returning to the discussion of possible labour market repercussions of a cut in the standard workweek in Sections 3.1 and 3.2 – as related to Figures 3.1 and 3.2 – an external market increase in the demand for available manhours (vacancies) relative to the supply of available manhours (unemployment) may stimulate an increase in quits. The only positive action so far attributed to firms as a means of stemming job loss in the face of a tightening of the labour market has been to reduce layoffs. It is perhaps unreasonable to suppose, however, that firms will not also take action directly to reduce quit rates. In particular, it is likely that firms with a relatively highly skilled labour force would show a tendency to protect their share of human capital investments by minimizing potential quits. An unanticipated rise in quits results in two types of labour cost increase. In the first place, the amortization period and, therefore, the expected return of specific investments are reduced. Secondly, the firm will need to replace at least some of the quits by new hires and this involves extra once-over increases in search, hiring and training expenditures.

Even in the absence of a stimulus to quits through a tightening of the labour market, an hours reduction by itself might induce a firm with significant fixed labour investments to reduce its existing quit rate. The idea is illustrated by means of the simplest possible case. Suppose that a given firm only works standard hours with no opportunity for overtime working. Further, assume that its only significant specific investment involves once-over training expenditure for a given proportion of its workforce. If there is no other slack time, its effective total working hours per period are equal to standard hours *adjusted for non-productive training time* multiplied by the size of the workforce. Of course, the training time itself has to be adjusted by the quit rate, as in (4.1), since a higher rate of quits, provided they are matched by new hires, involves a greater amount of total working time devoted to training. *The proportion of productive to total working time will be reduced if there is a cut in the standard workweek.* The firm's *effective wage rate*, that is, the rate per effective hour worked, would increase and there would be an incentive for the firm to attempt to offset this by reducing the rate of quits.

In summary, the firm may wish to take action concerning anticipated quit threats in the face of a tightening of the labour market following a reduction in standard hours. This latter possibility has been illustrated in Chapter 3 in relation to Figure 3.1 where no allowance is made for variations at the intensive margin. (See the discussion concerning Figure

5.2 for an equivalent example.) An increase in quits would increase its effective wage rate by increasing the per-period proportion of total manhours devoted to training rather than to productive activity. Even in the absence of increased excess demand, however, the working time reduction *per se* may induce the firm to reduce its quits below current rates in order to offset the increase in the effective wage rate through a loss of productive hours.

In order to take account of a firm's reactions to an increase in potential quit threats and/or the cost of quits, assumptions concerning wage setting behaviour need to be modified. In most of our discussion so far, we have assumed that the firm is a price-taker. A more suitable assumption in the present circumstances may be to treat individual firms as wage setters. In the spirit of Salop (1973, 1979), Schlicht (1978) and Okun (1981), each firm sets the wage rate in the awareness that the quit rate is a negative function of the firm's own wage rate relative to its competitors and a positive function of labour market tightness. Therefore, we introduce the quit function

$$q = q\left(\frac{w}{w^*}, \varrho\right) \qquad (5.16)$$

where q is the quit rate and $q_1 < 0$, $q_{11} > 0$, $q_2 > 0$, $q_{12} < 0$ and where w is the firm's wage, w^* is the comparable wage of other firms and ϱ is the probability of finding a job.

In an extremely interesting piece of work, Hoel and Vale (1985) have investigated the effects of an exogenous cut in working time on a representative wage setting and profit maximizing firm in a competitive market when the quit function in (5.16) is incorporated into its total labour cost expression. In order to capture explicitly the difference between actual and productive working time, the authors postulate a specific version of the labour services function in (4.3) that takes the form

$$L = (h - z_t q)N$$

where z_t is the exogenously determined hourly training time per new employee. Note that L is now defined as *effective* labour input.

113

The authors also treat h as exogenous, thereby abstracting from problems concerning the distinction between standard and overtime hours. The wage rate w is the only variable labour cost. The firm's profit, π, is thus given by

$$\pi = F(L,K) - whN - cK.$$

Quasi-fixed costs do not appear in the above representation of π since L is effective labour input and training (which is not directly productive) is the only fixed expenditure. Substituting for q and h from above allows profit to be written alternatively as

$$\pi = F(L,K) - \hat{w}(w,w^*,h,\varrho)L - cK \qquad (5.17)$$

where

$$\hat{w}(w,w^*,h,\varrho) = \frac{wh}{h - z_t q(w/w^*,\varrho)} \qquad (5.18)$$

is the effective wage rate.

In a two-stage optimization procedure, the firm first chooses w such that $\hat{w}$ is equal to $\hat{w}^0$, the minimum effective wage rate. It is easy to show that $\partial\hat{w}^0/\partial w^*$, $\partial\hat{w}^0/\partial\varrho > 0$, that is a rise in the competitive wage or the probability of finding a job increases the equilibrium effective wage. On the other hand, $\partial\hat{w}^0/\partial h < 0$, that is a cut in working hours increases the equilibrium effective wage. The second stage involves inserting $\hat{w} = \hat{w}^0$ into the profits function (5.17) and finding a maximum solution. Holding capital fixed in the short run, L is given by

$$F_L(L,\bar{K}) = \hat{w}^0(w^*,h,\varrho)$$

from which an explicit demand function for the total workforce N in terms of z_t, w^*, ϱ, (optimal) w, $\hat{w}_0$ and $\bar{K}$ can be derived.

Finally, the unemployment rate u_r is linked directly to ϱ such that

$$u_r \equiv \frac{M-N}{M} = u_r(\varrho), \quad u_r' < 0 \qquad (5.19)$$

where M is the supply of workers. Deriving (5.18) using u_r instead of ϱ and, on the assumption of identical firms, letting $(w/w^*) = 1$ in equilibrium, (5.18) provides an expression of unemployment as a unique function of working time. From this it is easy to show that (assuming M in (5.19) is fixed)

$$\frac{du_r}{dh} < 0$$

or a working time reduction will increase the rate of unemployment. The authors show that this result holds for the long run (where K is variable) as well as the short run. Also, they show that $dL/dh > 0$, or that effective labour input is reduced with a cut in working time, again in both the long and short run.

Hoel and Vale go on to derive a number of short and long run comparative static results concerning changes in working time as well as to consider dynamic aspects of their labour market system. We will not concern ourselves with these other aspects here except to note that they find that the effect of a change in h on the hourly wage rate w is ambiguous, although a reduction in h is more likely to lead to a fall in w the higher is the initial unemployment rate and the more significant are training costs.

The crux of the matter for our purposes, however, is the finding of a negative (positive) relationship between unemployment (effective labour input) and working time. The introduction of wage setting with the objective of minimizing costly quits would seem to have quite radical implications for our earlier model constructs. For example, in the models outlined in Section 5.2, the restriction $w(h) = w_s h$ (that is, there is no overtime) can lead to the outcome that a reduction in h increases employment. In the wage setting model here, given M is fixed in (5.19), the prediction is more firmly against a favourable employment response.

115

There are two main limitations with the Hoel and Vale approach. In the first place, if overtime working is allowed for, the firm has an alternative means of counteracting upward movements in the effective wage as expressed in (5.18). It can compare the cost of increasing effective hours through rises in overtime working with that of reducing quits through an increase in the standard wage rate. An exogenous reduction in working time, *ceteris paribus*, reduces the amortization period of fixed investments thereby increasing the effective discount rate. Periodic fixed labour costs increase and, as we have seen, there is an incentive for the firm to increase the utilization of labour on the intensive margin. This in turn offsets the initial rise in fixed costs – or the effective wage rate in the Hoel and Vale model – and thereby may well serve to reduce the sensitivity of quits.

The second point relates to Hoel and Vale's treatment of training costs. In particular, the authors fail to recognize that specific investments are *shared* investments. There is a well-known literature (for example, Hashimoto, 1975, 1981; Okun, 1981) that convincingly argues that it is in firm's and worker's mutual interest to share the quasi-rent accruing from specific training and other investments. Indeed, there may be advantages to both sides in drawing up quasi-long-term employment contracts, perhaps consisting of a seniority-based payment structure, with large elements of deferred compensation. In part, firms and workers attempt to insure against unanticipated quits and layoffs by designing a compensation formula that favours longevity within the firm. For their part, workers who make significant contributions to their own specific investments receive assurances concerning long-term employment prospects. In many instances, it seems far more reasonable to assume that the firm would seek to minimize quits through such a long-term contractual commitment rather than face the riskier process of reacting to quit threats as and when they occur through changes in the spot wage.

116

5.6 Wage Setting by Unions

Recent developments in the theory of trade unions (for example, Oswald, 1982; Sampson, 1983) have provided a conceptual framework for studying the effect of working time reductions in the situation where a large monopoly union controls wages while leaving it to the employer to set employment levels. This provides a stark contrast to the firm wage setting model just described. The adaptation of the theory of the trade union in order to analyse the effects of a cut in the workweek has recently been undertaken, in two reasonably similar approaches, by Calmfors (1985) and Hoel (1984) (see also Booth and Schiantarelli, 1985).

In the analysis of Calmfors (1985), utility of an individual union member is given by

$$V = V(C,h) \qquad (5.20)$$

where C is consumption and $V_C > 0$, $V_h < 0$, $V_{CC} < 0$, $V_{hh} < 0$ and $V_{Ch} \gtreqless 0$. If the worker is employed, he/she receives wage income wh, where w is the hourly wage. If M is the total number of economically active workers and N is the number of workers in employment then, assuming a random probability of selection, N/M and $(M-N)/M$ are the respective probabilities of being employed and unemployed. Assuming all income is spent this allows the expected utility of a given worker to be written

$$U(w,h) = \frac{N}{M}V(wh,h) + \frac{M-N}{M}\bar{V} \qquad (5.21)$$

where $\bar{V}$ represents the utility of an unemployed worker. If one imagines that there is only one trade union that organizes all M and that all workers are alike then the problem can be stated as one whereby the trade union maximizes expected utility per member as expressed in (5.21) and, if working time is assumed exogenous, this in turn amounts to choosing w to maximize utility.

117

Firms maximize profits, given by $\pi = H(h,N,K) - whN$, and they treat h and w as exogenously given variables. With K assumed fixed, the implicit demand function for labour is given by

$$N = N(h,w). \tag{5.22}$$

If h changes there is both a direct effect on N and an indirect effect since w will also be changed via the utility function. This can be expressed

$$\frac{dN}{dh} = N_h + N_w \frac{dw}{dh}. \tag{5.23}$$

It can be shown that, in (5.22), $N_w < 0$ but $N_h \gtreqless 0$. In order to concentrate on the union wage setting part of the model, Calmfors *assumes* $N_h < 0$ and proceeds to investigate sign (dw/dh) in (5.23).

Setting $M = 1$ in (5.21) by choice of units, the trade union chooses the wage that satisfies the first-order condition

$$\frac{\partial U}{\partial w} = U_w = hNV_C + N_w (V - \bar{V}) = 0 \tag{5.24}$$

where $U_{ww} < 0$ is assumed in order to satisfy the second-order condition for a maximum. A rise in w increases the consumption and therefore the utility of employed workers – this is given by the term hNV_C in (5.24). It also results in an offsetting fall in utility, however, since the fall in N for a rise in w reduces the utility of those randomly selected as unemployed given the assumption $V > \bar{V}$ – this is represented by the second term and the third expression in (5.24).

In order to examine the effect on w of a cut in working time, Calmfors differentiates (5.24) with respect to w and h to obtain

$$U_{wh}dh + U_{ww}dw = 0$$

or

$$\frac{dw}{dh} = - \frac{U_{wh}}{U_{ww}}. \tag{5.25}$$

Given the assumed second-order condition $U_{ww} < 0$, sign (dw/dh) in (5.25), is determined by sign (U_{wh}). If the latter sign is negative then $dw/dh < 0$. Differentiating (5.24) with respect to h gives

$$U_{wh} = NV_C + hN_hV_C + hNV_{Ch} + hNwV_{CC} + N_{wh}(V - \bar{V}) \\ + N_wV_h + N_wwV_C. \tag{5.26}$$

Given a reduction in h, several of the terms in (5.26) create an incentive to increase w while others serve to depress it. As examples of each influence, consider the *last* two terms. In the first of these (N_wV_h) a fall in h increases the leisure time of the employed, thereby producing a utility gain. There is thus an incentive to lower the wage because of a greater utility loss of becoming unemployed. In the second (N_wwV_C), the loss in wage income (wh) due to a fall in h acts to reduce the utility loss of an employed worker becoming unemployed. Accordingly, the negative effects on utility of increasing the wage (and thereby increasing the probability of unemployment) is reduced. The influence on the wage is, therefore, in the opposite direction.

Of the seven RHS terms in (5.26), Calmfors argues that three will tend to increase w, two will depress w while the remaining two have uncertain effects. Thus, it is impossible to sign dw/dh in (5.25) and, therefore, dN/dh in (5.23). Even if it is *assumed* that $dN/dh < 0$ in (5.23) this *may* be more than offset by a reduction in employment due to a net wage increase induced by the effect of the hours reduction on utility.

While using different labour demand and union utility functions, Hoel (1984) adopts the same general union wage setting approach to study the employment effects of workweek reductions. He does, however, provide an important extension by studying the implications of adding an endogenous stock of capital into the analysis. It will

119

suffice to outline briefly the simplest version of Hoel's model since this captures the central point.

In logarithmic form, the labour demand function is given by

$$h + n = k + \alpha - \beta \, (w{-}h), \quad \beta > 0$$

where h, n and k are, respectively, the logarithm of average weekly hours, number of workers and capital stock, and w is the monthly wage. The constant β is the demand elasticity of total labour input. In what follows, it is useful to rewrite the above expression in the form

$$n = \alpha + k + (\beta - 1)h - \beta w. \tag{5.27}$$

The union's utility function, with arguments also in logarithms is given in general form by

$$u = u(n,w,h), \quad u_n > 0, \; u_w > 0, \; u_h < 0. \tag{5.28}$$

As in Calmfors's study, the union chooses the value of w that maximizes (5.28) and, given exogenous h, n is determined through (5.27). An optimum (w,n) combination is shown in Figure 5.3 at point A where the indifference curve I (assuming conditions exist for the 'correct' curvature) is tangential to the demand curve, D: at this point $u_n/u_w = 1/\beta$. The expansion path E denotes the locus of (n, w) combinations for which u_n/u_w is constant for given values of h, assuming n and w are normal goods. We restrict attention to the assumption that u_n/u_w is independent of h (weak separability in the utility function) although Hoel also discusses both positive and negative association between these two variables.

Now, suppose h is reduced. If $\beta < 1$ in (5.27), D shifts outwards to D' and if $\beta > 1$ it shifts inwards to D''. Given the weak separability assumption, the respective new equilibrium points are at A' and A''. In the first case ($\beta < 1$), both n and w rise. The rise in the hourly wage is such that the monthly wage increases despite the fall in h. In the second case, both n and w fall. The monthly wage falls given

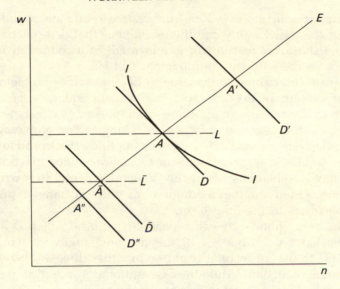

Figure 5.3 Wage and employment reactions to hours changes.

a less-than-offsetting rise in the hourly wage.

In this setting, Hoel introduces a return on capital k with long-run required value R^*. If $R < R^*$ then the capital stock will gradually decline and vice versa for $R > R^*$. The hourly wage rate is negatively related to R and $(w-h)^*$ corresponds to R^*. For given initial hours, let the monthly wage rate corresponding with R^* in Figure 5.3 be at L where L is the long-run labour demand and point A is now defined in terms of long-run equilibrium. As before, suppose h is reduced under the conditions $\beta < 1$ and $d(u_n/u_w)/dh = 0$. The new short-run equilibrium point is again at A' and D' with rises in w and n. But the long-run labour demand moves in the opposite direction, from D to $\bar{D}$, since in order to maintain $(w-h)^* = R^*$, an exogenous fall in h must be accompanied by a fall in w. Therefore, until long-run equilibrium at $\bar{A}$ is achieved, there will be a reduction in the capital stock, given $R < R^*$, which, through (5.27) implies a downward movement of the demand curve from D' to $\bar{D}$ (along E). In the long run, employment is reduced to below the initial equilibrium starting point.

121

The introduction of a long-run desired return on capital, given the stated utility conditions, implies that, irrespective of the short-run reaction of employment to a reduction in hours, in the long run employment will fall.

In an intertemporal treatment of the same problem, incorporating an explicit capital adjustment equation, Hoel finds that while the magnitudes of employment effects are changed, the directions of short- and long-run employment reactions remain unaltered. Further, he finds that replacing wage levels by wage changes in the union utility function produces ambiguous short-run unemployment, increased unemployment in the medium term and unchanged unemployment in the long term.

The assumption of weak separability, $d(u_n/u_w)/dh = 0$, is somewhat bold. Changes in the marginal utility of work relative to that of income could go in either direction given an hours reduction. While the assumption $d(u_n/u_w)/dh > 0$ is shown by Hoel generally to reinforce the employment effects described above, the opposite condition, $d(u_n/u_w)/dh < 0$, tends to increase the chances of more favourable employment outcomes.

5.7   Some Wider Considerations

It is emphasized in Chapter 1 that the primary purpose of this book is to concentrate on the employment (and unemployment) effects of working time changes within a labour market perspective. Of course, hours and factor price changes have implications for a wider set of economic relationships, within the macro economy, and these 'outside' influences may feed back into employment thereby serving to modify the foregoing partial labour market outcomes. While no attempt is made formally to integrate such possibilities, it is worthwhile to devote some attention to pinpointing relevant issues.

There are two obvious areas of interest within a broader economic setting. The first concerns an indirect influence on unemployment via the Phillips curve as hours changes have potential impacts on wage changes. In the longer term, the response of unemployment to changes in working time may not only be influenced by relative factor price changes but also by the underlying shape of the long-run relationship between wage changes and unemployment rates. A second issue concerns the possibility that relative labour cost changes due to hours reductions may have balance-of-payments implications and corrective action by monetary and fiscal authorities may again influence the longer-term employment–unemployment position.

Some authors (for example, Drèze and Modigliani, 1981; Strøm, 1983; Hoel, 1983, 1986) have considered working time reductions on a broader basis. In general, it is probably fair to conclude that, under most model specifications, the addition of inflation, balance-of-trade and other influences outside the immediate labour market, *tends to leave unchanged or to worsen* the employment–unemployment position obtained from the more narrowly based models.

Perhaps the best means of illustrating this is to select a simple demand specification that is particularly biased towards the result that a cut in standard hours has a beneficial effect on employment. A good example is that of the simple labour services function, $L = f(hN)$ – that is labour services are a function of manhours where hours are exogenous – within the context of the sort of labour demand framework presented in Section 5.2 and elsewhere. Strøm (1983) has used this labour services specification (as well as a more realistic alternative – see below) within a simple two-sector comparative static macroeconomic model in order to analyse the effects of a cut in hours. The two sectors are for a traded and a non-traded good. The price of the traded good is determined on the world market (the exchange rate multiplied by the world market price for the traded good) while the non-traded good's price is endogenously determined to a level compatible with the (instantaneous) clearance of the domestic market. Labour market disequilibrium is allowed for in that wages are rigid in the short run, adjusting slowly in the longer term in order to clear the market. In line with these wage assumptions, the adopted Phillips curve is one in which wage changes react to the level of unemployment and the expected rate of inflation. At each time period, the expected rate of inflation is equated with the rate of change of the price of tradables after adjusting for the change over time in the exchange rate. In the long run, no deviation is allowed between actual and expected outcomes and, in most of Strøm's examples, the assumption of a vertical long-run Phillips curve is imposed. Profit maximizing behaviour is assumed for producers while households maximize utility.

Against this background, Strøm considers the effect of an exogenous reduction in hours given the simple 'manhours' labour services function. The immediate short-run effect is for real wages and employment to increase. Assuming a constant labour supply, unemployment also decreases and this, via the Phillips curve, increases the rate of inflation thereby eroding the real wage gain. Given the assumptions concerning price determination, real wage rates in the tradable good's sector rise proportionately more than in the sector for the non-tradable good with the effect of switching consumption towards the former. In turn, the change in relative prices between the two sectors produces a deficit in the balance of payments. The rise in real wages has the gradual effect of reducing employment and (with fixed labour supply) the unemployment rate rises back to a level determined by the rate of world inflation and the long-run Phillips curve.

One of several modifications to this story introduced by Strøm is to postulate that the total supply of workers is a decreasing function of the length of the workday: for example, shorter working hours might enable more female labour to enter the labour force (see Chapter 7). This generates a short-run *increase* in the rate of unemployment and thus a fall in the inflation rate given normal Phillips curve assumptions. The resulting short-run fall in the domestic inflation rate relative to the world market inflation rate is gradually eliminated and employment in both sectors remains at a higher level than the initial starting values until the long-run Phillips curve is reached.

As a major alternative, Strøm considers the same type of scenario under the assumption that the labour services function is given by $L = hf(N)$. For this functional form, the

124

profit maximizing number of employees is independent of the length of working hours as long as the wage rate remains the same. In the short run, it is reasonable to regard the wage rate and the price of tradables as given. Therefore, there is no change in the number of workers employed in this sector. On the other hand, Strøm argues that it is probable, although not certain, that the wage rate in the non-tradable sector will increase thereby decreasing the number of workers here. Overall, this means that, assuming a fixed labour supply, the unemployment rate will increase with a resulting downward shift in domestic inflation. The balance-of-payments position is also predicted to improve. The main difference resulting from the change in labour services function (with the labour supply fixed) is that even the short-run unemployment rate might increase given that the exogenous fall in hours has a bigger negative impact on production. The longer term, as before, is controlled by the long-run Phillips curve and the world market inflation rate. Indeed, in all of Strøm's permutations and combinations of possibilities (he also considers upward wage revisions given hours cuts and continual government efforts to maintain a trade balance) the long-run unemployment position is always controlled in this way.

In a somewhat similar analysis, Hoel (1983) (see also Hoel, 1986) also adopts the above two basic types of labour services function. He argues, however, that it is perhaps more suitable to think of the simpler manhours' function as applying to the production of the non-tradable good while the more realistic function is a feature of the tradable good. Using this mixture, Hoel finds that the net effect of a reduction in working hours is to produce an increase in employment in the tradable good's sector which may be offset to a greater or lesser degree by a fall in employment in the non-tradable good's sector. The overall net impact on unemployment is uncertain.

Needless to say, government intervention to correct balance-of-payments deficits through influencing exchange rates or to counteract inflationary increases through monetary and/or fiscal policy might alter shorter-run and medium-run employment and unemployment trade-offs. However, these types of models seem to indicate that, at best, the government may serve merely to modify outcomes rather than radically to alter the net directions of change.

5.8 Summary

In their concluding comments, Hoel and Vale (1985) declare that a government action to reduce the length of the workweek 'is a very uncertain policy for reducing unemployment, as the effects might very well be the opposite of what is intended'. This view may reasonably be regarded as a fair approximation to the conclusions of *all* the analyses under discussion in this chapter. Indeed, if anything, the bulk of the work tends to go beyond merely expressing caution over outcomes and far more towards suggesting that, in likelihood, hours reductions may well impair employment–unemployment prospects.

The simple cost minimizing model of labour demand in Section 5.2(a) – incorporating a linear piecewise wage schedule, positive overtime working and a fixed capital stock – set the scene by providing unequivocal employment predictions. A reduction in standard hours increases the price of the labour stock input relative to labour utilization resulting in an increase in average premium hours combined with fewer workers. This is not the most gloomy employment prediction, however, since (as reported in Section 5.2(b)) in the equivalent profit maximization model the same substitution effect is obtained *as well as* a negative employment scale effect. If firms work the maximum permitted standard hours with no overtime, the other commonly observed case, then the standard hours reduction will produce a positive employment response for those firms that continue to work to the new standard hours limit. Otherwise, the outcome is uncertain.

Returning to the cost minimizing results with endogenous overtime, Santamäki's work, outlined in Sections 5.3(a) and 5.3(b) has shown that the workers–hours substitution predictions are sensitive both to the specification of the labour services and to the wage functions. Separating standard from overtime hours in the former and allowing for continuous increases in compensation with rising overtime in the latter provide generally ambiguous outcomes. It should be stressed that, even under these alternative specifications, it is by no means certain that the employment repercussions of cuts in the workweek would be favourable.

Further, as outlined in Section 5.4, the introduction of a variable capital stock does not improve the employment prospects since it provides an alternative substitution outlet given a relative worker cost increase due to the standard hours reduction. Nor does the ability of some firms to vary capacity utilization through changes in the number of shifts seem to help the employment position.

To this point, it appears that the only hope for any real optimism for employment gains arising from hours reduction is for those firms that work *only* (the full amount of) standard hours. Leaving aside problems associated with variations in capital and shiftworking as well as scale effects, such firms have no endogenous component of labour input that can be substituted for the loss of hours. As we have seen from two different types of modelling approach, however, this hope may be misplaced. In the first place, in models where the firm sets an efficient wage (see Section 5.5) there is a tendency for unfavourable employment and unemployment outcomes (in both the short and long term) to a workweek reduction even *when only exogenous hours are assumed*. Secondly, in union wage setting models (see Section 5.6), again incorporating only exogenous hours, the net employment effects are particularly difficult to decipher.

The introduction of long-run considerations, such as an optimum capital stock or Phillips curve trade-offs or balance-of-payments equilibria (see Sections 5.6 and 5.7), tends if anything to reinforce arguments to the effect that cuts in the workweek are either neutral or detrimental to employment and unemployment.

It should be noted that, at this stage, we have purposely avoided embracing 'other assumptions' that may serve to modify the direction of these labour market outcomes. The most obvious areas of additional interest are usefully brought together by Drèze and Modigliani (1981) when they state that 'shorter hours make sense, if and only if they permit some form of cost absorption, like productivity gains, wage restraint or selective subsidies'. We have discussed the general problem of productivity in Section 4.5 concluding that, *a priori*, no solid view of net effects can be derived from the theory. Outcomes can move in either direction and, accordingly, this topic is dealt with in the following empirically orientated chapter. The possibility of granting subsidies in order to encourage beneficial employment effects to accompany the introduction of shorter workweeks has been an issue of growing interest to several governments in recent years and this topic is discussed in some analytical detail in Chapter 9. Finally, in the chapter on collective bargaining (Chapter 11), the issue of wage reactions to working hours reductions is examined.

Appendix

In the following, an outline solution is given to several of the results shown in this chapter.

Section 5.2(a)

The cost minimization problem in (4.5), incorporating the general labour services function in (4.3) is

$$J = C_L + \lambda\{L - F(h,N)\}.$$

The determinant of the bordered Hessian matrix for this problem is given by

$$\Delta = \lambda\{F_h^2 F_{NN} + F_N^2 F_{hh} + (2F_h^2 F_N)/N - 2F_h F_N F_{Nh}\} \quad \text{(A5.1)}$$

where $\Delta < 0$ is assumed in order to satisfy the second-order conditions for minimization.

In Section 5.2(a), $F(h,N) = (h-s)^\varepsilon N^{1-\alpha}$ and so

$$F_h = \varepsilon F/(h-s) \quad \text{(A5.2a)}$$

$$F_N = \{(1-\alpha)F\}/N \qquad\qquad (A5.2b)$$

$$F_{hN} = F_{Nh} = \{(1-\alpha)\varepsilon F\}/\{(h-s)N\} \qquad\qquad (A5.2c)$$

$$F_{hh} = \{\varepsilon F(\varepsilon-1)\}/\{(h-s)^2\} \qquad\qquad (A5.2d)$$

$$F_{NN} = \{-\alpha F(1-\alpha)\}/N^2 \qquad\qquad (A5.2e)$$

$$\lambda = \{Paw_s N(h-s)\}/\varepsilon F \qquad\qquad (A5.2f)$$

where the last expression is found after substituting $w(h)$ and $g(h)$ used in Section 5.2(a) (see beginning of section) into (4.6a) and solving for λ. Substituting (A5.2a)–(A5.2f) into (A5.1) and simplifying produces the second-order condition shown in (5.2).

Section 5.3(a)

The first labour services function of this subsection is given by $L = N^{1-\alpha}h_s{}^{\gamma_1}(h/h_s)^{\gamma_2}$ and, on finding the equivalent derivatives and value of λ as in (A5.2a)–(A5.2f) and substituting into (A5.1), it is easy to show that the new second order condition requires that

$$\frac{(1-\alpha)Paw_s L^2}{Nh}\{\gamma_2-(1-\alpha)\} < 0$$

or $(1-\alpha) > \gamma_2$ as stated in the main text. Note that

$$L_{Nh_s} = \{(\gamma_1-\gamma_2)L_N\}/h_s \qquad\qquad (A5.3)$$

$$L_{hh_s} = \{(\gamma_1-\gamma_2)L_h\}/h_s \; . \qquad\qquad (A5.4)$$

Then, the fact that the value of the ratio of the marginal products of the labour inputs for a change in h_s is given by

$$d\left(\frac{L_h}{L_N}\right) \Big/ dh_s = \frac{L_N L_{hh_s} - L_h L_{Nh_s}}{(L_N)^2} = 0 \qquad (A5.5)$$

is easily checked on substituting (A5.3) and (A5.4) into (A5.5).

Finally, the second labour services function discussed in this subsection is $L = N^{1-\alpha}\{h_s + k(h-h_s)\}^\beta$. Using the same procedure as above, the second-order condition for this case is given by

$$\frac{(1-\alpha)Paw_s L^2 k}{N\{h_s + k(h-h_s)\}}\{\beta - (1-\alpha)\} < 0.$$

Section 5.4

Dividing (5.14c) by (5.14a) and substituting for $\bar{h}$ from (5.15) gives an equation for equilibrium capital stock in terms of equilibrium workers,

$$\bar{K} = \bar{N} \text{ (expression 5.15) } (\frac{\beta_2}{\beta_1})\,\frac{aw_s(1-v)}{c} \qquad (A5.6)$$

Ignoring purely constant expressions, an equation for $\bar{N}$ in terms of exogenous variables can now be derived after substituting for $\bar{h}$ from (5.15) and $\bar{K}$ from (A5.6) in (5.14d). This can be written

$$\bar{N} = Q^{\frac{1}{\psi}} \left[\frac{Z}{aw_s} + h_s\left(\frac{w_s}{aw_s} - 1\right) \right]^{\frac{-(\beta_1+\beta_3)}{\psi}} [aw_s(1+v)]^{\frac{-\beta_3}{\psi}} c^{\frac{\beta_3}{\psi}}$$
$$(A5.7)$$

where $\psi = \beta_2 + \beta_3$. Substituting (A5.7) back into (A5.6) allows us to identify equilibrium capital stock such that

$$\bar{K} = Q^{\frac{1}{\psi}} \left[\frac{Z}{aw_s} + h_s\left(\frac{w_s}{aw_s} - 1\right) \right]^{\frac{\beta_2+\beta_1}{\psi}} [aw_s(1+v)]^{\frac{\beta_2}{\psi}} c^{\frac{-\beta_2}{\psi}}$$
$$(A5.8)$$

Assuming $\beta_2 > \beta_1$ and given $v > 1$ and $a > 1$, the various partial derivatives with respect to $\bar{N}$ and $\bar{K}$ are then easily derived from (A5.7) and (A5.8).

CHAPTER SIX

Employment Effects of Workweek Reductions: Empirical Evidence

6.1 Introduction

This chapter reviews the empirical literature that is most closely related to the theory presented in the foregoing two chapters. An emphasis is given to examining the effects of changes in standard hours on employment and average total hours but also consideration is given to relative factor price, scale and hours productivity influences on these labour inputs.

Of the three types of theoretical approach outlined in Chapter 5 – labour demand models, efficiency wage models and union bargaining models – the first has promoted by far the greatest empirical interest. One main reason for this is that such models incorporate overtime working as an endogenous input and so square with the fact that many firms do indeed employ overtime working over long-run periods of time. In the literature to date, most versions of the other types of model treat hours of work as a purely exogenously determined input.

In Section 6.2 attention is concentrated on empirical findings from labour demand studies: all studies referred to are based on quite aggregative data. As the focal point of this discussion, some results from a pooled cross-section/time-series labour demand model of the FRG manufacturing sector are presented in Section 6.2(a). The model has been designed to match, as closely as possible, the main

131

comparative static framework of the demand analysis in Section 5.2. The results are then compared, in Section 6.2(b), with those derived from earlier, reasonably comparable, studies undertaken with respect to other economies.

One potential criticism of labour demand work is that it has been tested, in the main, using somewhat aggregative – economy-wide or industry-level – data while the underlying theory is at the firm level. Accordingly, in Section 6.3, some very recent micro evidence is presented.

In Section 4.5, and elsewhere, it has been explained why the employment effects of changes in hourly productivity are difficult to predict theoretically. Of course, this does not preclude the possibility that, empirically, such changes may have an important bearing on employment outcomes given hours reductions. Section 6.4 is devoted to discussing this issue, again reviewing the most important aspects of the relevant literature. The section is in two parts. In Section 6.4(a), evidence is assessed on the returns to hours of work in production and labour demand functions that separate workers and average total hours. Results from production functions, in which scheduled and overtime hours are separated, are then reported on briefly in Section 6.4(b).

Perhaps the most important aspect of the subject of hours productivity concerns the issue of labour hoarding. Some further reflections on this topic, in the light of empirical findings, are presented in Section 6.5.

Much interest on the empirical side has been given to simulating the effects of hours reductions within large-scale econometric models. A review of the main findings is undertaken in Section 6.6. Also in this section an attempt is made to account for differences in the findings between the macro and the more partial model systems.

Finally, in Section 6.7, we draw together the main conclusions.

6.2 Labour Demand Studies

There have been several well-known attempts to test empirically the 'conventional' labour demand model outlined in Sections 4.4 and 5.2. Two main types of approach to estimation are adopted. In the first, the comparative static theoretical framework is retained by testing the model on cross-sectional data. The study by Ehrenberg (1971) is perhaps the best-known example in this respect. In the second, time-series data are used, in which case it becomes necessary to take account of the type of interrelated dynamic factor adjustment reviewed in Section 4.7. The earliest example of this approach, by Brechling (1965), has retained a strong influence on the literature.

There are arguments for and against each approach. Cross-section studies allow for the measurement of the effects of hours and factor prices without contamination due to possible inadequate measurement of adjustment lags and cyclical influences. On the other hand, since standard or scheduled hours may vary little among cross-section units – especially if measured with respect to workweeks – and only change significantly at fairly long time-intervals (as, for example, in the UK metalworking industry in Figure 2.4) then relatively long time-series data may be needed in order to 'pick up' the most significant variations.

A third possibility, that allows both types of advantage to be achieved, is to pool cross-section and time-series data with relatively long time-intervals between each set of cross-section observations. By 'relatively long' is meant that sufficient time is allowed for full labour market adjustment to have taken place. A simple version of such a pooled model is estimated and presented below for FRG manufacturing industry. The results of this exercise are then compared with those existing (separate) cross-section or time-series models estimated for a number of OECD countries.

6.2(a) A Model of FRG Manufacturing Industries, 1969–1981

The equilibrium labour demand functions that arise from the cost minimizing and profit maximizing problems set out in Sections 4.4 and 5.2 may be written implicitly

$$\bar{h} = \bar{h} \;(h_s, \; z/v, \; q, \; \mathbf{X})$$
$$\phantom{\bar{h} = \bar{h} \;(h_s, \;} (?) \, (+) \, (+) \qquad\qquad (6.1)$$

$$\bar{N} = \bar{N} \;(h_s, \; z/v, \; q, \; Q, \; \mathbf{X})$$
$$\phantom{\bar{N} = \bar{N} \;(h_s, \;} (?) \, (-) \, (-) \, (+) \qquad\qquad (6.2)$$

where $\bar{h}$ is equilibrium average total per-period hours per operative, $\bar{N}$ is equilibrium number of operatives, z/v is the ratio of quasi-fixed to variable labour costs, q is quit rate, Q is output and $\mathbf{X}$ is a vector of control variables. The expected signs of the partial derivatives, derived in Section 5.2, are given in parentheses below each variable.

The FRG data do *not* distinguish between firms that employ overtime working and those that work only standard hours. Therefore, given the theory outlined with respect to Figures 5.1 and 5.2, the signs $\partial\bar{h}/\partial h_s$ and $\partial\bar{N}/\partial h_s$ are indeterminate. It would be expected, however, that $\partial\bar{h}/\partial h_s > 0$ since the incidence of overtime in the FRG is relatively small compared to several other European countries. On the basis of results presented by Rehyer *et al.* (1983), it can be estimated that overtime in the FRG between 1970 and 1982 comprised 6.3 per cent of actual hours worked, where actual hours (on an annualized basis) = normal hours + overtime – short-time – sickness – vacation – legal holidays – bad-weather – strikes. The elasticity, $\{(\partial\bar{h}/\partial h_s)\cdot(h_s/\bar{h})\}$, would be expected to lie between 0 and 1 (and near to 1) since a fall in h_s in all firms should be partially offset by an increase in $(h-h_s)$ in firms employing significant levels of overtime.

The selected control variables are

$$\mathbf{X} = (K, \; \text{SICK}, \; \text{FEM}) \qquad\qquad (6.3)$$

where K is capital stock, SICK is sickness payments as a proportion of total labour compensation and FEM is female employees as a proportion of the total labour force.

While recognizing the possible endogeneity of K in the regressions shown below, no attempt is made to specify a separate equation for the capital stock. It may be expected that $\partial\bar{N}/\partial K < 0$ in (6.2) although Brechling (1965, p. 202) argues that, in practice, it is often difficult to interpret the actual role played by K in this type of equation. No *a priori* view is taken with respect to the equivalent partial in (6.1), although $\partial \bar{h}/\partial K = 0$ may seem reasonable give scale-independence arguments. The main point, however, is that it is clearly important to include K in the regressions, especially given the cross-section dimension of the data.

The choice of the variable, SICK, is motivated by Ehrenberg's (1971) study and it is taken to represent a proxy for the absentee rate. In his (overtime) hours equation, Ehrenberg argues that its sign is ambiguous. He states that:

an increase in a certainty absentee rate would tend to increase overtime. On the other hand, under certain conditions, a stochastic absentee rate will lead to less observed overtime than the certainty equivalent. If the 'variability' of the absentee rate is not constant across firms, it is conceivable that the expected positive relationship between absenteeism and overtime per man will be obscured.

(Ehrenberg, 1971, pp. 60–1)

The variable FEM is an essential addition to the hours equation (6.1); clearly, we would expect $\partial \bar{h}/\partial$(FEM) < 0. The variable is retained in the worker equation (6.2), without any *a priori* judgement over its sign.

A fairly comprehensive measure of the ratio z/v was constructed from three-yearly FRG labour cost surveys carried out by the Central Statistical Office (Statistische Bundesamt). Unfortunately (an instrument of) this variable proved unsatisfactory in all regressions. The main reason is that it correlates strongly with the adopted proxy for quits – a wage ratio (see below) – and there is a serious collinearity problem when both variables are included together. In order to ease this problem, z/v was regressed on some simple explanatory variables in order to find a reasonable set of proxies that also reduced significantly the association with quits. The most satisfactory results were obtained for (pooled) log-linear regressions of the general equation (omitting time-series and cross-section subscripts):

$$z/v = f(\text{SKILL, LF}) \quad f_1' > 0, f_2' > 0 \qquad (6.4)$$

where SKILL is employees in highest skill category as a proportion of all employees and LF is large firms (over 1,000 employees) as a proportion of all firms (over 20 employees). The association with SKILL is self-evident. The variable LF is designed to capture the influence of private fringe benefits which contain both large fixity elements and a high proportion of deferred compensation. This form of compensation varies positively with firm size (Woodbury, 1983; Hart, 1984a). Several reasons can be advanced to explain this phenomenon (see Freeman, 1981). Large firms not only spread the fixed costs of implementing and running deferred compensation schemes but also they can expect to pay lower per-worker fees – due to group discounts – for management of the various funds. Further, the longer average tenure in larger firms due to better opportunities for internal mobility provides a greater incentive to instigate this form of compensation.

In the main regressions (see (6.6) and (6.7) below), SKILL and LF replace z/v.

Labour turnover data are unavailable for the industries and time periods included in our sample and so, following the sort of arguments in the efficiency wage model outlined in Section 5.5 (see the discussion with respect to equation (5.16)), the quit rate in the ith industry in period t is approximated by

$$q_{it} = g(w_i/\bar{w})_t, \quad g' < 0 \qquad (6.5)$$

where w_i is the hourly wage rate and $\bar{w} = \sum_i \theta_i w_i$ where $\theta_i = N_i/\sum_i N_i$.

No other reasonable measure of q is available and while (6.5) is a commonly used proxy, it prevents the use (see above) of z/v: relatively high wage firms also have relatively high fixed-to-variable cost ratios.

As mentioned above, K is treated as an endogenous variable. Ehrenberg and Schumann (1982) present arguments – connected with fringe benefit payments – as to why the ratio z/v is an endogenous inclusion in their (overtime) hours equation. For our equations, this problem is essentially avoided by using the proxies SKILL and LF from (6.4). As a precaution, however, instruments were obtained for these latter two variables but this does not alter the results. More obviously, the variable q_{it} in (6.5) should be regarded as being simultaneously determined with h and N following the sort of arguments advanced by Hoel and Vale (1985) that are discussed in detail in Section 5.5.

From the discussions in Sections 4.4 and 5.2, output (Q) is treated as either an exogenous or an endogenous variable depending on cost minimizing or profit maximizing assumptions, respectively. At an industrial (as opposed to a firm) level of aggregation it might be thought that endogeneity is the more appropriate assumption. In the event, regressions were attempted that treated output as either an exogenous or an endogenous variable. While the former proved somewhat better – and these are the ones that are shown below – reasonably similar results are obtained with the endogeneity assumption.

The data consist of $i = 1, \ldots , 25$ FRG manufacturing industries observed at three-yearly intervals, $t = 1, \ldots , 5$. A brief description of the data is given in an appendix to this chapter.

The log-linear estimating equations take the form

$$\ln h_{it} = \alpha_0 + \alpha_1 \ln h_{sit} + \alpha_2 \ln(\text{SKILL})_{it} + \alpha_3 \ln(\text{LF})_{it} + \alpha_4 \ln(w_i/\bar{w})_t$$
$$+ \alpha_5 \ln K_{it} + \alpha_6 \ln(\text{SICK})_{it} + \alpha_7 \ln(\text{FEM})_{it} + v_{it} \qquad (6.6)$$

$$\ln N_{it} = \beta_0 + \beta_1 \ln h_{sit} + \beta_2 \ln(\text{SKILL})_{it} + \beta_3 \ln(\text{LF})_{it} + \beta_4 \ln(w_i/\bar{w})_t$$
$$+ \beta_5 \ln Q_{it} + \beta_6 \ln(\text{SICK})_{it} + \beta_7 \ln(\text{FEM})_{it} + v_{it} \qquad (6.7)$$

Assuming a cross-sectionally correlated and timewise autoregressive error structure, we have

$$E(v_{it}^2) = v_{ii}, \ E(v_{it}v_{jt}) = \sigma_{ij}, \ v_{it} = \varrho_i v_{i,t-1} + u_{it}$$

where

$$u_{it} \sim N(0, \phi_{ii}), \ E(v_{i,t-1}u_{jt}) = 0, \ E(u_{it}u_{jt}) = \phi_{ij}, \ E(u_{it}u_{is}) = 0 \ (t \neq s)$$

and estimation is carried out by the appropriate generalized linear regression (GLS) model (for details, see Kmenta, 1971, pp. 512–14).

As mentioned above, $(w_i/\bar{w})$ and K are treated as endogenous variables in (6.6) and (6.7). Instruments were obtained by running separate pooled regressions of these variables on the current and lagged values of the exogenous variables and the lagged values of the endogenous variables. The estimates, $(\widehat{w_i/\bar{w}})$ and $\hat{K}$, are then incorporated into (6.6) and (6.7) as explanatory variables. Results are presented in Table 6.1 for the period 1969–81. (Data are available for 1966 thereby allowing the one-period lag in first-stage of the instrument equations.)

In relation to the theory, the performance of the scheduled hours variables, h_s, is only partially as expected. It is insignificant in the worker equation – a plausible outcome. A better

Table 6.1
Pooled GLS Results to Equations (6.6) and (6.7):
FRG Manufacturing Industries, 1969–81

Independent variables	Dependent variables	
	h	N
$\ln h_s$	1.209	−0.387
	(17.261)	(0.478)
$\ln(\text{SKILL})$	0.017	−0.351
	(1.025)	(1.835)
$\ln(\text{LF})$	0.006	−0.008
	(1.694)	(0.181)
$\ln(\widehat{w_i/\bar{w}})^*$	−0.177	−0.866
	(2.678)	(0.957)
$\ln Q$	–	0.319
		(4.448)
$\ln K^*$	−0.017	0.109
	(−1.025)	(1.168)
$\ln(\text{SICK})$	−0.000(3)	0.077
	(0.085)	(1.476)
$\ln(\text{FEM})$	−0.313	0.134
	(5.518)	(0.966)

Notes $|t|$ statistics in parentheses; * denote instrumental variables.

insight into its proper role depends on separating overtime from non-overtime industries (see Section 5.2(b)). While this is not possible with these data, some UK results along these lines are reported in Section 6.3. The equivalent hours equation result is contrary to theoretical prediction in that the total hours/standard hours elasticity is in excess of unity (1.21). This suggests that a reduction in scheduled hours results in a more than proportional fall in total hours, achieved through *less* overtime working. It is reported in the following sections that an elasticity less than unity is the common finding in UK studies. It should be noted that, while significant short-time working occurs for one of our time points (1975 – see Table 2.6), the hours data are corrected for short-time and so the high elasticity should not be influenced by variations in the amount of short-time working.

With the exception of *LF* in the worker equation, the proxies for *z/v* in (6.4) perform reasonably satisfactorily. Also, the quit-proxy from (6.5) is a strong addition in the hours equation, with the expected sign, although insignificant in the worker equation. Other clear support for *a priori* expected outcomes is provided by Q in the worker equation and *FEM* in the hours equation. The remaining two variables, K and SICK, are relatively weak: most surprising, perhaps, is the fact that SICK is insignificant in the hours equation.

6.2(b) Related Research

One of the earliest attempts to measure the influence of standard hours on employment was undertaken by Brechling (1965) who estimated an employment demand function using aggregate British manufacturing industry data observed at quarterly intervals, 1950(1) to 1963(4). Brechling employed a restricted version of the interrelated demand system discussed in Section 4.7 since adjustment was represented by including a lagged dependent variable within a single employment equation. In other words, cross-factor adjustment was ignored. Brechling's demand theory was also somewhat less general than the equivalent models here since labour services are defined simply as $L = hN$ (see the discussion in Section 4.4). In the event, this has no serious implication for the relevant part of the theory since Brechling predicts that the employment effects of a change in standard hours are the same as those derived in Section 5.2. In particular, since paid-for hours lie consistently above standard hours throughout Brechling's sample period, the expected result (see Section 5.2(a)) is that a reduction in standard hours would lead, *ceteris paribus*, to a lower level of employment. Contrary to expectations, however, Brechling obtains a significant *negative* coefficient on the standard hours variables in preliminary versions of his regressions.

One explanation offered for this finding is that equilibrium hours may include some guaranteed form of overtime working – often regarded as an important working hours phenomenon in the UK – and so industry may be operating at the 'kink' in its hours schedule since the 'normal' workweek would be expected to include *both* normal and overtime hours. This seems to be highly unlikely since the traditionally very high levels of overtime working in the UK can, at best, be only partially explained by implicit or explicit contractual overtime guarantees. In fact, on further testing, Brechling found that the result with respect to standard hours was not robust. Thus, when he included both standard hours and a capital stock term in the same equation he found that the role and significance of each was severely affected. In the event, he discovered a very strong positive correlation between standard hours and the capital stock.

One of Brechling's worries about the standard hours variable is that, for his sample period, such hours were virtually constant until 1958 and then declined somewhat thereafter. Naturally, a better test would have been to obtain a series with somewhat more variability. In the mid-1960s there were some quite large reductions in standard hours in UK industries (see, for example, Figure 2.4(a)) and when Hart and Sharot (1978) estimated a reasonably similar model on aggregate British manufacturing monthly data, 1961(10) and 1972(9), the standard hours variable is found to be insignificant in the worker equation. In their total hours equation, on the other hand, standard hours enters very significantly with a positive coefficient. Unlike the results in

140

Table 6.1, however, the hours coefficient is less than unity (approximately 0.9) indicating that part of the standard hours' reduction is compensated for by increased overtime working. These results are, at least, consistent with the theory.

Much more detailed UK empirical evidence on the influence of standard weekly hours in a total weekly hours demand equation is provided in a time-series study, 1948–77, of 40 separate industries (Neale and Wilson, 1985). Their estimates of long-run total hours/standard hours elasticities with respect to manual male workers (who are responsible for the bulk of overtime working in the UK) provide a weighted average elasticity across industries of 0.67; a reduction in standard hours results in a reduction in total hours of two-thirds the size. This is considered by the authors to reflect 'the tendency for the proportion of overtime working to increase as negotiated hours have fallen'. Reasonably similar elasticities are also obtained when all workers are taken together.

By contrast, Ehrenberg (1971) estimates an hours equation using cross-section data based on 2-digit US manufacturing industries. He concentrates specifically on average overtime working, his dependent variable, although several of the explanatory variables are the same as those in equations (6.6) and (6.7). Apart from a measure of standard hours, he includes a fixed-to-variable labour cost ratio, a wage ratio to represent the quit rate and the ratio of paid sick leave to total hours worked in order to proxy absenteeism. While the wage variables perform relatively well in relation to theoretical predictions (as in the results in Table 6.1), the standard hours variable displays decidedly mixed results and more often than not its sign is (contrary to expectations) significantly positive. The measurement of standard hours takes the form of a rather crude dummy variable with a value of one if the 'scheduled weekly hours' are greater than or equal to 40 and zero otherwise. The main explanation offered by Ehrenberg for the positive sign is that those industries that scheduled 40 or more hours per week may also be industries with high 'disequilibrium' overtime and so a spurious positive correlation may have resulted.

141

A somewhat more elaborate study has been undertaken more recently by de Regt (1984). The firm is assumed to be a long-run cost minimizer and its long-run production function allows for substitution between capital and labour services. Given relative factor prices, the firm selects an optimal capital intensity. Adjustment impediments prevent the firm from attaining optimal intensity in the short run and so de Regt differentiates between long-run and short-run production functions, linking the two through a partial adjustment mechanism. In the short run, capital and labour are treated as complementary inputs; for instance, in a recession employment falls below 'capacity employment' and the utilized capital stock falls below the available capital stock. De Regt incorporates a partial adjustment response in the short-run labour input to capture the likelihood of labour hoarding. The key exercise for our purposes is an attempt to estimate the elasticities of capacity employment with respect to shorter working time. Estimates are made under the assumptions of either a fixed capital stock or a stock that is adjusted to keep production capacity constant. (A similar type of differentiation is made in several large-scale econometric models that are used to investigate the employment effects of hours reductions – see Section 6.6.) Under a fixed capital stock, the working time reduction is found to have no effect. If capacity output is assumed to be given, on the other hand, the elasticity of capacity employment with respect to working time is found to be in the region of minus 1. These latter estimates are extremely weakly determined, however, and great caution should be exercised over the working time results in this study.

In summary, the employment–hours outcomes from these somewhat aggregate studies with respect to standard hours changes are *very* inconclusive. The effect of standard hours reductions on employment is found *either* to be insignificant (a result not inconsistent with the theory) *or* negative (contrary to the theory). With respect to the effect of standard hours reductions on overtime hours or total hours, the evidence is also very mixed. In the FRG analysis in Section 6.2(a) and in Ehrenberg's 1971 study, the results do not support the theory while the UK work provides a far more consistent set of results.

Perhaps the fundamental message behind the results, however, is that the micro theory should be tested with far more disaggregated data.

6.3 Micro Evidence

It is clearly preferable to test the labour demand theory in Chapter 5 using firm or (better) establishment-level data. This section reports the findings of two very recent studies undertaken with respect to establishment-level data within the UK. In general, their findings with respect to changes in working time give much better support to the underlying theory than the work reported in the previous section.

The first study consisted of a detailed questionnaire-type survey, undertaken in November 1981, of 218 establishments in industries that introduced shorter working hours through national agreements during the same year. The establishments were in the engineering, pharmaceutical, printing and construction industries. An examination of the first segment of Table 2.4, which covers a part of the relevant industries, reveals that a drop in standard hours took place at this time. The second survey, carried out in 1982/3, was a follow-up investigation. An attempt was made to quantify the *ex post* effects of shorter hours through examining production and accounting data from the establishments involved. The work is reported in White (1983) and White and Ghobadian (1984). The surveys are useful not only because they examine the workers–hours reactions to a cut in the standard workweek but also because they pay close attention to the impact of changes in labour productivity on these variables. It should be added that they refer to a period (1981/2) when there was output stability/slight growth in the industries in question. It is worth quoting a number of the main findings:

(i) There is no evidence . . . that reduction in working time leads to increased employment. This is mainly

143

because hourly productivity tends to increase to compensate for the reduction in working hours.

(ii) In some firms the response to shorter working time appeared to reduce employment as a means of obtaining some of the productivity increases needed to compensate for the reduction in working time.

(iii) Simple productivity improvements were still very common, for example the elimination of tea breaks, although the incidence of more complex changes in production methods are also found.

(iv) There was some evidence that overtime hours started to grow but it is unclear whether this was entirely due to the introduction of shorter hours.

(v) The survey found that shorter hours did not lead to lower wage settlements.

(vi) On balance, shorter hours led to higher labour costs, because the increases in productivity did not fully offset the reduction in working hours and because of additional overtime.

(White, 1983, p. 436)

The purpose of the second follow-up study was to allow time to elapse (between 6 and 9 months) in order for the effects of productivity changes to work through to employment and hours variables. It is not clear that the process had fully matured during this time but at least the indications were that the productivity offsets were not strong enough to result in employment increases. (See the discussion in Section 4.5.)

The issue of productivity impacts on hours changes is examined more closely in the following two sections and, here, we concentrate on the narrower finding in this survey that workweek reductions were associated with zero or negative employment effects and, possibly, increases in overtime working. This, of course, is very much in line with the predictions in the model outlined in Section 5.2(a).

The second study was designed to test equations of the form (6.1) and (6.2) using very detailed cross-sectional data on 52 enterprises in the UK metalworking industry. The data are based on results of a plant-level survey conducted in 1984/5 (Wilson, 1985). The data were obtained for a random sample of 52 enterprises engaged in metalworking (UK Standard Industrial Classification 310–70) with a size range of the establishments between 50 and 3,000 employees. The interview schedule consisted of nine main sections. The first asked for basic factual information about each enterprise. Further sections asked for details of the product, prevailing market conditions and market structure, production methods, the nature of the production process and technology. Detailed information on the composition of the labour force, turnover, training and working practices were obtained from personnel records. This also included information on unionization and collective bargaining arrangements, pay and incentives schemes, wage and non-wage labour costs and all key variables included in the labour demand equations (6.1) and (6.2). The data were obtained for five separate years for the period 1978–82.

Hart and Wilson (1986) report detailed results to equations of the form in (6.1) and (6.2), although a much more elaborate set of control variables are included. Reasonably strong support is obtained for the predicted signs of these equations. Here, however, comments are limited to a selection of estimates with respect to 'scheduled' hours, h_s. This latter variable refers to average *annual* hours actually worked minus annual overtime hours. Of the 52 enterprises, 43 worked some overtime in one or more years of the study: these are classified as 'overtime enterprises'. Cross-section estimates were obtained for each of the five separate years and the coefficients proved to be quite stable over the whole period. In Table 6.2, coefficient estimates of h_s are shown for 1980; the comparable results for other years are very similar. In order to differentiate between overtime and non-overtime enterprises, pooled cross-section/time-series estimates for the entire period were obtained by the same GLS technique reported in Section 6.2(a); pooling is necessary since the latter group of enterprises contained only nine annual observations.

For all enterprises (that is, the first row in Table 6.2), the estimated h_s elasticity is less than unity in the h-equation. A fall in scheduled hours produces a less than proportional fall

Table 6.2
Coefficient Estimates of h_s for 52 Enterprises
in UK Metalworking Industry, 1980

Sample/Date (estimation method)	Dependent variables h	$(h-h_s)$	N
All enterprises/1980 (OLS/TOBIT)	0.76 (10.02)*	−7.71† (2.48)	0.46 (0.65)
Overtime enterprises/ 1978–82 (Pooled GLS)	0.80 (29.95)	–	0.41 (1.96)
Non-overtime enterprises/ 1978–82 (Pooled GLS)	–	–	−0.59 (1.37)

* $|t|$ ratios
† TOBIT estimate
Source: Hart and Wilson, 1986

in total hours with magnitudes similar to those obtained by Neale and Wilson (1985) in their time-series estimation (see Section 6.2(b)). As a direct test of whether the shortfall in total hours is matched by an equivalent gain in overtime working, the same equation was estimated, replacing h by $(h-h_s)$. (A TOBIT estimator was used given $(h-h_s) = 0$ for some enterprises.) The equivalent estimated elasticity is −7.7. In 1980, the average value of h across all enterprises is 1850 hours per year, and the average for h_s is 1750. If h_s is reduced, say, by 175 hours (that is, 10 per cent), then h reduces by 141 hours (that is, $1850\left[\left(\frac{1575}{1750}\right)^{0.754}-1\right]$. The shortfall is $175-141 = 34$ hours. From the theory in section 5.2(b) (see Figure 5.2), we would expect the average non-overtime enterprise to make up for this deficiency by increasing its workforce. For the average overtime enterprise, we would expect a workforce reduction accompanied by a more-than-offsetting rise in overtime hours. Supporting evidence for such reactions is given in Table 6.2. A 10 per cent reduction in h_s in 1980 would produce an average rise in overtime per worker of 125 hours (that is, $100\left[\left(\frac{1575}{1750}\right)^{-7.71}-1\right]$ in enterprises employing some overtime. In the worker equations (third column), a reduction in h_s in the pooled regressions is predicted to *reduce* employment in the

146

overtime enterprises and *increase* employment in the non-overtime enterprises as expected. Note that, for all enterprises the coefficient on h_s in the N-pooled equation is insignificant, reflecting the opposing reactions between the two enterprise subsets.

One result, however, runs contrary to the basic theory. A fall in h_s produces a fall in h – albeit a less than proportional fall – in the overtime enterprises. A number of factors may help to explain this outcome. First, for those enterprises with relatively low incidences of overtime working, there may be little recourse, or opportunity, to effect a substantial substitution between internal and external margins. Secondly, if only a proportion of employees work overtime then, for those that work only standard hours – due perhaps to supply or technical constraints – the enterprise may have less opportunity to extend the utilization of its existing workforce. Thirdly, if actual overtime schedules are better approximated by wage functions such as (4.10), where premium payments are positively related to total hours, then the outcome in Table 6.2 may be compatible with theoretical prediction (see Section 5.3(b)).

6.4 The Productivity of Hours

6.4(a) Production and Labour Demand Functions

So far we have concentrated on the *direction* of the impact of a change in standard hours on employment and total hours. As discussed in Sections 4.5 and 5.3, the hours reductions are also likely to change labour productivity. In turn, this may lead to employment responses, through factor substitution and scale effects, which may serve to modify the results obtained with respect to pure demand influences.

The illustration of possible productivity effects in Section 4.5 is carried out with respect to a simple Cobb–Douglas production function. In fact, the majority of empirical studies on this topic have used a Cobb–Douglas formulation to calculate hours and employment elasticities. In terms of our usual notation, this function may be written simply as

WORKING TIME AND EMPLOYMENT

$$\ln Q = \eta_h \ln h + \eta_N \ln N + \ldots \qquad (6.8)$$

where η_h and η_N are the respective hours and employment elasticities and where, depending on particular specifications and data constructions, the omitted variables may include the capital stock, technological change and a capacity index, as well as industry and time dummies.

For our purposes, there are two main empirical points of interest. First, whether estimates of η_h reveal decreasing $(0 < \hat{\eta}_h < 1)$ or increasing $(\hat{\eta}_h > 1)$ returns to hours: recall that arguments exist to support either outcome. Secondly, whether or not it is found that $\hat{\eta}_h < \hat{\eta}_N$. As shown in equation (5.2), this latter inequality is required in order to satisfy the second-order condition for cost minimization. (See also the appendix to Chapter 5 where it is shown that it is also a requirement for other, closely related, models.)

The evidence from five studies, relating to four countries, is summarized in Table 6.3. To say the least, no uniform pattern emerges. Three studies find decreasing returns to hours but, among them, all possibilities $\hat{\eta}_h \gtreqless \hat{\eta}_N$ occur! The remaining two studies find markedly increasing returns to hours and, not surprisingly, $\hat{\eta}_h > \hat{\eta}_N$, which contradicts the necessary condition. While the wide variations in the estimates may be due to a large number of influences, a potentially important difference does occur between the studies that find decreasing returns and those that find increasing returns.

The three studies that find decreasing returns incorporate some measure of industry capital utilization into their basic production function. This may be defended on the following grounds. Since all the studies include paid-for, not actual, hours worked then, without some proxy of work intensity, the estimated returns to hours may well be upwardly biased (see Sections 4.2 and 6.6 for more detail, as well as Leslie and Wise, 1980). In fact, Hart and McGregor (1987) in their FRG study show that the result $\hat{\eta}_h < 1$ changes to $\hat{\eta}_h > 1$ when capacity utilization is excluded from their production function. In 'special cases' of his main formulation, Feldstein (1967) also includes capacity utilization variables and two of these – measures of multiple shiftworking and capital stock

148

Table 6.3
Estimates of Hours and Employment Elasticities
from Cobb–Douglas Production Functions

Study	Country	Data*	$\hat{\eta}_h$[†]	$\hat{\eta}_N$[†]
Åberg (1976)	Sweden	cs/ts	0.47–0.60	0.65
Craine (1973)	USA	ts	1.89–1.98	0.68–0.80
Feldstein (1967)	UK	cs	1.10–2.55	0.75–0.90
Hart and McGregor (1987)	FRG	cs/ts	0.81	0.31
Leslie and Wise (1980)	UK	cs/ts	0.64	0.64

*cs = cross-section; ts = time-series; cs/ts = pooled.
† where a range of values is shown, this indicates that no preferred specification is indicated.

growth – do reduce $\hat{\eta}_h$ although it remains greater than unity.

The most convincing evidence with respect to capacity utilization comes from a factor demand rather than a production function analysis. In their interrelated demand functions (for a general outline of this type of system, see Sections 4.6 and 4.7), Nadiri and Rosen (1969) include stock and utilization components of both labour and capital. Using the estimates of their full workers and hours equations – which include lagged values of all components of factor inputs – they derive output elasticities that exhibit both decreasing returns to total labour input (that is, $\hat{\eta}_h + \hat{\eta}_N$) and returns to hours *less* than returns to workers. When they repeat the experiment after excluding capacity utilization from these equations, they find *increasing* returns to total labour input. They conclude:

The reason for large returns to labour estimated from short run employment functions is due to omission of the rate of utilization of capital. These high estimates should not be considered as returns to labour alone, as most writers have done, but are more properly interpreted as short run returns to both labor and capital utilization.

(Nadiri and Rosen, 1969, p. 469)

149

It may also be the case that the removal of possible systematic differences in the length of working hours in firms or industries in the pooled models may have the effect of depressing the hours elasticity towards its 'true' value. In a purely cross-sectional analysis, as in the Feldstein (1967) work, the constant term in the production function is assumed to be the same for each cross-section unit. Suppose, however, that firms with relatively high specific human capital investments work longer per-period hours – for reasons easily inferred from earlier discussion – and also achieve relatively high marginal returns to hours. Then, it might be the case that the constant is positively related to hours, in which case, unless this association is removed, the regression estimate $\hat{\eta}_h$ would be upwardly biased. The Leslie and Wise paper is devoted to investigating this point. On the basis of 28 UK production industries observed at 21 yearly intervals, they obtain a value $\hat{\eta}_h = 1.61$ in the absence of industrial shift dummies and a measure of capacity utilization. When these latter variables are subsequently included, they obtain $\hat{\eta}_h = 0.64$ as reported in Table 6.2.

In all, although evidence on returns to hours is mixed, the studies that have found decreasing returns are perhaps the most convincing to date. Following the discussion in Section 4.5, a 1 per cent reduction in (standard) working hours produces a productivity increase of $(1-\hat{\eta}_h)$ per cent. Accordingly, if $\hat{\eta}_h < 1$ and providing there is a relatively high price elasticity of demand, then such positive productivity effects would be in favour of employment and may serve partially to offset unfavourable factor substitution effects. Of course, this assumes that there are *no* increases in hourly wage costs to compensate workers for reduced hours. (Discussion of this specific complication is left until Chapter 11.)

Brunstad and Holm (1984) simulate the employment effects of a reduction in Norwegian weekly hours from 40 to 37.5 on the basis of a factor demand model. In the simulations they use $\hat{\eta}_h = 1.4$ (that is, in the lower range of the Feldstein estimates) and $\hat{\eta}_h = 0.6$ (that is, the Åberg/ Leslie and Wise estimates). With no offsetting wage compensation, they find a 'trifling' employment increase of 4,000 jobs with the former elasticity and a 'more substantial' increase of 53,000 jobs with the latter. It should be added, however, that these employment calculations are almost certainly too high since no allowance is made for offsetting overtime increases in their model.

6.4(b) Production Functions Incorporating Separate Measures of Standard and Overtime Hours

As shown by Brunstad and Holm in making their above Norwegian calculations, inferences concerning the implications of hours productivity for the employment effects of workweek cuts depend on knowledge of a number of other key parameters. These include the elasticity of substitution between labour and capital, the product elasticity of demand and the product elasticity of capital. Even allowing that reasonable information is available, there remains an intrinsic difficulty over using estimates of hours elasticities based on the sort of work summarized in Table 6.3. In all these aggregate studies, marginal hours of work lie in the overtime region: that is, aggregate average total hours are in excess of standard hours. Invariably, however, the workweek cuts discussed in relation to these elasticities refer solely to standard hours. In order to use these studies to predict the productivity effects of standard workweek reductions, the implicit assumption has to be made that the estimated returns to hours are *the same* at *both* the overtime and standard hours margins. If the amount of overtime working is quite large then, given the sort of $g(h)$ schedule illustrated in Figure 4.1, this assumption appears to be rather bold.

In fact, a number of reasons are presented in Section 5.3(a) that support the need to design production functions that separate the two hours components. To date, little research work has been undertaken in this area although two pieces of evidence suggest that further investigations may prove to be well worth pursuing.

In the first, Tsujimura (1970) attempted to measure the separate standard and overtime hours effects on hourly per-worker productivity using Japanese manufacturing data for the 1960s. A typical result is

151

$$(Y/hN) = ah_s^{-1.71}h_p^{-0.37}(K/N)^{0.96}(h/h_s)^{7.54}$$

where h_s is the standard workweek, h_p is premium or overtime hours, K/N is the capital-to-labour ratio and h/h_s is the actual-to-standard hours ratio taken as a proxy for capacity utilization. Not only are the estimated productivity increases significantly different for the two types of hours reduction but standard hours reductions are predicted to entail much larger productivity impacts than overtime reductions.

As a second indication, Hart and McGregor (1987) incorporate the non-linear hours schedule specified in (4.12) and discussed in Section 5.3(a) into a pooled production function describing 20 FRG manufacturing industries observed over 20 half-yearly time periods, 1968(1)–1978(1). Their function may be written

$$\ln Y_{it} = A + \sum_{j=1}^{3} \alpha_j \ln X_{jit} + \beta \ln(h_s + kh_p)_{it} + u_{it}$$

$$i = 1, \ldots ,20, t = 1, \ldots ,20$$

where the X_js are numbers of workers, capacity utilization and the capital stock, k is taken to represent the productivity of a premium relative to a standard hour and u is a stochastic error term. The 'A' term contains the equation intercept as well as cross-section and time-series 'shift' dummies. Estimation, using an instrumental variable non-linear approach yielded:

	$\hat{\beta}$	$\hat{k}$
Including capacity utilization	0.87	0.02
Excluding capacity utilization	0.99	1.69

Unfortunately, the $\hat{k}$ estimates are very unstable (with very wide standard errors): not surprisingly, overtime hours are strongly positively correlated with capacity utilization and so the 'true' value of k could not be determined on this data set. The values of β, however, are significant and are somewhat larger than the elasticity on total average hours estimated on the same data set (see Table 6.3). This, at least, may indicate that the productivity effects estimated on the basis of average total hours should be treated with some caution.

6.5 More on Labour Hoarding

As discussed in Section 4.3, the use of paid-for hours in empirical work on production functions can give highly misleading estimates of returns to labour services. If such hours contain significant 'hoarded' elements during cyclical downturns, then output may vary more than proportionately to labour input simply because fluctuations in the latter are achieved partially by hoarding and dishoarding. Without correcting for this phenomenon, the estimated returns to labour inputs would not be expected to coincide with those for firms that are 'on' their production functions.

The potential seriousness of this problem has long been recognized and various authors have attempted to differentiate explicitly between effective and paid-for total hours in their work on labour demand and production functions (see, especially, Fair, 1969). A common procedure is to regard the effective production relationship as represented by a fitted trend through the peaks of output per total hours (that is, workers × paid-for hours) with the assumption that, at the peaks, effective and paid-for hours coincide. Then, the labour demand relationships can be 'adjusted' by taking account of the gap between actual and estimated points.

While this type of exercise clearly affects the estimates of returns, there was no *direct* evidence, until recently, that firms do hold labour inputs in excess of requirements during relatively depressed economic conditions. As indicated in Section 4.3, work by Fay and Medoff (1985) strongly suggests that significant hoarding does take place, at least among blue-collar workers in US manufacturing industry. Confirmation of the Fay and Medoff findings within an aggregate macro model of the US economy by Fair (1985 – see also, 1984) would appear to add to the force of the direct evidence (although a great weakness in the Fair methodology is a failure to distinguish between the *separate* returns to workers and hours).

Much more work is needed before the importance of labour hoarding in the present context is firmly established. The evidence so far suggests that those studies cited in Table 6.3 and elsewhere that do indirectly account for excess labour through some measure of capacity utilization provide the more convincing empirical estimates.

6.6   Macroeconometric Models

As pointed out by van Ginneken (1984) there appears to be a marked advantage in studying the employment effects of workweek reductions by simulation on large-scale econometric models. Not only can one study the direct employment effects, a prime concern of the present text, but *also* indirect influences on employment due to inflation, balance of payments, monetary policy, government budget constraints, investment and the level of aggregate demand (see Section 5.7). Van Ginneken himself reviews the results of simulating workweek reductions within seven large-scale European econometric models (two French, two Dutch, and one each from the FRG, Belgium and the UK). Added to this, Whitley and Wilson (1986) have extended the UK literature by studying workweek reductions within a multi-sectoral dynamic model of the economy. Other useful international comparative studies of the performance of such models can be found in Görres (1981, 1984) and Franz (1984).

The structure and performance of the various models, inevitably, display wide variations and it is not the intention here to give a detailed account of model similarities and differences. Rather, we will examine some broad findings and mention possible reasons for large discrepancies in the findings.

The study by van Ginneken is perhaps the most useful for our purposes since it attempts to standardize the results from the models under review by estimating the employment elasticity based on a 1 per cent reduction in the length of the workweek. Further, these elasticities are calculated under the hypothesis that there is no wage compensation for the reduction in hours and the hypothesis that there is *full* wage compensation. Also, for some of the models, the elasticities are presented on the basis of either unchanged or reduced production capacity. If there is full equivalent loss of production capacity then this assumes that a given percentage reduction in weekly hours will be represented as a comparable percentage loss in operating time thereby leading to higher capital costs per unit of production. With no loss of production capacity, it is implicitly assumed that workers accept shiftwork, rotation systems or better work organization so that capacity can be maintained and capital costs do not increase.

From a policy perspective, the results of van Ginneken's estimates are rather encouraging. In only one model – the Vintaf model for the Netherlands (Centraal Plan Bureau, 1979) – are negative employment elasticities found. Moreover, these only occur under the assumption of full wage compensation (with either a capacity reduction or the same capacity). The elasticities are in the range −0.08 to −0.19. At the positive end of the spectrum, employment elasticities in the region of 0.6 to 0.8 are found in the two French models (for more details of both see Oudiz *et al.*, 1979) and the West German model (see Henize, 1981). The UK model of Whitley and Wilson (1986) produces, under the author's preferred specification, an employment elasticity of 0.37. The other UK model, the Treasury model (see Allen, 1980), produces a relatively low elasticity (between 0.05 and 0.28) with modest forecasts for increased employment/reduced unemployment. The Treasury and FRG models also make allowances for changes in productivity resulting from reduced workweeks as well as for offsetting increases in overtime working: however, the assumed responses of these two variables diverge widely between the two models.

In the case of the three models that estimate high employment elasticities – that is, the two French and the FRG model – one should be highly sceptical about the results.

In the case of France, van Ginneken reports that a study undertaken by the National Institute of Statistics and Economic Studies (INSEE – see Marchand *et al.*, 1983 for more details) examined the employment consequences of an actual reduction in the standard workweek which took place in January 1982. The study found that, by September 1982, the hours fall led to between 10,000 and 20,000 new jobs in industry and between 4,000 and 8,000 new jobs in commerce; in the latter case these were mainly part-time jobs. It should be noted that enterprises paid full wage compensation. On a basis of the simulation from one of the French econometric models, the estimated employment increase after one year would amount to 143,000 new jobs – that is five to ten times higher than the INSEE findings. Even on the most favourable explanations of this divergence, van Ginneken cannot reduce the model estimates below 65,000 new jobs.

In the case of the West German estimates, the comparison is necessarily somewhat less direct. Henize (1980, 1981) estimates that between 800,000 and 1,120,000 new jobs would be created in the FRG given a 2-hour reduction in the workweek. The lower estimate stems partly from an assumption that wages are compensated by a productivity increase while the higher figure derives from an assumption that the government gives full wage compensation through reduced taxation. The main reason for this latter result is that the model, like one of the French models, postulates that investment depends solely on anticipated increases in demand (that is, a simple accelerator principle) while other models include profitability, capital utilization and interest rates in their investment functions. The simpler investment specifications almost certainly lead to an overestimation of investment and employment responses. While not directly comparable, the estimates by Henize seem nevertheless at odds with the questionnaire-type studies undertaken for West Germany. For example, Franz (1984) develops estimates obtained by the IFO-Institut (IFO-Institut für Wirtschaftsforschung, 1983) into the percentage of firms that planned to apply given measures as a result of a reduction in the workweek of two hours (within two years) assuming constant nominal incomes. The results are presented for production and administration and are based on a sample of 2,900 firms employing 24 per cent of all employees in these two sectors. By far and away the largest response came under the category 'additional measures of rationalization', which over 80 per cent of firms in both sectors indicated would take place. The next highest category was 'reorganization of shiftwork' with a 47 per cent response in the production and 28 per cent in the administrative sectors. Then came 'more overtime', with 19 per cent and 14 per cent respectively. As far as hiring full-time employees was concerned only 8 per cent of the production sector and 5 per cent of the administration sector indicated such a response. As Franz concludes: 'In the absence of a tremendous bias, these figures confirm . . . that a reduction in working hours at unchanged take-home pay will result in a minor expansion of employment, if any at all' (Franz, 1984, p. 645).

One of the main reasons for the much lower employment forecasts of the UK Treasury model is that it incorporates the interaction of a monetary sector in which interest rates are endogenously determined. (This is also the case with one of the Netherlands models.) If full wage compensation is allowed for, any resulting deficit in balance of payments and the government account would lead to an interest rate and/or exchange rate response and the resulting government action to offset this may produce negative employment repercussions. Whitley and Wilson (1986), while obtaining broadly similar results to the Treasury model, argue that their somewhat higher employment elasticity estimate is due to an overestimate in the Treasury model for the overtime reaction. This is due to the fact that the calculations of overtime in the latter model are estimated on the basis of manual workers who in fact account for most overtime working.

In general, van Ginneken and Whitley and Wilson provide convincing reasons for taking the results of the models with relatively low employment elasticities considerably more seriously than the other models.

Even in the case of models with modest forecasts, however, there is no reason to be other than highly cautious about the results. None of the models, for example, adequately measure differences in factor prices – that is, incorporate appropriate measures of wage and non-wage labour costs (fixed and variable) and full measures of user capital costs (such as in expression (4.17)). They come nowhere near, in other words, to modelling fully the labour market interactions emphasized in Chapters 3, 4 and 5. Indeed, even in the relatively sophisticated models, such as that by Whitley and Wilson (1986), the employment and hours equations are really quantity adjustment equations with no regard to the role of relative factor prices. This omission has two types of problem as far as such work is concerned. In the first place, introducing factor prices into the estimating equations may lead directly to divergences from the existing estimates. In the second place, they are indirectly important when considering changes in employment and unemployment resulting from a working time reduction. New workers, especially those taken from the unemployment register, have to be hired and trained and they may also involve fixed fringe benefit and social security contributions; these quasi-fixed labour costs have to be weighed against cost at the intensive margin associated with changes in shiftworking, improved work reorganization, increased utilization of existing workers, and so on. Almost invariably, the large-scale models fail to make these sorts of calculations.

Another potential defect with macro models, emphasized by Drèze (1985), is that simulations are usually undertaken with respect to estimates derived from long time series data. Yet inferences concerning workweek reductions usually refer to time periods of particularly depressed economic conditions. Drèze concludes:

> Too little is known about the elasticity of employment with respect to weekly hours *in a context of general recession* for these simulations to be reliable. Estimates of production functions where hours and number of employees appear as separate arguments, based on time series data covering the past thirty years, are not apt to measure that elasticity accurately.
>
> (Drèze, 1985, p. 38; emphasis in original)

It should be added that the same types of criticism attach to some of the labour demand models outlined in Section 6.2.

6.7 Concluding Comments

Depending on modelling assumptions, the comparative static theory of Chapter 5 shows that a reduction in standard hours may influence employment in either direction or leave it largely unchanged. Those models that predict that employment may actually fall gain some empirical support from two micro-level studies. At a more aggregate level, the equivalent results from partial equilibrium labour demand studies find little employment effect, one way or the other, resulting from standard hours changes. By contrast, simulation exercises using large-scale macroeconometric models tend to find positive employment responses to reductions in the workweek. Since the theory in Chapter 5 is largely micro-oriented, firm-level studies provide the most convincing tests and so the verdict must lean on the side of pessimism over potential employment responses. Added to this, reasons have been advanced (in Section 6.6) for being particularly sceptical about the more optimistic employment forecasts from some of the macro models.

In the case of standard hours effects on total average hours and/or overtime hours, empirical findings are also mixed. Most of the available data consist of observations on firms that exhibit a large variation in the degree of overtime working as well as on firms that employ no overtime working at all. Using such data in empirical tests, it would be expected from the theory that a reduction in standard hours would lead to a less than proportional reduction in average total hours due to an offsetting increase in overtime working. Estimates from West Germany and the USA tend to reject the theory while UK studies have generally provided strong support. This may be partly explained by the particularly high levels of overtime working in the latter country so that, in the UK, changes in overtime working is a much more feasible response to hours reductions. (Overtime working is also an important part of Japanese total hours and it would be interesting to discover if similar evidence to that of the UK is to be found there.) There is certainly strong reason for believing that the omission of overtime responses may be quite critical in estimation and simulation both with respect to determining the direction of total hours and employment responses as well as in the measurement of productivity impacts of hours reductions.

In line with the above observations, the various studies on hours productivity are no less heterogeneous in their findings. Some researchers have found increasing returns and others decreasing returns to hours. This chapter has come down quite strongly in favour of the latter studies since, in general, they tend to have accommodated the estimation problem, at least to some limited extent, of accounting for variations in the gap between paid-for and effective working hours. Usually, this involves incorporating some measure of capacity utilization within the production function. Recent US work on labour hoarding has provided further support for the appropriateness of this approach. If this view is correct, the evidence from work on productivity of hours would point to the conclusion that reductions in the workweek may well produce increases in productivity that might serve to modify negative or insignificant direct employment responses. Much more work is needed in this area together with further investigations into the separate role of standard and overtime hours within the production function. Two studies are cited, in Section 6.4(b), that suggest that the productivity responses may be quite different between these two components of total hours.

On the basis of the empirical information so far available, there is little reason to modify the general conclusion gained from the survey of theoretical models. Reductions in standard hours as a means of stimulating employment is a highly risky policy strategy.

Data Appendix

Table A6.1

Source and Description of Variables of Regressions in Table 6.1: FRG Manufacturing Industries, 1966–81

Variable	Name	Source	Calculation
Q	Sales	Statistisches Bundesamt, Fachserie D (to 1976) Fachserie 4 (from 1977)	Original values, adjusted for the period 1962–76
N	Number of workers (blue collar)	"	
h_s	Effective average monthly hours of (blue-collar) workers minus average monthly overtime	"	
$w_i/\bar{w}$	Wage ratio	"	Average wage per industry divided by average wage of all industries

continued

Table A.6.1 continued

Variable	Name	Source	Calculation
$h-h_s$	Overtime hours	Statistisches Bundesamt, Fachserie 16, Reihe 2.1	
FEM	Female employees as proportion of total labour force	"	
SKILL	Employees in highest skill category as proportion of all employees	"	Rate of skill-group 1 (of 3 skill-groups) in relation to all skill-groups
z/v	Fixed-to-variable labour cost ratio	Statistisches Bundesamt, Fachserie 16, 'Personal- und Personalnebenkosten'	Ratio of compensation components that are independent of hours worked to components that vary with hours
SICK	Sickness payments as a proportion of total labour compensation	"	
K	Capital stock	RWI, Kapitalbestandsrechnungen	Includes unpublished data
LF	Large firms as proportion of all firms	Statistisches Bundesamt, Fachserie 4	Rate of firms with 1000 and more employees in relation to all firms with more than 20 employees

Table A6.2
List of Industries for Regressions in Table 6.1

FRG code	Industry
22	Mineral oil refining
25	Extraction and manufacture of non-metallic mineral products
27	Iron and steel
28	Production of non-ferrous metals
31	Structural metal products
32	Mechanical engineering
33	Motor vehicle engines
34	Shipbuilding
35	Aerospace
36	Electrical engineering
37	Instrument engineering
38	Tools and finished metal goods
40	Chemicals
51	Fine ceramics
52	Glass and glassware
54	Timber and wood
55	Paper
56	Paper products
57	Printing and publishing
58	Plastics
59	Rubber
62	Leather goods
63	Textiles
64	Clothing
68	Food

CHAPTER SEVEN

Part-time Employment: The Demand and Supply of Workers and Hours

7.1 Introduction

It is quite clear from the descriptive statistics presented in Section 2.3(a) that a general analysis of working time and employment would be incomplete without significant attention devoted to part-time employment. In several major economies part-time employment constitutes a significant proportion of total employment. This largely reflects female employment since in the region of 90 per cent of part-time jobs are undertaken by females. This phenomenon is reflected in the fact that much of the work on part-time employment is subsumed in the extensive literature devoted to the participation decision and the supply of working hours of economically active females.

While the supply-side of the problem has been given considerable attention, demand aspects of part-time employment have been somewhat neglected. One of the aims of this chapter is to rectify the imbalance to some extent by giving a large weight of emphasis to demand-side analysis. In fact, neglect of the demand-side of the subject would seem to be particularly problematic in a climate of long-run, persistent unemployment. It may be the case that, under these conditions, there is an excess supply of part-time hours. If this is combined with some degree of downward rigidity in labour costs, demand may play *the* significant role

164

of determining numbers of part-time workers and the length of their weekly hours. The demand analysis is presented in Section 7.2. Then, in Section 7.3, attention is given to describing a supply-side model which offers a reasonably high degree of compatibility with the main demand issues. No attempt is made to integrate formally the demand and supply aspects of part-time employment into a unified model structure. However, some attention is given, in Section 7.4, to comparing and contrasting the main results from each side with respect to the changes in hours of work, fixed costs, wages and taxes.

7.2 The Demand-side

In this section, a labour demand model which distinguishes between part-time (PT) and full-time (FT) workers is outlined and discussed. A full technical development of the model can be found in FitzRoy and Hart (1986). A special problem for demand modelling, concerned with payroll tax wage ceilings, is then highlighted. Other related, though somewhat more partial, approaches can be found in Owen (1979), Disney and Szyszczak (1984) and Tegle (1985) and some mention is made of the empirical aspects of these publications.

Imagine a firm that can divide its available job slots and weekly hours per slot between PT hours and workers (h and n respectively) and FT hours and workers (H and N respectively). (*The use of small and capital letters in order to distinguish between PT and FT variables is used for presentational convenience in this chapter and in Section 10.3(b) only and should not be confused with labour and price variables elsewhere in the text that refer only to FT workers.*) It is assumed that it has the flexibility to switch at the margin into relatively more or less PT employment according to changes in the relative factor prices relating to the stock and flow dimensions of both types of labour input. Compared to the analyses of the previous chapters, the question of how price changes affect factor allocation is more complicated if only for the reason that we have doubled the elements of labour input.

For reasons of continuity and comparability, it would be

useful to approach the demand analysis of PT working as closely as possible along the lines of the 'conventional' FT demand models discussed in Section 5.2. Accordingly, although emphasis is now switched to profit maximization, an attempt is made to expand on that type of framework. Therefore, a number of necessary ingredients suggest themselves. First, it is important to retain the distinction, for FT workers, between exogenously given standard hours (H_s) and endogenously determined overtime hours ($H-H_s$, $H >$ H_s). Since an important feature of the whole text is to examine quite broadly the question of the employment effects of workweek reductions, this particular subject should certainly be broached within the context of PT working. For example, in the FT demand models in Section 5.2, a cut in H_s, given overtime working, produces an hours–worker substitution response: the reduction in H_s has the effect of increasing the marginal costs of employing a new worker more than proportionately to changing hours per worker. (There are also negative employment scale effects in the profit maximizing case.) In the new situation, we might suppose, intuitively, that the possibility of substituting into more PT working provides another option to the firm since (feasible) reductions in standard hours have no immediate bearing on the marginal costs of employing PT labour. Secondly, in preparation for later developments, we have stressed the distinction between quasi-fixed and variable labour costs in the earlier models and, again, this separation of costs should be carried over into the analysis of PT working. One important reason for this is that recent actual and planned legislation in the area of employment protection for PT workers has a potentially significant bearing on the quasi-fixed costs of PT work and so some insights into the demand repercussions of this type of activity is essential to an overall evaluation of the merits of PT employment. These and other distinctions that were earlier made with respect to FT labour demand are incorporated in the model here.

In the first instance, the firm's total cost function (TC) is quite easily extended to include PT labour input. It may be written as

$$TC = whnp+nz+W_sH_sNP+W(H-H_s)NP+NZ+cK \quad (7.1)$$

where lower-case letters refer to PT labour inputs and prices except for user capital costs, c. Thus, w and W are marginal wage rates, $p = 1+\hat{p}$, $P = 1+\hat{P}$ are payroll taxes (rates) and z, Z are quasi-fixed costs for PT and FT workers respectively.

It is assumed, as in earlier models, that the payroll taxes apply to the *complete* wages schedule; in other words, there are no per-period wages for an individual worker for which payroll taxes are zero-rated. Since, by definition, PT employees work less than standard (weekly) hours, then W_s, H_s are the standard FT wage rate and hours, respectively. In line with Section 5.2(a), we adopt the piecewise linear wage schedule from (4.9) and so

$$W = aW_s, \; a > 1, \quad H_s < H. \quad (7.2)$$

The specification of the production function is not so straightforward. Ignoring the stock of capital K for the moment, we may write the function in general form as

$$Q = Q(h,n,H,N).$$

In the equivalent FT production function, we chose a Cobb–Douglas specification as a convenient and not un-reasonable special case on which to base the analysis. This option is not open in the present case since, with no PT working, we would have $Q = Q(0,0,H,N) = 0$ which is clearly not acceptable. The choice of function should allow for the possibilities

$$Q(0,0,H,N) > 0$$

and

$$Q(h,n,0,0) > 0.$$

It should also possess two other desirable properties. In the first place, the marginal product of the four parts of labour input should be positive and decreasing, or

167

$$Q_x > 0, \; Q_{xx} < 0, \quad x = h,n,H,N$$

denoting partials by subscripts. In the second place, the marginal products of PT (FT) labour should *decline* with FT (PT) inputs, or

$$Q_{hx}, \; Q_{nx} < 0, \; x = H,N$$

$$Q_{Hx}, \; Q_{Nx} < 0, \; x = h,n.$$

Reintroducing the capital stock, FitzRoy and Hart adopt the following production function as a means of meeting these various conditions:

$$Q = K^{1-\beta\delta}\{h^{\alpha}n^{\beta}+H^{\varepsilon}N^{\beta}\}^{\delta} \tag{7.3}$$

where $0 < \alpha,\beta,\delta,\varepsilon < 1$ and, in line with the second-order conditions equivalent to (5.2) (since they also apply here), it is assumed that $\alpha < \beta$ and $\varepsilon < \beta$. Note further that the simplifying assumptions of constant returns to total employment $(n+N)$ and capital (K) are made since this avoids problems related to firm size, fixed capital costs and number of firms.

The function in (7.3) retains a reasonable degree of simplicity but it does entail one drawback: the marginal product of either kind of labour input (that is, hours or workers) tends to infinity as the input quantity reduces to zero. This is also a property of our equivalent FT model but clearly a far less likely event in that case. For PT inputs, corner solutions are of more serious concern. Since a number of useful insights are gained from the present structure, however, we proceed 'as if' this possibility does not arise for the typical firm. Some reference is made to corner solutions in later discussion, however.

The profit maximizing firm has the objective

$$\max \pi = Q-TC \tag{7.4}$$

where π is profit and Q and TC are defined respectively in (7.3) and (7.1).

168

Assuming that second-order conditions for a maximum are satisfied, the implicit equilibrium labour demand functions are

$$\bar{x} = \bar{x}(H_s,z,Z,w,W,p,P,a) \qquad (7.5)$$

where $\bar{x}(\bar{x} = \bar{h},\bar{n},\bar{H},\bar{N})$ refers to the equilibrium value of each component of labour input. Comparative static results with respect to these demand functions are summarized in Table 7.1 where

$$\bar{R} = \bar{n}/\bar{N}$$

represents the equilibrium ratio of PT to FT workers.

In the equivalent FT model, outlined in Section 5.2, a fall in standard hours produces hours–worker substitution. The comparable results with respect to the present model are shown in the first column of Table 7.1. In the case of FT workers and hours the same substitution effect carries over; a reduction in H_s produces an $\bar{H}$–$\bar{N}$ substitution. The fall in H_s, however, has no effect on PT equilibrium hours ($\bar{h}$) and an ambiguous effect on the equilibrium PT workforce ($\bar{n}$). On the other hand, there is, as might be expected, a rise in the equilibrium ratio of PT to FT workers ($\bar{R}$). This ratio effect could be achieved by the fall in $\bar{N}$ being associated *either* with a rise *or* a less-than-proportionate fall in $\bar{n}$. In all, therefore, there is some reason to suppose that the intuitively appealing view that PT employment provides an

Table 7.1
Responses of Equilibrium Labour Inputs to Changes in Factor Prices and Standard Hours

Labour inputs	ΔH_s	Δz	ΔZ	Δw	ΔW	Δp	ΔP	Δa
$\bar{h}$	0	+	0	−	0	−	0	0
$\bar{n}$	?	−	+	?	?	?	?	?
$\bar{H}$	−	0	+	0	−	0	−	−
$\bar{N}$	+	+	−	+	+	+	+	+
$\bar{R}(= \bar{n}/\bar{N})$	−	−	+	−	?	−	?	−

alternative adjustment mode to FT hours (that is, through overtime rises), given a cut in H_s, has some degree of consistency with the present structure. Again, as discussed in Section 5.3(b), these results are partly contingent on the specification of the simple linear overtime schedule in (7.2) and alternative specifications may yield alternative outcomes.

The other main results with respect to FT employment in Section 5.2 concern changes in relative factor prices. Thus, from (5.5), (5.6) and (5.7), an increase in variable relative to fixed labour costs produces an equilibrium employment–hours substitution. A rise in PT workers' fixed costs (z) relative to variable costs (w and p) increases PT equilibrium hours ($\bar{h}$). The same response holds with respect to FT workers' equilibrium hours ($\bar{H}$) given comparable changes in their own factor prices. These outcomes are fully in accord with our findings in the 'conventional' FT model; the firm offsets the rise in fixed costs by increasing the utilization of the given input. Note that, with respect to both fixed and variable cost changes, there are zero cross-price effects between PT and FT hours, a result comparable to that found in interrelated factor demand models that distinguish between utilization rates of labour and capital inputs (for example, Nadiri and Rosen, 1973).

The effects of changes in relative factor prices on equilibrium PT and FT numbers of workers are somewhat more complicated to evaluate. The most clear-cut results are found with respect to fixed costs. A rise in PT fixed costs (z) produces both PT hours–worker substitution *and* FT–PT employment substitution. There is a fall in the equilibrium ratio $\bar{R}$ comprised of both a decrease in $\bar{n}$ and an increase in $\bar{N}$. A rise in FT fixed costs (Z) produces both FT hours–workers *and* PT–FT employment substitution. In other words, compared to the FT model, a substitution out of workers and into hours for a rise in fixed costs is now reinforced by substitution between type of worker depending on the relative change in the ratio z/Z. As we might expect, an increase in the variable costs of PT workers (that is, w or p) reduces the ratio $\bar{R}$. While there is an unambiguous rise in $\bar{N}$, however, the effect on $\bar{n}$ is indeterminate. An increase in PT variable costs raises the price of $\bar{h}$ more than proportionately to $\bar{n}$. In the absence of

FT workers this would result in a simple $\bar{n}-\bar{h}$ substitution effect. With both categories of worker, the cost rise of $\bar{h}$ relative to $\bar{N}$ is even greater since it is assumed that changes in w or p are independent of $\bar{N}$. Accordingly $\bar{N}$ is substituted for $\bar{h}$ while the direction of change in $\bar{n}$ could go either way depending on specific relative elasticities. As in the 'conventional' model, a rise in FT variable costs (W or P) produces an unambiguous $\bar{N}-\bar{H}$ substitution. On the other hand, effects on $\bar{n}$ and $\bar{R}$ are ambiguous. It is shown in FitzRoy and Hart (1986) that the sign of $\bar{R}_W$ depends on the size of Z and is positive if $Z > PH_s(W-\varepsilon W_s)/\varepsilon$. Finally, a rise in the overtime pay premium (a) produces an FT workers–hours substitution as in the equivalent FT model. While the effect on $\bar{n}$ is ambiguous, the ratio $\bar{R}$ will decline. The rise in $\bar{N}$, therefore, is accompanied by a less-than-proportionate rise or a fall in $\bar{n}$.

At this point, it is worth noting another result with respect to wages that is not explicitly modelled in the system under discussion. Suppose that the firm faces an exogenously imposed minimum wage. Intuitively, we might expect that the relative demand effect on PT and FT workers if the minimum wage were to rise would depend on whether or not PT workers are covered by the minimum. If PT workers *are not covered* then $\bar{R}$ would be expected to rise given an upward minimum wage revision; if they *are covered* then $\bar{R}$ should fall. In the case where both types of worker are covered by minimum wage legislation, McKee and West (1984) obtain some support for this hypothesis with respect to a sample of Canadian employees.

It is difficult to obtain empirical evidence on the full range of these results, and especially on the predictions concerning H_s. Indeed, in general, there is a dearth of quantitative research on the demand-side of PT employment. Some information is available, however. Using cross-section US data for 1973 covering 200 occupational groups taken from 20 major industries and 10 major occupations, Owen (1979) estimated the demand equation

$$R = R\left(\frac{w}{W}, C^1, \frac{\hat{N}}{N}\right), \quad R_1, R_2 < 0, R_3 > 0$$

where R and w/W follow our earlier notation, C^I is an 'index of indirect costs' (an hourly wage index adjusted for differences in education and experience) and $\hat{N}/N$ is the proportion of FT workers employed at non-standard times of the working day.

Owen argues that the index C^I will vary positively with the degree of investment in specific human capital. Further, we might reasonably view C^I as a rough proxy for z/Z. The higher the value of C^I for a given occupational group then the greater the disincentive to hire and train PT workers since they provide a lower expected amortization period over which to recover the initial fixed expenditures. The ratio $\hat{N}/N$ lies outside our theoretical model but its interpretation is quite simple. Thus, the more 'lumpy' the distribution of demand over the workweek then the more effectively can capacity be utilized by employing PT workers.

In his estimation, Owen derives an instrumental variable estimate of C^I in order to purge it of the obvious association with w/W. Also, he specifies a supply function for C^I given the classical simultaneity problem that w/W is determined within a demand *and* supply system. Then, using two-stage least squares, he estimates the above demand function obtaining generally strongly supportive results of his maintained hypotheses. Perhaps the most interesting result is that the elasticity of substitution between FT and PT workers to changes in w/W is over 4: in fact, it is over 5 when industries with very low proportions of PT workers are excluded from the sample.

By contrast, Disney and Szyszczak (1984) attempt a time-series analysis of the demand for PT employment. They set themselves two broad objectives. First, using a somewhat restricted version of the adjustment system outlined in Section 4.7, they investigate such topics as relative adjustment speeds of PT and FT workers, the effect of PT employment protection legislation both on the adjustment speeds as well as directly on the desired demand for PT employment, and the effects of changes in PT and FT social security contributions by employers. In a second, particularly interesting, exercise these authors seek to measure the degree to which employment protection legislation alters the degree of substitutability between employment and hours of work.

Disney and Szyszczak carry out their empirical work using UK annual aggregate data for the 1970s and early 1980s. The work is hampered in two main ways. First, there are relatively few degrees of freedom and, secondly, unlike Owen, they make no attempt to unravel demand and supply influences. Thus, in this latter respect, the authors obtain a positive coefficient on w/W in their 'demand' equation where PT employment (n) is the dependent variable. They argue, therefore, that the relative wage variable is primarily representing supply influences. The results to their first set of tests are decidedly mixed with little evidence, for example, that employment protection legislation either alters adjustment speeds or the desired demand for PT employment. The only significant result in the expected direction is that the employers' contribution rate for PT social security has a marked negative influence on the demand for PT employment. This influence is represented by p in (7.1) and gives some information on the ambiguous outcome reported in Table 7.1. More interesting are the findings relating to their second type of question. Before the UK Employment Protection Act 1975, there was relatively little protection for PT workers who worked less than 21 hours a week. In this period, therefore, the adjustment costs of such workers were significantly smaller than equivalent FT workers. After the Act, the gap was considerably narrowed. Accordingly, Disney and Szyszczak find that varying PT employment appears to be a substitute for varying average hours as a means of labour force adjustment prior to 1975 while, after 1975, the differential adjustment between FT and PT employment was eliminated.

While the comparative static model outlined in (7.1)–(7.5) provides some useful insights into possible effects of factor price and working hours changes on PT/FT employment, it none the less abstracts from two important problems. First, it only allows for interior solutions since the marginal products of both hours and workers tend to infinity as the input quantity reduces to zero. Perhaps, however, the possibilities of corner solutions are most apparent on the supply-side of the labour market and so we will leave further discussion of this subject until the following section. Secondly, we have assumed implicitly that the labour part of the total cost function in (7.1) is continuously differentiable when, in fact, the payroll tax structures in several countries produce functional discontinuities. Where payroll taxes are not eligible until some lower ceiling level of wage earnings, there is a 'kink' in the cost function that produces the possibility of multiple optimum solutions. This latter problem is illustrated for the case of a single individual working PT hours with the aid of Figure 7.1.

We assume that PT fixed costs (z) and variable costs (w and p) are held constant. Initially, the individual's per-period earnings are at the ceiling limit and expressed as wh_c where h_c are the per-period ceiling hours for the given wage rate. Labour costs, c_0 are given by

$$c_0 = z + wh_c.$$

Suppose that hours rise to h_1. As far as the new labour cost is concerned, two possibilities now arise. First, the

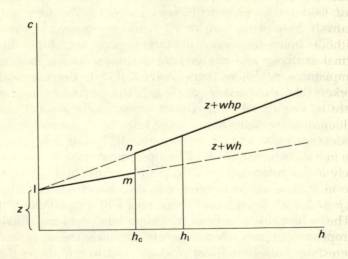

Figure 7.1 Lower wage ceilings and labour cost functions.

174

payroll tax p is only eligible for $h > h_c$ in which case the new cost c_1 is given by

$$c_1 = z + w(h_c + \Delta hp)$$

where $\Delta h = h_1 - h_c$ and, recall, $p = 1 + \hat{p}$. Thus, the change in costs is given simply by

$$\Delta c = w\Delta hp \qquad (7.6)$$

Alternatively, once h_c is exceeded the payroll tax may apply to the whole interval $[0, h_1]$. Here, the new cost c_1 is given by

$$c_1 = z + wh_1 p$$

and the change in cost is given by

$$\Delta c = w\Delta hp + wh_c\hat{p} \qquad (7.7)$$

where the last expression, $wh_c\hat{p}$, is represented by $1-m-n$ in Figure 7.1.

The essential difference between (7.6) and (7.7) is that, under the latter type of tax schedule, the employer incurs a *fixed* labour cost $wh_c\hat{p}$ in the sense that this payment is incurred irrespective of the size of the change in hours. Without attempting to integrate this outcome within the formal analysis, one can at least anticipate one additional complication it provides. Thus, suppose the firm employs n PT workers who are working equilibrium hours $\bar{h} < h_c$. Suppose there is a cut in the payroll tax rate $\hat{p}$. Disregarding the influence of the ceiling, the predictions from the foregoing model (see Table 7.1) are that $\bar{h}$ and $\bar{R}$ both rise. Now if the rise in h is such that, in the new equilibrium, $\bar{h} > h_c$ then the likely $\bar{h}$–$\bar{n}$ substitution for a fall in p may be *reinforced* by a rise in fixed costs (equivalent to z in Table 7.1) – equal to $wh_c\hat{p}\cdot n$ – which would tend to depress $\bar{n}$ and raise $\bar{h}$.

The second type of cost schedule operates in several European countries, including the FRG, and involves an interesting possible additional implication. If the interval $[0, h_c]$ is relatively small so that, for many firms, PT working is not feasible below h_c then the fixed cost effect illustrated in (7.7) may result in firms only considering employing PT hours that are significantly above zero. This would produce an analytical problem that closely parallels the implications of fixed labour supply costs on the supply of working hours (see Section 7.3 below).

Clearly, the introduction of the payroll tax wage ceiling produces greater uncertainty over several of the comparative static outcomes derived from the PT–FT demand model.

7.3 The Supply-side

From the viewpoint of the supply of PT hours and workers, the initial task is to choose a suitable model framework from the extensive labour supply literature. As a simplifying step, attention will be concentrated purely on a one-period model thereby ignoring life cycle influences (as developed in the work of Heckman and MaCurdy, 1980 and elsewhere).

Tegle (1985) argues persuasively that an analysis based on a household with two adults, one of whom is an FT worker, would be representative of a very significant part of the total PT labour supply. In the case of Sweden, he shows that over 80 per cent of all PT workers are married and that over 70 (90) per cent of total (female) PT workers have a spouse that undertakes FT work. (On a related note, the high growth of married female labour force participation relative to total female participation since the mid-1960s appears to be a phenomenon that is general to almost all industrialized economies – see Mincer, 1985, Table 1, p. S2.)

A well-known model incorporating a utility function that describes a household with two adults is that of Ashenfelter and Heckman (1974). Their utility function is given by

$$U = U(l_1, l_2, X) \tag{7.8}$$

where l_i ($i = 1,2$) are the amounts of time spent in non-market activity per period by each adult household member and X is the household's composite of all consumption goods based on the assumption of fixed relative prices of individual goods. The family budget constraint is given by

$$\Sigma w_i(T-l_i)+I = C_pX, \quad i = 1,2 \qquad (7.9)$$

where w_i is the ith member's wage rate, C_p is the price of consumption goods, I is non-labour income and T is a fixed total time constraint. Given that the utility function is twice continuously differentiable and assuming interior solutions, the first-order conditions from the maximization of (7.8) subject to (7.9) produce

$$\frac{\partial U}{\partial l_1} \bigg/ \frac{\partial I}{\partial l_2} = \frac{w_1}{w_2} \qquad (7.10)$$

and

$$\frac{\partial U}{\partial X} = \lambda C_p \qquad (7.11)$$

where the Lagrange multiplier λ represents the marginal utility of income. From (7.10), we have that the optimum household marginal rate of substitution is equal to the ratio of each person's wage. The equilibrium supply of labour function for each household member is given by

$$\bar{h}_i = \bar{h}_i (w_1, w_2, C_p, I), \quad i = 1,2 \qquad (7.12)$$

where $\bar{h}_i \equiv T-l_i$. As shown by Ashenfelter and Heckman the only unambiguous partial derivative in (7.12) is $\partial \bar{h}_i/\partial I < 0$; an increase in non-labour income reduces the family members' work effort.

Taxes and transfers are quite easily added into the utility function in (7.8) and the budget constraint in (7.9) (see Killingsworth, 1983, pp. 332–5, 340–3).

By introducing several restrictions and increasing the range of variables, this system can be modified so that the supply equations in (7.12) compare more closely with the equivalent demand functions in (7.5).

One point of emphasis on the demand-side has been to consider the implications of changing standard hours on the relative demand for PT/FT labour services. In particular, since only FT employees work total per-period standard hours, a reduction in standard hours, given fixed labour costs, alters the relative prices of PT and FT workers and thus produces PT–FT labour substitution. A reasonably similar situation on the supply-side may also arise. Suppose we were to assume that one household member works exogenously determined FT standard hours (that is, ignoring overtime, short-time, and so on) while the other member is free to choose both whether or not to participate in the labour force and the length of per-period working hours. A cut in the workweek would increase the FT worker's non-market time input into the household. This may, in turn, influence the household demand for the market time of the other adult member, the direction of which would be dependent on assumptions concerning substitutability or complementarity of non-market time between members.

The role of fixed labour costs also played a prominent part in the demand story. Much recent work has been devoted to fixed costs associated with labour supply (for example, Hausman, 1980; Cogan, 1981). These involve time and money costs incurred when changing from non-work to work activity that are independent of the length of hours worked. Their inclusion produces a discontinuous labour supply schedule given that individuals facing such costs will only commence work activity at hours significantly above zero in order to recover the initial fixed outlays. As shown by Cogan (1981), for those at work an increase in money costs will tend to increase hours of work if leisure is a normal good while an increase in time costs will reduce working hours if income is a normal good. On the other hand, an increase in time costs has ambiguous effects on the entry decision of non-workers while a money cost increase would tend to raise the minimum working hours required before entry is undertaken.

Incorporating fixed costs and the assumption that one adult household member works exogenously determined standard hours, Tegle (1985) derives supply of hours and participation equations for the other member. For simplicity, a special case of (7.8), that of independent utilities for each household member is assumed; that is,

$$U^i(l_i, X); \quad i = 1,2; \; U_j' > 0, \; U_j'' < 0; \; j = l_i, X \quad (7.13)$$

where $i = 1$ refers to the person working standard hours. He also incorporates the assumption that *overemployment* exists in the model. The point is an important one. Given that standard hours are fixed then there is no guarantee that working hours will be in equilibrium in the sense that the individual's value of time at the margin is equal to the real wage rate. Overemployment exists if the individual's value of time exceeds the real wage. If the wage rate does not rise to compensate, then the individual is effectively rationed in his or her demand for leisure time. In the case of underemployment, the real wage exceeds the value of time and, with no wage adjustment, work supply is rationed.

The time restrictions are given by

$$T_i - l_i = h_i; \quad i = 1,2 \quad (7.14)$$

where $h_1 = H_s$ (that is, using the notation of the previous section, FT exogenously determined standard hours). Avoiding unnecessary detail, the budget constraint is given by

$$C_P X < E_1 + (1-t_2)w_2 h_2 - F_2 - S_H + B + I$$

$$- \text{('pseudo tax transfer' for person 2)} \quad (7.15)$$

where E_1 is person 1's net earnings, that is, $w_1 h_s \times$ (taxes person 1); F_2 is person 2's fixed money costs of labour market entry; S_H is the household subsistence level; and B is the household gross income dependent public transfers. The 'pseudo tax transfer' expression is a means of linearizing the piecewise budget constraint (see Tegle, 1985, p. 137, for particular application, and Macrae and Yezev, 1976, for general methodology).

Maximizing U^2 in (7.13) over l_2 and X subject to (7.14) and (7.15), Tegle derives the supply of hours function for household member 2:

$$h_2 = h_2 (H_s, F_2, E_1, w_2, t_2, I, \; S_H, B, \dots)$$
$$\quad (-) \; (+)(-)(?) \; (-)(-) \; (+) \; (-) \quad (7.16)$$

179

where the signs of partial derivatives are shown in parentheses and where we ignore 'pseudo tax' terms.

A rise in h_2 in (7.16) is interpreted as a supply of less PT and more FT work. With this in mind, perhaps the most interesting result from our viewpoint is that the supply of PT work will decrease (FT work increases) when H_s is reduced. This is by no means a hard and fast outcome, however; it depends on the assumptions that person 1 is overemployed and that non-market time inputs of the two adult household members are substitutes. In line with expectation, PT work supply also decreases if fixed money costs of entry (F_2) increase. A rise in household subsistence (S_H) has the same direction of effect. On the other hand, the supply of PT work increases if the net earnings of person 1, non-wage household income and public transfers increase. The effect of a change in w_2, the wage rate of person 2, cannot be signed without further restrictions. Tegle explains in some formal detail that a rise in w_2 will decrease PT work supply if preferences are 'goods-intensive' and increase the supply of PT work if preferences are 'leisure-intensive'. Finally, a fall in the marginal tax rate (t_2) of person 2 will reduce the supply of PT work.

Equation (7.16) refers to the supply of hours of person 2 given that he/she is *already participating* in the labour market. Where this is not the case, changes in one or more of the RHS variables would bear on the participation decision. Person 2 participates in the market if the conditions

(1) $\mathrm{MRS}(X, l_2) < (1 - t_2)w_2$

(2) $F_2 <$ (pseudo tax transfer $+ B/h$) $\qquad$ (7.17)

are satisfied simultaneously. MRS( ) is the marginal rate of substitution between X and l_2.

Suppose fixed entry costs, F_2, rise. Given the values of the other parameters in (7.17) this would serve to raise the minimum number of hours, under condition (2) at which labour market entry would occur. Also, through (7.16) it would serve to raise the PT hours supplied of those persons already participating.

180

While Tegle's supply system is useful in that it permits some interesting comparisons to be made between demand and supply outcomes (see next section), his econometric tests of the supply equation (7.16) prove to be very unsatisfactory. Of course, there exist a large number of empirical studies that attempt to estimate reasonably similar hours equations (see, for example, Hausman, 1980; Layard *et al.*, 1980; and special issue of *Journal of Labor Economics*, 1985), many of which appear to perform quite satisfactorily.

Despite this, it should be added that it is difficult to make a proper evaluation of many of the supply-oriented studies since they often fail completely to take account of the extent to which some of the empirical outcomes may have been the result of demand influences. It is especially interesting to note in this context that Tegle achieves more statistical success with his demand compared to his supply estimation. As noted in Section 7.1, it is hard to ignore the role played by firms' demand for PT labour services during times of considerable excess supplies of hours in the labour market.

7.4 Assessment

While the demand and supply models outlined in the previous sections share a number of variables in common, they have not been derived along strictly compatible lines and so it would be unwise to draw other than tentative conclusions when undertaking comparisons. One obvious drawback is that the demand model of FitzRoy and Hart assumes that overtime is worked in equilibrium while in Tegle's supply model overtime working is precluded for the FT household member 1. None the less, it is useful to undertake some comparative demand and supply assessment of the employment effects induced by changes in given exogenous variables. At least, such an exercise serves to highlight the necessity of investigating the interactive roles of demand and supply in this area of research work.

In the demand model, a reduction in the standard workweek increases the ratio of PT to FT workers employed by the firm although the direction of change in the absolute number of PT workers is uncertain. A cut in the standard

181

workweek in the supply model produces a reduction in PT hours (and an increase in FT hours) supplied by households. Both sets of results are open to, perhaps quite strong, qualifications. As we have seen in Section 5.3(b), the impact on employment of reductions in standard hours is sensitive to the construction of the wage schedule. Here, we have employed the simplest piecewise schedule and other specifications may well produce divergent outcomes. Notwithstanding this type of problem, it is not at all improbable that, providing PT employees work hours significantly below standard hours, a cut in the workweek would increase the marginal cost of FT relative to PT employment. On the demand-side, it would seem reasonably safe to regard the outcomes in Table 7.1 with respect to a change in H_s, and especially the effect on the PT/FT ratio, to be fairly general. The equivalent supply of hours result in (7.16) is largely contingent on two assumptions. One of them, that the market time inputs of the two adult household members are substitutes, is reasonably easy to accept as having quite wide validity. The other, that overemployment exists because person 1's value of time exceeds the real wage, is somewhat more difficult to defend without a great deal of further information.

There would appear to be little or no empirical information on the effects of workweek cuts on the demand and supply of PT employment. On the somewhat bold assumption that the outcomes predicted from the two models here are generally valid, then the policy conclusion is quite interesting. On the demand-side, the inclusion of PT employment serves to modify the negative employment reaction predicted in the equivalent FT model in Section 5.2. While there is still a substitution of FT hours for workers this negative effect on the size of the workforce *may be offset by a rise in the demand for PT employment*. The supply-side story, on the other hand, tends to run contrary to this scenario. A reduction in the standard workweek increases the non-market time input into the household of the FT family member 1 and this, given non-market time substitution, may induce the other adult member to seek longer working hours. On aggregate, therefore, there will be an increased (decreased) supply of FT (PT) hours of work. The combined demand and supply effects, given a cut in the standard workweek, may produce proportionately more PT employees working longer PT average hours.

We have already mentioned that there was probably a significant rise in the ratio z/Z in the UK in the mid-1970s following the introduction of statutory employment protection for PT workers. Other countries have achieved similar legislation (Robinson, 1984) and high-level discussion is continuing over new initiatives (see Commission of the European Communities, 1982). The prediction from the demand-side is that an increase in the ratio z/Z will increase PT average hours and FT vacancies at the expense of some existing PT jobs. This result is in line with the work of Nickell (1979) who concentrates on the impact of greater employment protection legislation on flows into (and duration of) unemployment *vis-à-vis* average hours variations. Note that Disney and Szyszczak (1984) also investigate a more cyclically oriented reaction against PT employment if the fixed cost ratio rises. Simply, if employers incur increased hiring costs of PT workers given protection legislation, *then PT employment will have less of a comparative advantage compared to hours of work in meeting a relatively short-term cyclical change in product demand.*

It may also be the case that a relative rise in the fixed costs of PT workers on the demand-side is treated, on the supply-side, as an effective increase in the net earnings of the household. This may occur for a number of reasons. First, an increase in training expenditures on PT workers would be expected to enhance their share of the periodic rent arising from specific investments. Secondly, non-wages are enhanced by fringe benefits with a high fixity element or by employment protection which, in effect, lengthens the discount period over which wage expectations are formed. In equation (7.16) the effect of household member 2's wages on the supply of hours of work is uncertain but if preferences are 'goods-intensive', then a rise in w_2 (equivalent to an increase in the above types of non-wage income) will increase the supply of FT work and reduce the supply of PT work. This result is fully compatible with the intentions on the demand-side since, in line with several earlier models, employers will be relatively content to offset the fixed (that is, hours-independent) costs of employment protection with longer average hours per worker. This will serve to reduce the discounted per-period value of the increase in fixed labour expenditures.

A number of other issues relating to the analysis of PT employment are raised in later chapters. In Chapter 10, we will consider worksharing through 'partial retirement' whereby an older worker shares her/his job with a young recruit on a joint PT basis. Further, some collective bargaining aspects of PT employment are mentioned in Chapter 11.

CHAPTER EIGHT

Hours, Layoffs and Implicit Contracts

8.1 Introduction

The optimization process behind most of the theoretical and empirical models previously outlined takes place somewhat myopically in that the employer unilaterally determines employment and utilization levels and, moreover, bases the employment decision on influences that are not contingent on outside events. Some justification for the seeming narrowness of approach in this respect is provided by Hall and Lilien (1979) (see also Hall and Lazear, 1984) who discuss efficient wage bargains under significant uncertainty with respect both to product demand (on the firm-side) and employment opportunity costs (in households). Potential problems concerned with moral hazard, costly legal disputes and the reliability of outside statistical indicators limit the practicability of enforcing wage contracts that are contingent on outside events. The authors argue that, under these conditions, such relatively fixed mechanisms as overtime and shift premium payments schedules can generate efficient layoffs in response to short-term fluctuations and that any cumulation of inefficiencies may be dealt with through periodic contract renegotiation. From casual observation, there seems to be some justification for adopting this stance. None the less, the demand models so far discussed clearly do omit any explanation of a number of important labour market phenomena that are linked with the issues of hours of work and employment. Perhaps the most important of these, especially in the context of the US economy, is that many layoffs are not once-for-all separations between workers and firms but consist of short spells of unemployment followed by re-engagement with the original employer. The quantitative significance of such *temporary layoff* unemployment in the USA is well documented (see Feldstein, 1973, 1978; Topel and Welch, 1980; Topel, 1982). The usual means of attempting to explain this type of short-term unemployment involves an extension of the conventional type of labour demand model to embrace implicit wage contracts that provide some degree of wage and employment insurance to workers. Specifically, the employment and wage decisions of an optimizing firm that provides such insurance would involve consideration of workers' utility. As a consequence, the effects of state subsidies to wage income within the total employment/ hours of work decision are directly integrated into the model (see, especially, the seminal contributions of Feldstein, 1976, and Baily, 1977). It is this latter aspect of the implicit contract literature that is of most concern to the developments here. (For excellent general critiques of the literature, see Stiglitz, 1984, and Rosen, 1985.)

The main implications stemming from the implicit contract approach to the effects of changes in unemployment subsidies on the firm's allocation among workers, hours per worker and layoffs form the subject of Section 8.2. Some mention is also made of modifications with respect to unionized firms. A specific implicit contract model is outlined in Section 8.3 which not only illustrates the way in which the earlier myopic models are generalized but also provides a number of fiscal extensions to the earlier literature. The section emphasizes, however, a number of shortcomings of implicit contract theory in this area of research.

Section 8.3 also highlights several unresolved puzzles. One of these relates to the fact that there remain less-than-complete explanations of why firms and workers favour temporary layoffs rather than worksharing as a response to, for example, unanticipated fluctuations in product demand.

A possible form of worksharing at such times is to employ short-time work schedules which represent a labour utilization equivalent to temporary layoffs. In many OECD countries, and particularly in Europe, short-time working is eligible for government subsidy in more or less the same manner as temporary layoffs are subsidized in the USA. Some discussion of short-time working, in relation to quasi-fixed cost and contract theory, is undertaken in Section 8.4. Very brief concluding remarks are made in Section 8.5.

8.2 Implicit Contract Models and Unemployment Subsidies

In the sort of optimizing problem represented by equations (4.23) and (4.24), the firm maximizes revenue net of costs subject to an additional constraint with respect to workers' utility. What is the rationale for adopting this type of approach? Within the context of temporary layoff unemployment, two basic hypotheses are usually advanced, one of which pertains to the implicit contract literature in general while the other specifically concerns the existence of subsidies to unemployment.

The general hypothesis is that workers are risk-averse and, with the possible exception of wage indexation against inflation, they cannot easily obtain insurance against fluctuations in their wage income. Some firms, however, may be willing to provide a degree of wage and employment insurance through implicit contracts given that they have both relatively greater access to capital markets and less risk-averse attitudes. Such firms can trade off more insurance for a wage that is lower than that of firms that do not offer such insurance. The optimizing strategy of firms providing insurance, therefore, would involve some account being taken of the employment/income aspirations of employees as represented by their utility functions. Workers' utility would include work income, leisure *and* social security subsidies.

The potential subsidy that is of most interest to the study of temporary layoffs is unemployment benefits. If workers are laid off and receive benefit then this subsidizes the firm and its workforce to the extent that their unemployment contributions do not represent the true actuarial value of their own layoff experience. The more specific type of hypothesis is that an increase in the value of the subsidy will lead to a utility gain, provided leisure is a normal good, that can be realized by more workers experiencing unemployment spells and then returning to their previous employment before such time that their level of benefits would be reduced. Intuitively a number of other related outcomes would be expected to hold. First, given less than fully experienced rated benefits, an unforeseen change in product demand is likely to result *ceteris paribus* in a tendency for employment to fluctuate more than proportionately to hours of work. Secondly, a decrease in the degree of experienced rating, tantamount to an increase in subsidy, is likely to exacerbate this employment/hours fluctuation differential as well as to increase the layoff response to a given rise in benefit. Less experience rating constitutes a greater degree of subsidy and, therefore, leads to a higher propensity to realize the utility gain this represents.

These expected outcomes are generally supported theoretically in the formal models of Feldstein (1976) and Baily (1977). For example, Feldstein develops a two-period model for a competitive firm with a production function that distinguishes between workers and hours per worker. Over a given fraction of the year, its product price falls below the normal level. If workers are laid off as a result of the fall, they would receive unemployment benefits that are less than fully experience-rated. Excluding ownership of assets, each employee's expected net income at the beginning of the year, assuming an equal probability of becoming unemployed, is the after-tax wage income per 'normal' employee (that is, with reference to the number of employees engaged when the price is at its normal level) plus the after-tax unemployment benefit per 'normal' employee. A representative worker's utility is a function of this expected net income and the expected hours of work. This latter variable (assuming strong separability in utility) is in three parts. First, the employee works 'normal' hours during that expected fraction of the year that prices are normal. Second, the employee works 'revised' hours for the fraction of the year that prices fall multiplied by the probability of remaining in employment. Thirdly, the employee works zero hours for the period of time during which prices fall multiplied by the probability of being laid off. The problem for the firm in a competitive labour market is to choose values of normal hours, revised hours and revised employment that maximize this utility.

While Feldstein deals with the special case of institutionally fixed hours over the two periods, obtaining generally unambiguous results, he also allows both components of labour input to be determined endogenously. Thus, the firm may choose a policy of reduced employment or shorter working time or a combination of both as a reaction to a fall in demand. In fact, the optimum combination of labour inputs may involve an *increase* in one of the component parts. As expected, he finds that a rise in the amount of unemployment subsidy decreases employment. Interestingly, the existence of a subsidy serves to increase average hours per worker during the demand downturn. In general, a subsidy provides an incentive to resort to a layoff rather than a worksharing strategy as a means of effecting a reduction in manhours. The effect of a change in demand cannot, given variable hours, be unambiguously determined: however, the model does suggest that, during a demand fall, both the likelihood and the resulting magnitude of an employment cutback would probably be magnified. One additional result is worth noting. Feldstein finds that the existence of an unemployment subsidy makes it worthwhile for the firm and its workers to have periods of 'feigned unemployment' even if there is no fall in demand.

The unemployment insurance system in the United States and elsewhere effectively subsidizes layoffs because the benefit receipts are not taxed as ordinary income and because tax contributions are less than fully experience-rated. The rating system in the USA is a complicated one, varying from state to state, although relatively concise descriptions of prevalent schemes can be found in Topel and Welch (1980) and Brechling (1977). The limited degree of experience rating in many states is illustrated by the former authors who estimate the implicit subsidy given to a high-layoff compared to a low-layoff firm. The state of Michigan provides a typical example. They calculate that a firm with an average layoff rate of 3 per cent (where the percentage figure is the estimated unemployment insurance subsidy per worker relative to 52 times the average weekly payroll – and thus representing about one week per year per worker) receives a subsidy of 0.3 per cent of its labour costs. By contrast, a firm with a 15 per cent layoff rate (equivalent to roughly eight weeks layoff per employee per year) receives a subsidy of 7.5 per cent. Moreover, firms with high average layoff rates account for a disproportionate amount of total benefit receipt. In Michigan in 1967, firms with taxable payrolls that represented 3.6 per cent of total taxable payrolls received 34.8 per cent of benefits. While estimates of the effect on temporary layoffs of changes in unemployment benefit can be found in a number of sources (for example, Feldstein, 1978; Medoff, 1979), the only comprehensive study, unravelling tax effects from benefit effects is provided by Brechling (1981). He estimates the impacts of changes in both unemployment benefits and experience rating on layoffs and hours of work as well as on re-hires and layoff duration. His data refer to US manufacturing industries within states that operate the (dominant) reserve ratio method of rating. In fact, he finds that the tax influences on the dependent variables are considerably stronger than those of the benefits although there are some question marks over certain aspects of his findings (see Hamermesh, 1981).

Of course, there remain large elements of risk to the firm and its workers in adopting a temporary layoff strategy, especially if the laid-off workers are endowed with significant levels of specific human capital investments. Although subsidies to unemployment make the option of temporary layoff more attractive as a quantity adjustment mode, they do not remove the possibility of an eventual permanent separation between the parties. For example, the firm may underestimate the length and severity of a given fall in demand and, therefore, overestimate the degree to which it is able to recall workers. For their part, workers are clearly free to search for alternative employment while laid off. A higher recourse to the use of temporary layoffs increases the costs associated with unanticipated permanent layoffs and quits. Moreover, given that the information to each side is liable to be asymmetrical then questions of moral hazard also arise. It would seem to follow that it is in the interest of both firms and workers to attempt to seek means of minimizing such separations. The likelihood that the parties will endeavour to avoid the costs associated with such risks gives rise to two further issues concerning temporary layoffs.

The first concerns the type of worker that is most likely to be laid off on a temporary basis. For the firm's part, it can most effectively safeguard against quits if it lays off those workers who have the greatest vested interest in returning to the firm. Possibilities would include workers with wages above comparable market rates, workers with special seniority privileges and workers with high proportions of non-vested pensions and other fringe benefits within total compensation. As for the workers, they are more likely to agree to temporary layoff if they have negotiated contracts that stipulate that re-employment by the firm would take place before job offers are made elsewhere. The obvious group of workers who, in general, would seem to satisfy the requirements of *both* parties are union members.

Empirical findings by Medoff (1979) for both two-digit and three-digit US industries suggest strongly that unionized firms, when trying to achieve labour reductions, exhibit a much higher propensity to use layoffs rather than to rely on quits, real wage cuts, average hours reductions and discharges. This contrasts with labour adjustment in non-unionized firms which exhibit a higher propensity to use quits/re-hires rather than layoffs/recalls. It is interesting to note that the seeming preference for layoffs as opposed to worksharing among American unions was not apparent in earlier times. Medoff (1979) compares hour-reduction provisions in major union contracts in effect in 1954–5 with those in 1970–1. He notes the following:

191

In 1954–55, only 5 per cent of the 28 per cent of the major contract workforce covered by hour-reduction provisions had agreements stating that layoff proceedings would begin when hours worked were below normal for four or less weeks. By 1970–71, a dramatic change had occurred: 43 per cent of the 28 per cent covered by hour-reduction provisions had contracts under which layoff proceedings would commence after four or less short workweeks.

(Medoff, 1979, p. 388)

Also, Medoff notes that, in the latter period, the 72 per cent of workers covered by reduction-in-hours provisions had negotiated a right of union participation over the choice between reduced hours and immediate layoffs; this compared with a comparable figure of 31 per cent in the earlier period. Evidence is given to support the view that this change was due in part to the increased desire by unions to have more control in circumventing reduced hour provisions and, instead, to initiate layoffs.

While the unionization argument goes some way towards explaining the pattern of temporary layoffs, it has nevertheless a somewhat limited role. Less than 20 per cent of the US workforce is currently unionized and not all unionized workers enjoy the type of privilege that fits neatly with the layoff story.

A second explanation of the pattern of temporary layoffs that also seeks to emphasize the need to avoid losses of specific investments has perhaps somewhat more appeal. The idea finds its roots in the reserve labour hypothesis (see Miller, 1971). Some firms may regard the possibility of inventory accumulation as an alternative to holding buffer stocks of labour, through hoarding or temporary layoff, during unforeseen recessionary periods. The degree to which they use inventories, hours of work or temporary layoffs as a means of achieving desired sales variation is a function of their relative costs. The three strategies are interdependent and can be treated in much the same way as the (interrelated) factor demand system represented in Sections 4.6 and 4.7. A higher recourse to inventory accumulation may be expected in those firms with higher specific labour investments. Such firms are more likely to 'ride out' temporary falls in product demand by attempting to utilize their labour as fully as possible. In his demand system, Topel (1982) finds some evidence of such inventory–hours–employment substitution on the basis of a limited sample of US manufacturing industries.

In all, that part of implicit contract theory that has concentrated on integrating the role of unemployment insurance systems within labour demand analysis would appear to enrich the myopic demand approaches outlined earlier. This is particularly the case in so far as temporary layoff unemployment is quantitatively important since the myopic models simply do not explain this phenomenon. In more recent times, however, questions have arisen not only over the importance of temporary layoffs within total unemployment but also over the fact that, on an inter-national basis, the incidence of temporary layoffs is not well predicted by the contract models. These issues are the subject of the following section.

8.3   Problems and Extensions

The work of Feldstein, Baily and others provides one type of support for the so-called 'new view' of unemployment. Two aspects of unemployment are particularly emphasized. First, workers in a given firm who are laid off due to, say, a temporary fall in product demand can be regarded as *voluntarily* unemployed since, *ex post*, utility is independent of their employment status. Secondly, the unemployment characterized by this activity is essentially of *short-term duration*: temporary layoffs represent flows of persons experiencing unemployment for short periods rather than stocks of long-term unemployed. In relatively recent times, the significance of this 'new view' has been vigorously challenged from a number of different perspectives.

The first type of challenge, which we will deal with quite briefly here, concentrates primarily on the specific predic-tions arising directly from models like that of Feldstein (1976) although it also forms a part of a much wider criticism

193

of the ability of implicit contract theory in general to predict important labour market phenomena (see, especially, Stiglitz, 1984). For example, the implicit contract model predicts, given subsidies to unemployment, that it would be to the benefit of the firm and its employees to arrange spells of unemployment *even if demand was at normal levels* in order simply to take advantage of the subsidy. In practice, over a relatively long period of stable demand, this would be achieved by a system of 'rotating layoffs' whereby each worker would take advantage of a spell of unemployment that was not long enough to affect his/her level of unemployment benefit or eligibility for future benefits. There would appear to be no evidence that such rotation plays a significant part in short spells of unemployment. Another seeming anomaly (see Stiglitz, 1984, pp. 39–41 for a fuller discussion) is that, under not preposterous assumptions about forms and shapes of utility functions, the contract theory predicts that laid-off workers can be better off than those retained by the firm.

While certain theoretical anomalies do occur, as in almost any other quite general theory, a number of the central propositions arising from the implicit contract literature with respect to temporary layoffs have been tested with some success, especially with respect to US data. A second type of criticism, which is potentially much more damaging, is that the quantitative significance of temporary layoffs has been overstated in the early contract literature. Here we will mention two, albeit related, arguments along these lines. In the first, it has been shown that, in the USA and elsewhere, temporary layoff unemployment is a quantitatively much smaller part of the total amount of unemployment than Feldstein and others had implied. In the second, a basic anomaly arises since in several major OECD countries, temporary layoffs are relatively uncommon and yet the conditions, à la implicit contract theory, for encouraging temporary layoffs are at least as strong, if not stronger, than in the USA. We deal with each issue in turn devoting rather more attention to the second since it provides a useful link to the following chapter on social security funding.

The 'new view' on unemployment has been directly or

indirectly challenged in an important internationally oriented literature dealing with the measurement of unemployment (for example, Freiburghaus, 1978; Clark and Summers, 1979; Akerlof, 1979; Akerlof and Main, 1980; Main 1981). The essential point is that advocates of the importance of temporary layoff unemployment had tended to report on the *average interrupted spell length* of unemployment, so called because it measures the average unemployment spells of those currently unemployed: it is equivalent, in demographic terms, to the average age of a population. With respect to a given individual this measure will clearly differ from the *expected* length of unemployment. The fact that it records the length of unemployment before the spell is completed produces a significant downward bias of spell length: in fact, on average in the steady state it is half the actual spell length. An offsetting upward bias also occurs, however, since longer spell lengths are over-represented in observation because of the associated greater probability of being observed at each discrete point of measurement. It is perhaps more meaningful to obtain a statistical measure that is equivalent to the expected life at birth. Such a statistic, referred to as the *terminations-weighted spell length*, would measure the average duration of all completed spell lengths within a given time interval. Since the majority of spells of unemployment are of relatively short duration, this particular measure may not lie outside the bounds which seem to be generally acceptable to the 'new view'. Main (1981) and others have argued that since this second type of statistic abstracts from persons actually experiencing unemployment, focusing rather on the average length of all spells, then its welfare implications may be somewhat misleading. A third statistic, the *experienced-weighted spell length* gets round this problem by representing the average length of completed spell of the currently employed: it measures the average length of spell in which unemployment is spent and is analogous to the average age at death of the current population.

The challenge to the 'new view' in terms of the distinction between these last two statistics compared to the first can best be summarized by quoting Akerlof:

195

The 'new view' has correctly pointed out that most spells of unemployment are fairly short. It has, however, failed to point out that most unemployed persons are unemployed for rather long periods. Over the post-war period the average spell of unemployment in the United States has been only about six weeks. On the other hand, persons who were currently unemployed at any given time over the post-war period in the United States were unemployed (in the sense of the duration of their completed spells) for an average period of close to six months.

(Akerlof, 1979, pp. 227–8)

In Britain too the average length of completed spells was in the order of six weeks in the early 1960s but, by the late 1970s, this figure had reached around 20 weeks (Main, 1981 provides an extensive survey of the British literature). By contrast, the experienced-weighted spell length has averaged between 60 and 80 weeks over this period and also displayed considerably less variability.

Although the initial fervour of support for the quantitative significance of temporary layoff unemployment in the USA has dulled somewhat in the light of this subsequent work, it is none the less an important source of unemployment in certain sectors of the economy such as in unionized firms or certain firms with relatively low specific labour investments. From a strictly US perspective, it would appear that the main challenge to the implicit contract theory in relation to unemployment subsidies has not been with respect to its consistency with observed phenomena but rather with the overall labour market significance of the phenomena themselves. If one goes beyond the US economy to other countries within the OECD bloc, however, somewhat more fundamental problems arise.

In Western Europe and Japan there is relatively little recourse to the use of temporary layoffs compared to the USA. By contrast, as highlighted in Tables 2.1 and 2.2, these countries are relatively more prone to vary hours of work in response to cyclical fluctuations in demand. Leaving aside for the moment special national institutional features that may serve to weigh the balance more towards hours rather than employment as a means of adjustment, the relative paucity of temporary layoffs does not fit at all comfortably with the predictions from the contract models. The subsidy element of unemployment benefits through less-than-full experience rating is more obvious in Western European countries than in the USA since little attempt is made to link benefits to firms' layoff histories. This comparative advantage is then enhanced both by the fact that unemployment benefits and social security provisions are more generous in Europe than in the USA (see Kaufman, 1980) as well as the fact that, especially in recent times, a greater proportion of the unemployed are eligible for benefit in Europe. Moreover, given Medoff's (1979) finding that within firms covered by collective bargaining agreements, 'layoffs are a much more important adjustment mechanism relative to quits, cuts in (the growth of) real wage rates, reduction in average hours, and discharges than in comparable firms that are non-union', then European countries, with a much more widely and deeply developed union sector, would perhaps be expected to experience a distinctly greater number of temporary layoffs than in fact occur.

A number of institutionally oriented arguments are typically advanced to explain differences in the layoff and hours of work experiences between Europe and the USA. For example, it is claimed that there are more severe legal barriers to layoffs in Europe while the European unemployment insurance system often encourages hours variability since short-time working is eligible, in some countries, for unemployment insurance assistance (see Moy and Sorrentino, 1981, for arguments along these lines). West Germany provides an excellent example on which to represent these European differences; not only does its federal labour law protect against arbitrary or 'unfair' dismissal but also its potential subsidies to short-time working are among the most generous in Europe. As pointed out by FitzRoy and Hart (1985), however, the case of West Germany does *not* provide convincing explanations for the differences. In the first place, it is noted that if temporary layoffs really do represent efficiency considerations then it is difficult to understand why the relatively powerful German trade union movement, with its close ties to the Social Democratic Party (SPD), has not exerted pressure to develop a temporary layoff system within the extensive West German labour legislation. Moreover, the authors point out that in most European countries layoffs are explicitly permitted and legislation simply serves to protect against arbitrary or 'unfair' dismissal. Nor does the West German experience of short-time working provide a convincing case that such a working time arrangement provides an important alternative. As we have seen in Chapter 2 (see Table 2.6) short-time working accounts for relatively little of the West German days-not-worked statistics.

FitzRoy and Hart (1985) develop a simple efficient contract model as well as a 'myopic' model (of the type illustrated in Section 5.2) in order to investigate a fiscal explanation of the difference in hours/layoff experience (see also Hart, 1982). They examine the consequences of differences in the payroll tax system of funding unemployment benefits between the United States and elsewhere for the allocation of hours and layoffs. This aspect of the work is developed further here since it is particularly useful to later developments (see especially Section 9.3).

Let workers' utility be represented by expression (4.23) that is,

$$V = U(wh) - D(h)$$

where, as usual, w is the wage rate and h is hours per worker and U', D', $D'' \geq 0$ but $U'' \leq 0$. A unit of 'permanent' labour force actually employed in demand-state θ is given by $n = n(\theta)$ and so the constraint

$$0 \leq n(\theta) \leq 1 \tag{8.1}$$

must always hold. Laid-off workers receive unemployment benefit B although short-time working is assumed not to be eligible. Assuming layoffs are randomly made, expected utility is given by

$$EV = EnU(wh) - nD(h) + (1-n)U(B) \qquad (8.2)$$

where we set $D(0) = 0$ and hours vary with θ.

For simplicity, it is assumed that there are only three types of non-wage labour costs, each associated with either unemployment insurance funding or layoffs. These are:

(1) unemployment contributions, $P \geq 1$, that vary directly with the size of the payroll and, therefore, wh (health and pension contributions and other variable non-wage costs are ignored);
(2) unemployment contributions T that depend *only* on the size of the workforce (thus, T is defined more narrowly than earlier in (4.2) and other quasi-fixed costs, such as Z in (4.1), are ignored);
(3) a direct payment to laid-off workers, T_d.

Therefore, total labour costs per labour unit, c_L may be written

$$c_L = whnP + nT + (1-n)T_d$$

where $(1-n)$ is the number of layoffs in a unit workforce.

Profit is now defined as

$$\pi = \theta L - whnP - nT - (1-n)T_d \qquad (8.3)$$

where θ is a random productivity (or price) shift and $L = g(h)N^{1-\alpha}$ from (4.4).

Following the optimization rule in (4.24) (and replacing C_L by c_L), the firm chooses an efficient contract by maximizing profit holding utility constant, or

$$J = E\pi + \lambda(EV - c_L) \qquad (8.4)$$

Letting $\bar{x}_y$ denote the partial derivative of the optimal factor input (that is, $\bar{x} = h, \bar{n}$) with respect to unemployment benefits and contributions (that is, $y = B, T_d, T, P$), then FitzRoy and Hart show that in the special case of risk

199

neutrality, or $U'' = 0$ in (8.2), the solutions to the problem in (8.4) produce

$$\bar{h}_B > 0, \ \bar{n}_B < 0 \tag{8.5}$$

$$\bar{h}_{T_d} < 0, \ \bar{n}_{T_d} > 0 \tag{8.6}$$

$$\bar{h}_T > 0, \ \bar{n}_T < 0 \tag{8.7}$$

$$\left.\begin{array}{c} \bar{h}_p < 0 \text{ if } T > T_d, \ \bar{h}_p > 0 \text{ if } T < T_d \\[2mm] \bar{n}_p > 0 \text{ if } T > T_d \text{ } and \text{ } P \text{ large enough} \\[2mm] \bar{n}_p < 0 \text{ if } T < T_d \end{array}\right\} \tag{8.8}$$

The results with respect to unemployment benefits in (8.5) are familiar to the contract literature of Feldstein and others mentioned above; a rise in unemployment benefit *ceteris paribus* leads to an increase in layoffs and average hours per worker. Not surprisingly, an increase in payments to laid-off workers, perhaps through collective bargaining agreements, induces, as in (8.6), the reverse outcome; the firm would reduce layoffs and average hours per worker.

Of somewhat more interest for our present (and later) purposes are the outcomes with respect to the different types of social security contribution. The results in (8.7) indicate that a rise in contributions that are independent of hours worked would induce the firm to increase both layoffs and average hours per worker. This is fully in line with earlier theoretical results in Chapter 5 and elsewhere. In effect, such taxes serve to increase the fixed costs of labour relative to variable costs thereby inducing a substitution on to the intensive and away from the extensive margin. Accordingly, we would expect the opposite result to hold for a *ceteris paribus* rise in hours-related contributions. In fact, as can be seen in (8.8), these outcomes only hold in the case of $T > T_d$ in the case of hours and in the case of $T > T_d$ *and* for large P in the case of layoffs (for low P values, the outcome is ambiguous). If $T < T_d$ then the hours–layoffs reaction to a change in contributions is the same as in the previous case in (8.7), a somewhat surprising result.

FitzRoy and Hart go on to investigate the last two results with respect to a 'myopic' maximizing model: in this case no account is taken of workers' utility. In effect, we already have investigated these results in the basic model introduced in Section 4.4 and analysed, especially, in Section 5.2. Thus, it has been shown that a rise in fixed to variable labour costs, through (5.7), induces a substitution of longer average hours for fewer workers. Since the unemployment contributions simply add to fixed costs, in the case of T, and variable costs, in the case of P, this simple direction of substitution holds in both cases.

In summary, conditions may exist with respect to the efficient contract model whereby a change in worker-related contributions *may* have the *opposite* effect on hours and layoffs compared to a variable payroll tax. In the equivalent myopic model the opposite effects of the different types of tax change hold unambiguously.

Comparing the results in (8.5) with those in (8.7) we see that if increased benefits are funded, in part, by increased contributions of an hours-independent type then the implications for working hours and layoffs are the same. Both benefit and tax rises would be predicted to produce an increase in layoffs and longer average working hours. If, on the other hand, benefit increases are funded by increases in variable contributions, it may be the case that the greater propensity to resort to layoffs on the benefit side would be *offset* on the contribution side by an inducement in the opposite direction. It so happens (see Hart, 1982, and 1984a) that firms' contributions to unemployment insurance in the USA are, in general, comprised of hours-independent taxes while those in Europe and Japan are overwhelmingly of the variable type. One explanation, therefore, of the different layoff experience might lie in the method of funding.

Another insight into possible reasons for differences in hours/layoff experiences among countries can be gleaned from the above contract model. This topic is also discussed in a similar model presented by Rosen (1985, pp. 1162–5); see also Baily (1977).

Take h, n and $y = wh$ as choice variables in the

maximization problem expressed in (8.4). From the first-order condition $J_y = 0$, we obtain $\lambda = P/U'(y)$, so optimal income $\bar{y} = wh$ is state-independent for all states. Combining this result with that derived from the condition $J_h = 0$ gives

$$\bar{n}^\alpha = \theta g' U'(\bar{y})/PD' \tag{8.9}$$

and combining the results from the conditions $J_h = J_n = 0$ gives

$$(1-\alpha)GPD' = (\bar{y}P + T - T_d)U' - P[U(\bar{y}) - U(B) - D] \tag{8.10}$$

where $G = g(h)/g'(h)$. (Note that the first-order conditions are given for θ such that (8.1) is not binding.)

In principle (8.10) can be solved for optimal hours, $\bar{h}$; as with $\bar{y}$, $\bar{h}$ is state-independent. Since $\bar{n}'(\theta) > 0$, there must exist a maximal layoff state $\bar{\theta}$ for which the constraint in (8.1) is binding, or $\bar{n}(\theta) = 1$. For layoff states $\theta < \bar{\theta}$, h does not vary with θ while by (8.9) $\bar{n}(\theta) < 1$ and there are layoffs in almost all layoff states. For non-layoff states $\theta > \bar{\theta}$, $\bar{n}(\theta) = 1$ and, through (8.9), $\bar{h}$ varies with θ. (In such states $J_n > 1$ and so the respective first-order condition no longer holds.) Therefore, there are two distinct regimes: for states $\theta < \bar{\theta}$ optimal layoffs vary with θ and optimal hours are constant while for states $\theta > \bar{\theta}$ optimal hours vary with θ and optimal layoffs are constant.

It should also be added that in layoff states $\theta < \bar{\theta}$ the optimal wage is rigid; that is, it is independent of θ. This result depends essentially on the assumption of separable technology with a constant employment elasticity.

The layoff/hours dichotomy leads Rosen (1985) to speculate concerning the observed fluctuations of hours and employment in the USA. Recall from the information presented in Section 2.2 that US employment has a far more pronounced cyclical pattern than that of hours of work. In normal times the mean of θ may be greater than $\bar{\theta}$, in which case hours per worker account for most of the fluctuation in manhours; there is relatively little recourse to the use of layoffs during such periods. When the mean of θ falls below $\bar{\theta}$, during poor economic conditions, layoffs provide the main form of manhour adjustment while hours are downwardly rigid. On first reflection, this appears to provide a valuable clue towards explaining the different hours/layoff behaviour. When considered against the statistical evidence, however, it might more realistically be regarded as the first step along one possible avenue of investigation. The international fluctuations in hours and employment in Figures 2.1 and 2.2 reveal that the US experience is by no means a general phenomenon. Moreover, the annual regression results for the USA in Table 2.1 tend to show that employment varies more than proportionately to hours per worker in *both* prosperous and stagnating time periods.

This does not preclude the possibility that the above contract approach may be a useful device towards explaining some of the observed behaviour. Examining hours and layoffs on a more disaggregate cross-section/time-series basis within countries as well as pinpointing relevant economic and other differences among countries (see Section 2.2) may help to bring the contract approach more into play.

8.4 Short-time Working

The foregoing contract model emphasizes a particular form of quantity adjustment as the means of responding to a cyclical downturn in economic activity. The tendency is for layoffs to increase with both hours and wages downwardly rigid. These results are basically pre-conditioned by three assumptions: (1) there is a separable production technology with a constant employment elasticity, (2) unemployment benefits are not (fully) experience-rated and (3) worksharing is not eligible. With respect to (1), the introduction of other production can lead to quite different outcomes, such as that of state-dependent (first-best) wages. We do not consider this here, however. As for (2), it is interesting to speculate over the conditions that may lead to a preference for worksharing rather than layoffs *if* unemployment benefits were fully experience-rated. Finally, under (3), it is worthwhile noting that, especially in Europe, a special form of worksharing, that is short-time working, is eligible for subsidy. These latter two issues are discussed here.

By 'worksharing' in the present context is meant trading off the employment of more workers for fewer hours per worker during cyclical trough periods. One possibility in this latter respect is to reduce overtime working. For many workers, however, overtime is not an available option. Moreover, others may regard (significant levels of) overtime as unanticipated 'bonus' compensation during relatively strong demand conditions and thus prefer to use the standard weekly wage as the basis of long-term, explicit or implicit, contractual agreements. It is perhaps more appropriate, therefore, to consider 'short-time' working as the realistic worksharing alternative to temporary layoffs. This definition of worksharing is adopted for the discussion in this section. Short-time working schedules involve average weekly working hours in the firm that are significantly less than standard or normal hours. As we mentioned in Chapter 2, short-time working in Europe is often subsidized in the same way as temporary layoffs in the USA and elsewhere and this helps to strengthen this particular comparison of extensive and intensive margins.

In the complete absence of 'labour adjustment subsidies', the decision of all workers in a given firm to accept short-time working as opposed to some workers being laid off, is closely analogous to the decision to accept a cut in the wage rate. Allowing for possible utility and productivity changes due to shorter hours, the firm and its workforce may be largely indifferent between fewer weekly hours at the same hourly rate and a lower rate for the same weekly hours. The former strategy may be chosen by the 'Keynesian' firm that treats demand as given while the latter may be more applicable to its 'classical' counterpart. Also, technological constraints may influence the choice of adjustment mode.

One approach towards assessing the likelihood of a price or quantity adjustment made during downturns in demand is achieved through a rather simple extension of quasi-fixed cost theory. Hashimoto (1975) has provided a rationale for firms and workers to agree to wage reductions rather than layoffs as a means of adjusting to an unanticipated fall in demand. Firms and workers share the periodic rent that accrues to human capital investment. The worker's wage reflects both the compensation that would have been attained in the best alternative employment, the opportunity wage, and part of the gap between his/her marginal product and the opportunity wage. The firm's gain to specific investments, on the other hand, is the discounted difference between the marginal product and the wage. For contractual or other reasons we may imagine that the typical worker does not experience a wage reduction due to the fall in demand while the firm receives a lower return due to a reduction in marginal product. Now the fall in demand might be so severe that the absolute amount of the decrease in return to the firm is *greater* than the worker's share of specific investment. The combined net gain would be negative and it would pay both firm and worker to separate, although, in this situation, layoff is more likely than quit. The possibility may arise, however, that the firm's net gain is negative but, when combined with the worker's, the *combined* gain is positive. It would now pay both parties to come to an agreement whereby the worker experiences a wage fall (although still leaving some positive rent) *or* increases his/her marginal product by working fewer hours without a full offset in wage compensation for the loss in time. Refinements and generalizations of this basic idea within a fuller contract theory that embraces informational asymmetries and questions of moral hazard can be found in Hashimoto and Yu (1980) and Hashimoto (1981).

Outside these immediate arguments, however, there are potential disadvantages in adopting a worksharing rather than a layoff strategy. For example, higher quality workers are more likely to quit given worksharing than other workers: layoffs on the other hand may be used in a more discriminatory way (see Arnott *et al.*, 1983). But even where the firm has less control over the choice of layoffs, worksharing may provide the more costly adjustment alternative. We noted in Section 8.2 that the US evidence suggests that *both* employers and workers may prefer layoffs to be experienced by relatively senior workers with strong vested interests to remain with the firm. For its part the firm obtains a higher expected present value of specific investments by increasing the probability of re-hire in the event of future layoff due to a temporary fall in demand. Of course, the investment discount period has both an extensive and an intensive dimension: it is a function both of the length of period the worker remains with the firm *and* the length of effective working hours per period. In adopting short-time working, the latter dimension is shortened but without the accompanying advantage of being confined to an optimum 'self-selected' group of workers. A full examination of the gains and losses with respect to specific investments through a strategy of layoff or short-time working or hoarding can be found in Sheldon (1986).

A lack of flexibility in the wage and work schedules due to information and moral hazard problems will naturally lead to some degree of non-optimal separations. Some workers will quit or be laid off when in fact a wage or hours adjustment would have allowed both parties to receive positive periodic rents. To the extent that this is a problem then, perhaps, there is some reason for governments to subsidize short-time working.

In many European countries, it is possible for workers to receive a government subsidy, funded in several cases through the unemployment insurance system, for loss of earnings due to periods of enforced short-time working. The fundamental problem faced by such schemes is the difficulty in ascertaining to what extent the firm and its workforce are receiving subsidies for manhours that would have been hoarded (for the sorts of reasons outlined in Section 4.3) in the absence of the subsidy. If firms are not required to pay the actuarial value of their own propensities to work short-time, this is the same type of problem on the intensive margin as that associated with 'feigning layoffs' due to incomplete experience rating of unemployment benefits on the extensive margin. It is clearly not possible for a government agency accurately to assess the firm's and its workers' expectations over the size of the periodic rent and, therefore, the degree to which both parties would attempt to avoid a separation in the absence of a subsidy. For these sorts of reasons several governments may have 'erred on the side of safety' since, as noted in Section 2.3(b), firms requesting such subsidies often face quite stringent qualification rules and conditions.

Since the regulations that govern short-time working subsidies differ from those concerning unemployment benefits, it is not possible to compare their relative effectiveness *vis-à-vis* intended policy goals. There is little justification for the claim made in some theoretical work that layoffs alone represent an efficient second-best response to uncertainty when the wage is predetermined. Several well-known contract models have excluded the possibility of hours variability and no serious attempt has yet been made to integrate both unemployment *and* worksharing subsidies into a complete contract model. On the demand-side, layoffs may provide the advantage of allowing the firm some discretion over which part of its labour stock should bear the brunt of economic hardship. On the supply-side, certain union members and/or senior workers may perceive advantages in selective layoff. Despite this, it is hard to imagine that significant groups of workers would not realize welfare advantages if emphasis was switched from wage to job protection.

8.5 Concluding Remarks

The implicit contract theory provides a fairly persuasive means of rationalizing the phenomenon of temporary layoff unemployment given the existence of unemployment subsidies. Added to this it offers, on the basis of models that (correctly) differentiate between the intensive and extensive labour markets, some explanation of the type of aggregate hours/employment behaviour experienced in the USA (see Tables 2.1 and 2.2). Unfortunately, in a wider international context, the generality of the predictions are found to be wanting. Temporary layoffs are less common in Europe and Japan and yet, if anything, the necessary conditions for such short-term unemployment spells are more obviously apparent there. Further, in countries like Japan (see Tables 2.1 and 2.2), the hours/employment patterns are radically different from the USA and, therefore, do not rest well with the theory.

This is not to suggest that refinements to the theory will not succeed in capturing more of the empirical observations. One attempt, outlined in Section 8.3, has been to integrate more fiscal detail into the general model. It would also be interesting to analyse explicitly the fact that, in several major OECD countries, subsidies are available to unemployed manhours on *both* the intensive and extensive margins.

CHAPTER NINE

Labour Subsidies and Social Security Funding

9.1 Introduction

In the earlier theoretical models that incorporate overtime as an endogenous variable, the key to understanding the effects of a reduction in the standard workweek is to establish the relative cost change on the extensive relative to the intensive margin. Exogenous changes in (standard) hours of work alter relative factor prices and therefore lead to substitution between inputs. We have seen that, in the majority of these simple models, a reduction in the standard workweek has the effect of increasing the price of a new worker relative to an additional (overtime) hour of work. However, even in the absence of variability in labour utilization, several different types of model have been shown to predict negative employment reactions to work-week reductions.

In the 'real' world, governments may well obtain signals concerning such employment effects as, for example, employers' associations argue that reductions in standard hours, especially with full wage compensation, will increase the relative price of the labour stock input and lead to scale and substitution effects that run against the primary goal of creating new jobs. One possible counter-reaction could be for the government to offset unfavourable price responses by offering marginal employment subsidies that accompany workweek reductions. For example, following the cut in

209

hours, the firm would receive a per-capita wage (or non-wage) subsidy for each new job created over and above the number of workers on the payroll at the time of the policy change. Naturally, such intervention has wider macro-economic implications, some of which we will consider later, but the strategy may appear to be sound at the micro level. Indeed, this type of policy approach has been followed in several countries. The best-known example in Europe is that of the French solidarity contracts (see Hart, 1984c), although in this case the standard workweek cuts were encouraged *on a voluntary basis* by contingent marginal employment subsidies with respect to social security contributions. Drèze (1985) reports on a similar scheme introduced in Belgium.

The aim of this chapter is to discuss the consequences of actions by governments to alter relative factor prices with the aim of redistributing the mix of total manhours more towards the labour stock dimension and away from utiliz-ation. Two kinds of policy intervention are discussed. The first, as in the French solidarity contracts, involves subsidies that are designed to reinforce the employment goals of workweek reductions. The second, which concentrates on social security funding, deals with somewhat more general attempts to increase employment through tax intervention that is not contingent on other policy initiatives.

Section 9.2 considers the use of a marginal employment subsidy as an instrument for achieving employment expan-sion both in its own right as well as in relation to exogenous hours reductions. As in Chapter 5 and elsewhere, the analysis concentrates on the micro level of the firm but also embraces some wider macroeconomic considerations.

As mentioned above, governments may consider more general labour market initiatives designed to alter relative factor prices in favour of employment. Perhaps the most obvious action in this respect is to instigate general incomes policies whereby wages and salaries, and perhaps consumer prices, are held at target rates of growth in order to depress unit labour costs with the aim of preserving existing, or creating new, jobs. Some discussion of this type of strategy is given in Section 11.4. Here, attention is concentrated on one aspect of government labour cost intervention that has received considerable interest in very recent years. While governments often find it difficult, for a variety of well-known reasons, to control direct wages and prices beyond the short term, they do have a potentially more effective long-term means of altering total average labour costs. Specifically, they have some degrees of freedom in controlling firms' relative share of funding social security programmes. (The possibility that full tax shifting takes place is discounted given the empirical evidence.) As is shown in Hart (1984a), such taxes are an important part of total labour costs – amounting to between 10 and 15 per cent for the average firm in the OECD – and provide a possible means of inducing significant changes in the costs of workers relative to hours as well as the costs of labour relative to capital. This topic is the subject of Section 9.3 and, again, the potential importance of the distinction between the stock and utilization dimensions of the labour input is established. Some policy conclusions are presented in Section 9.4.

9.2 Marginal Employment Subsidies and Workweek Reductions

The adopted approach here is to derive some comparative static implications of standard hours reductions accompanied by marginal employment subsidies within the confines of a simple labour demand model taken from Section 4.4. The developments are similar to those in Hart (1984b) and Rosen (1978); further, a somewhat more detailed analysis can be found in Hart (1986). The results will then be considered in a broader economic perspective. This includes both extensions to the labour demand model itself as well as the impact of non-labour market variables from a wider macroeconomic structure.

Consider a firm with an equilibrium work force of $\bar{N}_0$ employees that is required to reduce its standard hours. If it responds to the reduction by employing $N > \bar{N}_0$, it receives a subsidy ϕ on its variable labour costs with respect to the marginal increment to its workforce, $N - \bar{N}_0$. No subsidy is given for an outcome $N \leq \bar{N}_0$, however. Modifying the simple cost function in (4.1), labour costs may now be written

$$C_L = \{Pw(h)+Z+T\}N - \phi\, Pw(h)\{\max (0,N-\bar{N}_0)\};\ 0 < \phi < 1. \tag{9.1}$$

Suppose, in equilibrium, $\bar{h} > h_s$ and the piecewise linear wage schedule in (4.9) applies; thus

$$w(h) = W = w_s h_s + a w_s(h-h_s)\quad h > h_s,\ a > 1. \tag{9.2}$$

Substituting (9.2) into (9.1) with $\phi > 0$ gives

$$N = \frac{C_L/P-\phi W N_0}{\{\tau+(1-\phi)W\}}$$

Where, as earlier, $\tau = (Z+T)/P$. Then, for given C_L, we obtain

$$\frac{dN}{dh} = \frac{-W'\{\phi\tau N_0+(1-\phi)C_L/P\}}{\{\tau+(1-\phi)W\}^2} < 0 \tag{9.3}$$

where $W' = dW/dh$. Differentiating (9.3) with respect to h gives

$$\frac{d^2N}{dh^2} = \frac{-[2(1-\phi)aw_s\{\tau+(1-\phi)aw_s h\}][-W'\{\phi\tau N_0+(1-\phi)C_L/P\}]}{[\tau+(1-\phi)W]^4} > 0 \tag{9.4}$$

using the definition of W in (9.2). Note that in (9.3) we have

$$\frac{dN}{dh} \to \frac{-W'C_L/P}{(\tau+W)^2} = \frac{-W'PN^2}{C_L} < 0 \text{ as } \phi \to 0 \tag{9.5}$$

and, again, $d^2N/dh^2 > 0$.

Expression (9.3) corresponds to the slope of the firm's cost curve if it is in receipt of a subsidy, that is, if $(N-\bar{N}_0) > 0$ in (9.1). The curve is convex, as shown by (9.4). The slope of the equivalent curve in the absence of a subsidy, or $(N-\bar{N}_0) \leq 0$ in (9.1), is given by expression (9.5).

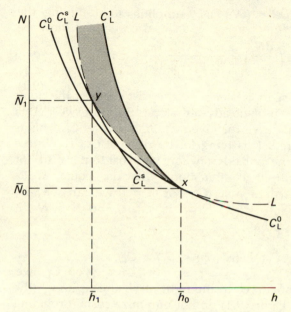

Figure 9.1 Equilibrium workers and hours reactions to changes in marginal employment subsidies.

Suppose that, initially, the firm is in equilibrium employing $N = \bar{N}_0$ workers. This is illustrated in Figure 9.1 at the point x where the 'subsidy-off' cost curve $C_L^0 C_L^0$ (that is, with $\phi = 0$) is tangential to the labour services function LL (see expression (4.8)). For convenience the 'pivots' in the cost functions at h_s (see Figure 5.1) are not shown; thus, Figure 9.1 is confined to points $h > h_s$. A marginal employment subsidy is now introduced that follows the rules indicated in (9.1). At this point, no other changes are considered. Perhaps the best way of understanding the implications of the introduction of $\phi > 0$ for $N > \bar{N}_0$ is to evaluate the effect on the slope of the cost curve of a marginal change in ϕ at the point $N = \bar{N}_0$ and for *given* C_L, h and N. Differentiating (9.3) with respect to ϕ, we obtain

$$\frac{\partial}{\partial \phi}\left(\frac{dN}{dh}\right) = \frac{-W'[\tau+(1-\phi)W]\{[\tau+(1-\phi)W](\tau\bar{N}_0-C_L/P)+2W[\phi\tau\bar{N}_0+(1-\phi)C_L/P]\}}{[\tau+(1-\phi)W]^4}$$

213

which, using $C_L/P = (W+\tau)\bar{N}_0$, simplifies to

$$\frac{\partial}{\partial\phi}\left(\frac{dN}{dh}\right) = \frac{-W'W\bar{N}_0}{[\tau+(1-\phi)W]^2} < 0. \qquad (9.6)$$

Thus, an increase in ϕ 'steepens' the cost curve at the point $\bar{N}_0$ compared to its 'subsidy-off' slope. Suppose we define the 'subsidy-on' curve for given C_L, h and N as C_L^1. This is shown in Figure 9.1 as lying to the right of C_L^0. The curve xC_L^1 represents the 'subsidy-on' constant cost to the firm, for varying $h-N$ input combinations, that is, equal to its 'subsidy-off' constant cost xC_L^0. For $\phi = 0$ we can set $\hat{h}(N)$ such that $C_L(N,h,0) = C_L^0$. Now, if $\phi > 0$ and $N > \bar{N}_0$, it must be the case that

$$C_L(N,\hat{h}(N),\ \phi) < C_L^0) = C_L^1).$$

All possible cost curves to the right of xL and up to C_L^1 (the shaded area in Figure 9.1) do not minimize costs. Providing

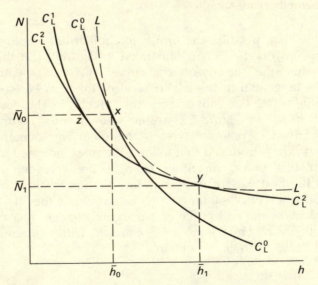

Figure 9.2 Equilibrium workers and hours reactions to joint changes in marginal employment subsidies and standard hours.

214

a tangency point exists, the 'subsidy-on' cost curve that does minimize costs clearly involves $N > \bar{N}_0$ and $h < \bar{h}_0$. Such a curve is illustrated in Figure 9.2 as $C_L^s C_L^s$ which at the tangent y gives a new equilibrium manhours combination, $\bar{h}_1 \bar{N}_1$. Employment is increased and average hours are reduced as a result of the subsidy.

It is easy to show that the same outcomes arise if quasi-fixed costs $Z+T$ in (9.1) rather than variable costs are subsidized. For example, the government may agree to subsidize a part of the firm's initial training costs in order to encourage the recruitment of young persons.

We now examine the effects of such marginal employment subsidies when made available in conjunction with a cut in the standard workweek.

In Figure 9.2, the firm is again in equilibrium at point x, with an $\bar{h}_0 \bar{N}_0$ combination of manhours on the 'subsidy-off' cost curve $C_L^0 C_L^0$. Suppose, *ceteris paribus*, that standard hours (h_s) are reduced. The slope of the new cost curve is found by differentiating (9.5) with respect to the h_s for given h and N. (See also the discussion in relation to Figure 5.1.) This produces

$$\frac{\partial}{\partial h_s}\left(\frac{dN}{dh}\right) = \frac{(1-a)w_s P^2 W' N^3}{C_L^2} < 0. \qquad (9.7)$$

The fall in h_s (algebraically) increases the slope of $C_L^0 C_L^0$; this is shown by the cost function $C_L^2 C_L^2$ in Figure 9.2. As we have already seen in Section 5.2(a) and (b) for this model, a cut in h_s leads to an $\bar{h} - \bar{N}$ substitution – that is, from $\bar{h}_0 \bar{N}_0$ to $\bar{h}_1 \bar{N}_1$ (x to y) in Figure 9.2.

Therefore, at least with respect to the present model, the direction of the substitution effect between $\bar{h}$ and $\bar{N}$ for an increase in marginal employment subsidy is *opposite* to that of a fall in standard hours. Without further information, the direction of the substitution effect of a subsidy that is conditional on a workweek reduction is indeterminate. Note from Figure 9.2 that the steeper 'subsidy-on' curve for $N > \bar{N}_0$ is given by zC_L^1. If this curve lies always to the left of LL (as in the figure) then point y represents the cheapest cost combination of inputs, and employment reductions would result. If, on the other hand, zC_L^1 crosses LL then there may exist a cost curve to the left of C_L^1 that provides a tangency point with LL thereby providing cost minimization at some point corresponding to $N > \bar{N}_0$ and $h < \bar{h}_0$.

It is worth commenting briefly on the implications of the above changes for a firm at an initial equilibrium corner solution at $\bar{h} = h_s$ with $W = w_s \bar{h}$ in (9.2) (for more detail, see Hart, 1986). It is recalled that (see the discussion in relation to Figure 5.2) a *ceteris paribus* reduction in h_s *may* produce an increase in employment. In this case, therefore, the hours and subsidy effects work in the same direction. What is not clear, however, is whether the employment substitution effect due to the subsidy is greater than that with respect to the hours reduction alone. Referring to Figure 5.2, the equilibrium position with respect to the reduced standard hours h'_s is at the corner solution y on $C_L^! C_L^!$. The equivalent 'subsidy-on' cost curve (which lies above $C_L^! C_L^!$ at points above $\bar{N}$) also pivots at $h_s^!$ and so it might well be the case that the post-tax cost minimizing curve may also be at the corner solution at y. In this case there is no net employment advantage in providing the marginal employment subsidy.

These conclusions are subject to much the same qualifications that are made to the comparable models, without subsidies, that appeared in Sections 5.2(a) and (b). For example, no mention has been made of scale effects. In the equivalent profit maximizing model, adverse (beneficial) substitution effects may be offset (enhanced) by positive employment scale responses to labour cost reductions. Also, alternative wage specifications, as in Section 5.3(b), may limit the adverse $\bar{h}-\bar{N}$ substitution response depicted in Figure 5.2.

Where scale arguments are thought to be potentially important then this may appear to be a reason for providing *general*, as opposed to marginal, subsidies to employment. Great caution should be exercised here, however. The most likely type of general subsidy would apply to *variable* labour compensation; this is equivalent to the subsidy in (9.1) *but applying to total N*. The two obvious examples are subsidies to direct wages or subsidies (as under the second version of the French solidarity contracts; see Hart, 1984c) to variable social security payments. Subsidies to fixed labour costs are not nearly so common. As we have seen in Chapter 5 and elsewhere, a reduction of variable relative to fixed labour costs, while possibly bringing about positive scale effects, would be predicted (see (5.7)) to have a *negative* impact on employment as far as substitution is concerned. Increases in per-unit fixed costs should influence the cost minimizing firm in the direction of substituting, at the margin, more hours for fewer workers. The relative advantage of the marginal employment subsidy is that *both* substitution and scale effects may be positive with a subsidy to variable costs.

Since the labour market implications of general changes in payroll tax rate and tax ceilings with respect to social security funding are currently under significant policy scrutiny in several countries, a more detailed analysis of this subject is presented in the following section.

Any major deviations from the above outcomes are likely to stem from the sort of wider macroeconomic considerations outlined in Section 5.7. Layard and Nickell (1980) have compared and contrasted the effects of general and marginal employment subsidies within a Keynesian macroeconomic comparative static model. Their analysis comes out firmly in favour of the marginal approach. One of their main arguments is concerned with international trade effects. (They discount the effects of employment subsidies on the domestic side since price reductions are constrained not to fall below the average cost of the marginal firm and so the resulting low price elasticity of aggregate demand will produce relatively little stimulus.) They argue that, in a small open economy like the UK, many firms are price-takers in markets where goods are internationally traded. If a given subsidy is concentrated at the margin then, for firms increasing employment, the fall in marginal cost of producing goods will be far greater than if they received general subsidies since these would have to be spread more thinly. This in turn could have an appreciable effect on the quantity of goods sold either as exports or import substitutes thereby improving the balance of payments. Further, the *net* increase in the total workforce would be expected to have a limited negative effect on the budget deficit since unemployment expenditure would be cut and additional tax revenue forthcoming. By contrast, a general reflation, through tax cuts or expenditure increases or general employment subsidies, are likely to produce adverse effects on the balance of payments as well as the budget deficit and prices.

Two aspects of Layard and Nickell's analytical approach seem to be quite critical. First, they acknowledge that it may in practice be extremely difficult to administer a marginal employment subsidy that provides payments to firms that increase employment purely as a result of the subsidy itself. In the simple comparative static model in this chapter, the starting level of employment is set, rather conveniently, at the equilibrium level and employment growth is treated simply as a *ceteris paribus* comparative static response to the subsidy. In practice, with other related variables and dynamic considerations playing a part, it would not be a simple matter to ascertain the pure subsidy effect on employment, let alone for employers and the government to agree on its value. In other words, problems of measurement and moral hazard would appear to render the introduction of this form of marginal employment subsidy to be somewhat impracticable. As a result, Layard and Nickell concentrate their attention on a scheme whereby *all* net new jobs receive a subsidy irrespective of the reason for their creation.

In the second place, as in our partial equilibrium analysis, Layard and Nickell's approach to modelling abstracts from dynamic considerations. Yet in their case, they are implicitly interested in employment adjustment speeds since they argue for the merits of a subsidy that applies to additional jobs created within two years of its initiation in the hope that this 'would encourage firms to bring forward their expansion plans so as to qualify for the subsidy, and quite substantial employment effects might be secured by relatively small expenditures of public money' (Layard and Nickell, 1980, p. 52). In this respect, therefore, it would seem to be quite critical to have some quantitative idea of the average adjustment lag between subsidies allocated and subsequent employment realized.

Whitley and Wilson (1983) have tested the macroeconomic implications of dynamic versions of the Layard and Nickell system for the UK economy using the Cambridge Growth Project multisectoral dynamic model. They find qualified support for the marginal employment subsidy effects claimed by Layard and Nickell. Their simulations are clearly sensitive to the starting assumptions over the initial employment base with which employment changes are compared. They use either the *expected* level of employment (on the basis of their model) in the absence of a subsidy or, more simply, the level of employment at some base year. On their estimates, the suggestion that the scheme should be designed to achieve relatively speedy employment responses obtains weak support since it is found that a period in excess of two years is required before maximum employment impacts are realized.

The most important conclusion from the Whitley and Wilson study, with respect to the discussion here, is that they are not able to find a significant employment advantage in using a marginal subsidy as opposed to general reflationary measures. This led them, given the inevitable high costs of running such a marginal scheme, to be somewhat sceptical over the claims for unique advantages.

Through distinguishing between the stock and utilization dimensions of the labour input, the results of our approach lean firmly towards the Layard and Nickell position. While these authors claim, correctly, that 'if the subsidy were a flat rate for each extra worker, it would encourage firms to produce extra output by employing extra men, rather than by lengthening the hours of those already employed' (p. 52), they do not in fact integrate the labour utilization dimension into their model. This is a major weakness which also recurs in the Whitley and Wilson work. In fact, the latter authors express agreement with Layard and Nickell that it is the demand stimulus of lower prices that produces the major employment effects rather than changes in relative factor prices. This conclusion is hard to take very seriously, however, since the relative price effect with respect to workers and hours is simply ignored.

9.3   Payroll Taxes and Ceilings

Unless there exists full payroll tax shifting, governments may also attempt to influence firms' factor allocation through statutory changes in social security contributions. The empirical evidence on tax shifting suggests, fairly comprehensively, that a significant proportion of tax payments are *not* shifted. Unfortunately, the bulk of this literature contains a serious specification error since it fails to differentiate between stock and utilization dimensions of the labour input. Not only is the importance of this distinction illustrated in what follows but also it is shown that, unlike in earlier studies, a correct specification of the labour input allows for a form of tax shifting that is integral to the analysis itself.

This section is concerned with the consequences for factor demand of exogenous changes in firms' social security contributions. In Section 8.3, it is shown that the direction of hours–worker substitution given changes in payroll taxes related to unemployment insurance depends on the system of funding. Taxes that are wage-related may be expected to work differently from those incurred on a per-worker basis. These ideas are pursued further here both by describing a more broadly defined operational model as well as providing some empirical evidence. The section is based on work by Hart and Kawasaki (1986).

9.3(a)   Comparative Statics

Most national statutory social security contribution systems within OECD have the same general structure. Firms contribute to each item of social security (that is, health, pensions and unemployment insurance) in the form of a payroll tax which, for a given period of time, varies directly with earnings up to a ceiling cut-off limit. For each worker with earnings *above* the ceiling, the contribution per period is calculated simply as the tax rate multiplied by the ceiling wage. In these cases, the contributions represent per-worker, or 'fixed', labour costs in the sense that a change in

per-period wage earnings due to a change either in the wage
rate or in working hours involves no alteration – providing
ceilings are not 'crossed' – in contribution.

In order to simplify matters, suppose there is only one
payroll tax rate, t, that applies to all items of social security.
This involves no significant loss of detail. For ease of
exposition, the contribution per worker applies to average
monthly wage earnings

$$W = wh \qquad (9.8)$$

where w is the average hourly wage and h is average
(effective) monthly hours worked.

In terms of a given firm, suppose W in (9.8) has a
probability density function $\Phi(W)$ with $E(W) = \bar{W}$. The
distribution may reflect, for example, occupational, skill and
sex differences among workers. Such a density is represented in Figure 9.3 which relates $N(W)/N$ (where N is the
number of workers, $\{N(W)/N\}dW$ is the percentage of

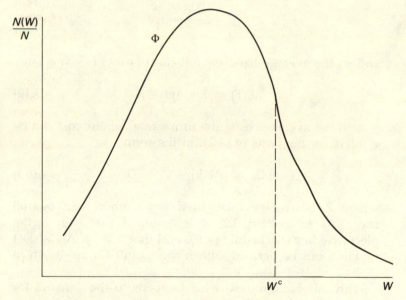

Figure 9.3 Wage distribution and ceiling limit.

workers earning a wage between W and $W+dW$ and where $\int_0^\infty \{N(W)/N\}dW = 1$) to W. The point, W^c in the figure represents the monthly wage ceiling that marks the upper tax limit. For $W > W^c$ the monthly wage is zero-tax-rated. (We ignore here the possibility of lower ceilings, below which wages are zero-rated, although these do apply in most countries.)

A number of simple definitions can now be made in relation to Figure 9.3.

First, the average hourly wage per worker can be expressed

$$E(w) = \bar{w} = \left\{ \int_0^\infty W \frac{N(W)}{N} dW \right\}/h. \qquad (9.9)$$

Average hourly *variable* payroll contribution is given by

$$E(P) = \bar{P} = \left\{ \int_0^{W^c} W \frac{N(W)}{N} t dW \right\} /h. \qquad (9.10)$$

Let p be the proportion of workers with $W > W^c$, then

$$p = \int_{W^c}^\infty \frac{N(W)}{N} dW \qquad (9.11)$$

and so the average fixed payroll contribution is given by

$$E(T) = \bar{T} = (ptW^c). \qquad (9.12)$$

At these average costs, the firm's total labour cost can be written, on the basis of (4.2), in the form

$$C_L = \{\bar{P}\bar{w}(h) + \bar{Z} + \bar{T}\} \qquad (9.13)$$

where $\bar{Z}$ is average quasi-fixed costs other than payroll taxes. As in Section 5.2, it is assumed that $w(h)$ is the piecewise linear schedule (4.10) and that $h > h_s$. An isocost function can be derived with respect to (9.13) as shown in (5.9).

With this background, what happens to the demand for workers and hours if the firm experiences an exogenous

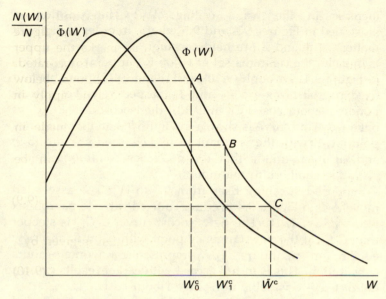

Figure 9.4 Wage distributions and ceiling changes.

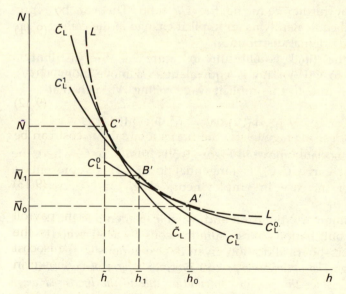

Figure 9.5 Equilibrium workers and hours reactions to ceiling changes.

increase in the wage ceiling, W^c? The position is illustrated in Figures 9.4 and 9.5 where, in order to simplify matters, t, $\bar{w}$ and $\bar{Z}$ are held constant.

Initially, the ceiling is set at $W^c = W_0^c$ at point A on $\Phi(W)$ in Figure 9.4. Through (9.10), (9.11) and (9.12), variable and fixed payroll taxes are $\bar{P}_0$ and $\bar{T}_0$, respectively. For corresponding labour costs, C_L^0 in (9.13), the isocost curve $C_L^0 C_L^0$ is obtained. This curve is shown in Figure 9.5 and its tangency point at A' with the isoquant locus LL – see (5.8) and (5.9) and, again assuming that the necessary conditions hold – gives the equilibrium manhours, $\bar{h}_0 \bar{N}_0$.

Suppose the ceiling rises from W_0^c to W_1^c. The associated move $A–B$ in Figure 9.4 produces a fixed/variable payroll tax ratio $\bar{T}_1 / \bar{P}_1 < \bar{T}_0 / \bar{P}_0$. The new isocost curve, $C_L^1 C_L^1$, is steeper than $C_L^0 C_L^0$ at the new tangency point with LL at B' and new equilibrium manhours, $\bar{h}_1 \bar{N}_1$, represents a workers–hours substitution. This is in full accord with earlier results given a fall in fixed-to-variable non-wage labour costs.

Assuming that the fall in hours is uniformly distributed over $\Phi(W)$, the effect is to shift the distribution to the left thereby further reducing the $\bar{T}/\bar{P}$ ratio. This can be represented equivalently as an implicit change in the ceiling wage on the original distribution.

In the 'final' equilibrium in figure 9.4, the distribution shifts to $\hat{\Phi}(W)$. This is equivalent to a move along $\Phi(W)$, from B to C to the implicit wage ceiling $\hat{W}^c$ such that

$$\int_{W_1^c}^{\infty} \hat{\Phi}(W)dW = \int_{\hat{W}^c}^{\infty} \Phi(W)dW.$$

The associated move in Figure 9.5 is from B' to C' where the isocost curve $\hat{C}_L \hat{C}_L$ is tangential to LL. This represents a further increase in employment, $\hat{N} - N_1$ and decrease in hours $h_1 - \hat{h}$.

In summary, the fixed and variable elements of the payroll tax contributions are simultaneously determined with workers–hours allocation given the exogenous change in the ceiling. *The optimizing process involves a form of backward tax shifting since the rise in contribution due to the increased wage ceiling is borne in part through a reduction in monthly wage earnings of the existing labour force.* This type of reaction is invariably absent from studies on tax shifting.

Due to the definitions of payroll taxes in (9.10), (9.11) and (9.12), a change in the payroll tax, t, leaves the ratio $\bar{T}/\bar{P}$ unchanged. In more realistic models, however, the simple ratio does not apply (see Hart and Kawasaki, 1986) and a change in t would be expected to alter the relative sizes of $\bar{T}$ and $\bar{P}$ with associated factor allocation and feedback effects.

9.3(b) Empirical Outcomes from an Extended Model Structure

In order to understand the employment–hours effects of changes in payroll tax rates and tax ceiling limits, given the prevailing social security systems, it is necessary to work in terms of wage distributions as in Figure 9.3. Payroll taxes cannot be considered exogenous in this framework; the simple illustration above establishes that they are functionally related to the parameters that describe the wage distributions. In terms of Figure 9.3, we have

$$\bar{P} = \bar{P}(h,N,t,W^c,w) \tag{9.14}$$

and

$$\bar{T} = \bar{T}(h,N,t,W^c,w). \tag{9.15}$$

Hart and Kawasaki incorporate the payroll tax expressions in (9.14) and (9.15) into a factor demand model that embraces effective working hours, workers and the capital stock. Their user cost of capital expression is identical to that in (4.15). One objective of the work is to measure the relative effectiveness in stimulating employment through exogenous changes in user cost (c) subsidies and tax rates (that is, k, δ and u in expression (4.15)) compared to changes in payroll tax rates and ceiling limits.

The demand equation for the desired level of the ith input factor, Y_i^* (where $i = 1,2,3$ refers to effective hours, workers and the capital stock) is given by

$$Y_i^* = Y_i^* [\bar{P}( ),\bar{T}( ),\bar{Z},t,W^c,w,c,Q] \tag{9.16}$$

where Q is output. Actual and desired values of the Y_is are related through the adjustment process given in (4.22).

For ease of exposition, the discussion with respect to Figure 9.5 has been couched in terms of the cost minimizing model of an individual firm. In fact, a profit maximizing framework is more appropriate in the present context since output exogeneity is an unrealistic assumption within the economy-wide policy context of payroll tax legislation. Besides, the results reported below are based on national-level data. It will be recalled from Section 5.2(b) that while factor substitution responses are the same in both types of model, profit maximization additionally involves the complications of scale responses. It will suffice here to report that the results reported below are based on an empirical model in which output is treated as an endogenous variable.

The wage distributions, comparable to Figure 9.3, are fitted statistically (to FRG data) using a rational spline technique and so this determines the functional forms of $\bar{P}(\ )$ and $\bar{T}(\ )$ in (9.14), (9.15) and (9.16). It is shown that introducing these functions into a standard profit maximizing problem introduces severe nonlinearities into the system. Apart from dealing with tax and output endogeneity, exact modelling is not attempted.

The factor demand equations are estimated using aggregate FRG manufacturing data, 1951–81. There are three payroll tax rates – for pensions, health and unemployment/ short-time working insurance – and three respective wage ceilings. Incorporating these makes no difference to the general methodology, however. Other special features of the FRG social security system are accommodated although these are not reported here. Of most interest for present purposes are the results of the simulations that are carried out, with respect to the year 1981, on the basis of the factor demand estimates. The simulations were designed to answer three basic questions:

(1) What are the factor demand implications of changes in payroll tax ceiling limits?
(2) What are the factor demand implications of changes in payroll tax rates?

226

(3) What would be the required change in capital subsidy, from its 1981 level, to produce the equivalent effects on employment as each given wage ceiling and tax rate change?

One important point to establish is that, in 1981, the ceilings (in common with those of most other OECD countries) were situated towards the extreme right tail of the distribution in Figure 9.3. (For their data set, Hart and Kawasaki estimate values, as a percentage of total labour costs, of $\bar{P} = 11.8$ per cent, $\bar{T} = 1.2$ per cent and $\bar{Z} = 11.8$ per cent in 1981.)

Attention is concentrated on simulation (2), that is, with respect to the payroll tax rates since this is the potential change that has received most policy attention. The results are summarized in Table 9.1 for tax rate changes at 5 per cent intervals in the range −15 to +15 per cent.

Table 9.1
Simulated Effects of Payroll Tax Changes on Factor Demand; FRG Manufacturing Industry, 1981

Percentage changes in payroll tax rates	Estimated percentage changes in factor input		
	h	N	K
− 5.00	0.86	−0.27	0.12
−10.00	1.78	−0.56	0.24
−15.00	2.76	−0.86	0.37
+ 5.00	−0.81	0.26	−0.11
+10.00	−1.58	0.51	−0.22
+15.00	−2.32	0.74	−0.31

On the evidence of these results, payroll tax cuts have the effect of increasing labour utilization and the stock of capital and reducing the number of workers. For tax rate reductions in the range 5 to 15 per cent, the magnitudes of the respective employment decreases lie between 16,000 and 28,000 workers (from a sample population of 5.8 million workers) while the respective hours increases lie between 1.2 and 3.8 hours per month (from an average of 138.5 hours).

Therefore, although there is an indication that payroll tax

reductions may stimulate a positive labour response, the labour increase is *only with respect to the utilization dimension*. The result is not surprising since, as indicated above, payroll taxes in 1981 constituted primarily variable labour costs. It has already been shown with respect to an efficient contract model (see (8.8)) and a simpler cost minimizing model (see 5.7)) that a fall in $\bar{P}$, *ceteris paribus*, may stimulate hours–worker substitution.

As might be expected, given the location of the tax ceilings in 1981, −15 to +15 percentage changes in the ceilings (simulation (1)) were estimated to have very small effects on both stock and utilization variables. Finally, with respect to simulation (3), the total capital subsidies (that is, tax and depreciation allowances) reduced user costs from their unsubsidized price by 9.7 per cent in 1981. It was found that even to produce the modest employment gain of 0.65 per cent – equivalent to a 5 per cent reduction in the wage ceiling – the capital subsidies would need to be reduced by one-half. For more substantial employment effects, the required capital subsidy changes were estimated to be so large as to be outside the bounds of a credible policy strategy.

9.4 Policy Conclusions

In this chapter we have touched on four main types of government intervention designed to encourage worksharing. These are

(1) marginal employment subsidies,
(2) general employment subsidies,
(3) reductions in payroll taxes (rates and ceilings),
(4) reductions in capital subsidies.

Of these, there is no doubt on the basis of the micro approach adopted here that option (1) provides the most encouraging strategy. If subsidies are to be given at all, then there would appear to be some quite sound logic behind offering labour cost reductions to firms that produce net increases in their workforces. It is, nevertheless, a type of policy that should be approached with extreme caution. In the first place, as emphasized by Layard and Nickell (1980), it may be prohibitively costly to measure the extent to which the observed employment gains result directly from the subsidy itself. The fact that the subsidy would almost certainly have to be paid to all newly created jobs, irrespective of the exact stimulus, does tend to limit the policy's cost effectiveness. In the second place, it is necessary to return to a point that is given prominence in Drèze (1985). Marginal employment subsidies are most likely to be forthcoming during relatively depressed economic conditions. For those firms that are hoarding labour at such times, the offer of marginal labour cost reductions is probably of very limited appeal. If such firms are not recovering the full periodic (sunk) costs of specific investments then the offer of reduced labour costs at the margin are unlikely to provide a potent employment stimulus. (Recall that the analysis in Section 9.2 is carried out under the assumption that the paid-for and effective working hours are equal.) This type of argument is very persuasive and it suggests that *marginal employment subsidies might be aimed at new firms or at existing firms with a recent history of expansion.* Finally, as we have attempted to show systematically in Section 9.2, marginal employment subsidies should be provided *without* the additional constraint of mandatory workweek reductions. This latter condition serves almost certainly to counteract the effectiveness of the subsidy.

In the case of general wage subsidies, it is clear from the analysis here that while positive scale impacts may provide beneficial employment effects, these may well be offset by hours–worker substitution since variable labour costs would reduce relative to quasi-fixed costs. Also they seem to involve potentially greater inflationary consequences at the macro level.

A very similar conclusion to that concerning general wage subsidies applies to reductions in payroll tax rates. Since these represent variable labour costs to the typical firm, a reduction may well have the effect of providing a relative cost advantage at the intensive rather than the extensive margin. Not only have we provided theoretical results to support this conclusion from a number of earlier models but also, in Section 9.3, corroborating empirical evidence is also provided.

Far less stress should be given to conclusions concerning the relative effectiveness of reductions in capital subsidies in stimulating new jobs. On the basis of one empirical analysis, this does not appear to be an encouraging avenue to pursue. Much more work is required on this topic, however.

CHAPTER TEN

Retirement and Employment

10.1 Introduction

The intervals of working time so far referred to are of relatively short length. In this chapter, the emphasis is switched towards examining the consequences for employment and work intensity of changes both in the length of working lifetime and in the financial provision for periods of non-labour market activity outside working lifetime. Attention is focused solely on the upper bound of the working age spectrum; that is, on working time issues related to retirement. While acknowledging increasing interest in topics at the lower bound – such as the length of schooling, youth training and special demographic features of the younger population – this area is largely ignored here. The one exception is where the subjects of youth training and retirement become interrelated.

The employment effects of changes in retirement policy, while involving somewhat different background modelling techniques, embrace broadly similar economic considerations to earlier chapters. Two examples serve to illustrate this. First, if the productivity of older workers differs significantly from the average for the entire workforce, then an evaluation of the effects of a reduction in the age of retirement involves related employment issues to those associated with weekly or annual hours reductions on hourly productivity. Secondly, alterations in the social security provision of retirees have implications not only for expected rates of retirement at given ages, but also for the levels of social security financing. The latter, in turn, may affect factor allocation via the type of payroll tax analysis presented in Section 9.3. An attempt is made to capitalize on these types of similarity by linking, as far as possible, the present discussion to earlier developments.

Three types of retirement are delineated in the chapter: these are mandatory, full- and partial-early retirement, discussed in Sections 10.2, 10.3(a) and 10.3(b), respectively. A brief general assessment is then undertaken in Section 10.4.

10.2 Mandatory Retirement

In most OECD countries, a high proportion of private firms and public organizations stipulate a mandatory age of retirement in their long-term employment contracts. Often this retirement age differs significantly between men and women but, otherwise, it usually has a remarkably narrow variation. Mandatory retirement does not preclude workers from re-entering the labour force and, as indicated in Table 2.7, a proportion of them, varying from country to country, continue actively to participate.

In Europe, there has been a great deal of recent interest in the possibility of reducing the mandatory retirement age in order to provide job opportunities for the younger unemployed population. This type of strategy has received strong support from European trade unions (see European Trade Union Institute, 1978). Under somewhat favourable assumptions, such as high replacement rates, the unemployment reducing potential of significant cuts in the mandatory retirement age has been calculated to be quite significant (for UK calculations, see Department of Employment, 1978). By contrast, an amendment to the Age Discrimination in Employment Act passed by Congress in 1979 raised the mandatory retirement age in the USA from 65 to 70. There has also been a marked recent tendency for the mandatory age to rise in Japan although, as mentioned in Chapter 2, from an existing average age base that is considerably lower than elsewhere.

It does appear that mandatory retirement *per se* encourages people to retire once and for all (see, for example, Zabalza *et al.*, 1980). Apart from relatively crude estimates, however, little is known about the quantitative effects of falls or rises in the mandatory retirement age on employment and unemployment. A full assessment of likely outcomes involves a complex set of economic and other considerations. In this section an attempt is made to outline some of the central considerations involved under three headings which, taken together, capture the main areas of interest in the relevant theoretical and empirical work.

10.2(a) Productivity of Older Workers

Perhaps the most common explanation (and defence) of the necessity for a mandatory age of retirement is that it serves as a formal contractual means of recognizing that there is a period in average working lifetime after which productivity declines markedly. It thereby provides the employer with an offsetting employment adjustment mode. Increasing ill health is the main reason advanced for the productivity decline, but it may also include occupational inertia and the growing inability to accept and integrate new work methods and practices.

A few simple reflections serve to blunt the force of this type of argument. First, on a cross-sectional international basis, there is a wide variation in the mandatory retirement modal ages – 55–60 in Japan, 60–5 in Europe, 70 in the USA – which do not relate to the respective international variations in health profiles. (A narrower example relates to the fact that Western European females have significantly longer average life expectancy than their male counterparts and yet, in most countries, experience a lower average mandatory retirement age.) Secondly, health and life expectancy have improved systematically over time throughout the OECD without a corresponding adjustment in mandatory retirement ages. Thirdly, psychological studies tend to produce little evidence of a strong systematic relationship

233

between chronological age and work performance (see Kreps, 1977).

Clearly, given the vast heterogeneity of the older work-force and its related occupational structure, a simple retirement rule provides a grossly inefficient device for eliminating significant productivity declines due to old age. Notwithstanding, evidence does exist that a commonly stated reason for retirement, although not necessarily at the mandatory age, is that of ill health (see, for example, Gordon and Blinder, 1980) and so it is fair to assume that a change in the mandatory retirement age would involve some change in marginal labour productivity for the typical firm. In order to evaluate the resulting implications for employment brings us back into the territory of Sections 4.5 and 6.4 where the labour productivity effects of weekly hours reductions are assessed. Factors such as product elasticity of demand and the elasticity of substitution between labour and capital again become important.

If a typical firm's hourly productivity is enhanced through a reduction in the mandatory retirement age then, allowing for high product elasticity of demand and/or a high price elasticity of substitution between labour and capital, new hires may result. The change may also alter the firm's private or (if the reduction is general to many firms) statutory pension contributions. Further, the wage profiles of the *existing* workforce may be significantly affected. The implications for employment with respect to pensions and wages, as discussed below, may not necessarily conform with those related to labour productivity.

10.2(b) Social Security

For given contributions, the asset values of many types of private and state pension are age-related and impose an actuarial penalty on those who remain in employment after the mandatory retirement age. Without this penalty, it may be expected that a higher proportion of the older age-groups would remain in work thereby, perhaps, reducing employment opportunities for younger persons. Gustman and Steinmeier (1985) find some evidence for this following a

234

recent US reform to the social security system that, among other features, sought to remove such disadvantages on the labour supply of older workers.

It may seem to follow that one indirect way of inducing more once-for-all retirement and (depending on replacement rates) increasing employment in the younger age-groups would be for governments and individual firms to increase the costs to the individual of deciding to remain at work after the official retirement date. Further, early retirement may be encouraged (see next section) by ensuring no actuarial loss of benefit for certain types of worker who wish to retire before the mandatory deadline. Unfortunately, the employment implications of such measures are by no means clear-cut.

Four complications are mentioned here (see also Ehrenberg, 1979). In the first place, if we consider that workers act, at least to some extent, with respect to the expected present value of their income stream over their lifetimes, then they may adjust *current* work patterns in anticipation of social security penalties in later years. This possibility has been studied for the USA by Burkhauser and Turner (1978, 1982 – see also Smith, 1975) using a life cycle asset maximization approach to modelling. These authors are particularly interested in understanding the implications on pre-retirement working behaviour of both social security benefits that actuarially penalize older workers and 'earnings tests' that reduce the net wage of those who accept social security benefits. Burkhauser and Turner estimate that life cycle reallocation of work effort due to social security penalties on the retirement years in the USA have increased the workweek by more than two hours for prime age males. They suggest that this finding ties in with the fact that hours per worker (see Table 2.1) have changed relatively little in the United States since the Second World War while activity rates of older workers (see Table 2.7) have declined quite dramatically. Therefore, it may be the case that a policy of attempting to stimulate new employment through a stronger and (perhaps earlier) encouragement to retire may have the effect of producing a relatively larger response at the intensive as opposed to the extensive margin. It should be added, as qualification, that the importance of earnings tests as an influence on the retirement decision has been queried elsewhere; see Blinder *et al.* (1980) for the USA and Zabalza *et al.* (1980) for the UK.

As a second consideration, increased pension benefits as an inducement to retire would almost certainly be matched by increased employer and worker social security contributions. Given less-than-full tax-shifting, the increased cost to the typical employer would be in the form of higher variable payroll tax contributions. While this may produce negative scale effects on employment, it may also involve favourable substitution effects – in line with the analysis in Section 9.3 – in the form of reduced labour utilization and increased stocks of employment and capital.

As pointed out by Ehrenberg (1979), there may also be a distributional effect following contribution increases. For a given payroll tax ceiling, the cost of low-wage employees would rise relative to high-wage employees. Therefore, not only might the worker–hours substitution effects differ *within* the two groups but also substitution *between* the groups may occur. Given these complications, together with technical constraints and job mismatching, employment responses may be impeded. Two further considerations serve to limit the importance of this aspect of the problem, however. First, relative wages may adjust to offset the differential cost effects. Secondly, and of more importance, current earnings/ceiling ratios throughout OECD are relatively high and only very small proportions of workers are exempted from contribution increases.

In the third place, potential increases in contributions in order to provide more attractive retirement benefits have to be considered in a climate of increasing pressure on pension financing due to adverse demographic factors in many countries (see the discussion in Section 2.4). In other words, the effect of policy may be to magnify existing strong pressures on rates of social security contributions and thereby provide a strong marginal incentive to introduce plans designed to substitute capital for labour. There are also other pressures from so-called 'cohort crowding'; for a wider discussion see Wachter (1977) and Duggan (1984).

Fourthly, net increases in social security contributions financed under pay-as-you-go systems (which are prevalent in most OECD countries) rather than through funded schemes may serve to depress private savings (Feldstein, 1974, 1977). In the longer term, this may lead to capital shortages, especially given the adverse demographic trends, and thus to reduced growth rates of output, productivity and employment. It should be noted, however, that the force of this argument has been challenged by Modigliani and Sterling (1983) and others.

10.2(c) Lifetime Wage and Productivity Profiles

As has already been mentioned in relation to the work of Burkhauser and Turner, workers may adjust current work patterns in relation to changes in social security retirement provisions in accord with a strategy of maximizing the present value of their wage stream over their lifetimes. Similarly, firms may act in relation to the expected stream of workers' marginal products over their life in the firm. An equilibrium wage path in relation to an individual worker is one where the present values of the wage and the marginal product are equated. One simple means of achieving such an equilibrium would be to pay the worker the spot value of marginal product (VMP) at each point in time. Under the so-called 'agency hypothesis', Lazear (1979) presents arguments as to why it is preferable for both workers and firms to agree to an alternative lifetime compensation schedule such that wages are less than VMP in early years of work and greater in later years (see also Lazear, 1981). This form of deferred compensation would be expected to reduce shirking and to encourage workers to aspire to higher occupational levels through improved work application and effort. Both firms and workers would be expected to prefer such a high-wage/high-marginal product combination. Given this interpretation, the mandatory retirement age can be viewed as a device that ensures retirement, on the average, at the (jointly) optimal age. Without a contractually binding termination date, workers who are nearing retirement may attempt to remain in their jobs since the wage exceeds VMP.

Under these circumstances suppose that, following legislation, the mandatory age of retirement is reduced in a given firm. The present value of VMP would now exceed the present value of the wage and there would be an incentive for workers to claim higher real wages. Therefore, any potential for employment expansion due to increased retirement may be offset by negative scale effects of increased labour costs. Moreover, since it is argued by Lazear that the 'agency' interpretation of the economic role of mandatory retirement is more likely to refer to relatively high-skilled/long-tenured workers, then the firm itself may also encourage greater utilization of its existing employees so as to counteract shortened expected lengths of amortization periods.

10.3   Early Retirement

In Section 2.4, it is indicated that considerable recent interest has been shown in Europe towards encouraging early retirement in the hope of creating new jobs, particularly for young unemployed persons. In this section some economic points are raised pertaining to early retirement, differentiating between those retirees who give up paid employment completely and those who retain part-time employment.

10.3(a) Full-time Early Retirement

As summarized in Section 2.4, the most common European schemes involve subsidized early retirement accompanied by mandatory job-replacement provisions. Usually, the early retiree loses no pension rights and receives an additional allowance for the period between actual and 'official' retirement ages. The schemes have been rather successful, involving relatively large numbers of workers and reasonably low net replacement costs.

On first reflection, the recent European experience with early retirement experiments is somewhat at odds with the main drift of argument in the previous section. Both the personal and the general fiscal costs of early retirement may be expected to be quite substantial thereby providing large disincentives for both individual and government participation. Of course, with mandatory replacement, the fiscal costs of early retirement are reduced to the extent that there is an exchequer saving on unemployment benefit and other social security cover. Further, for certain individuals, the necessary inducement to retire may be quite modest. It is well established in the literature, that deteriorating health plays a large part in the decision to retire irrespective of benefit inducements. Also, tastes for leisure and income are likely to vary considerably both across workers in a given firm and across firms themselves (see Mitchell and Fields, 1984). From the firm's viewpoint, there may be some gain to the extent that the productivity of older workers is less than average productivity.

The main conceptual difficulty would seem to lie with Lazear's notion of lifetime wage and productivity profiles. To the extent that workers receive a wage in later working life that is higher than VMP, then it is surprising that the take-up of early retirement opportunities has been quite strong. The point about the agency hypothesis, however, is that it is most likely to apply to high occupational status, long-tenure workers rather than lower skilled, more mobile workers. In the latter case, the wage might more closely reflect their spot marginal product and so the potential costs of 'persuading' the workers to retire early would be substantially reduced. Indeed, there is evidence that wages are depressed by age for significant groups of workers (see Gordon and Blinder, 1980).

The likelihood is, therefore, that the type of worker who would be encouraged to retire early would tend to have a relatively low occupational status and less current employment stability. It may be argued that these are the very workers, from an unemployment perspective, that are best encouraged to retire early since they provide the closest match to the potential occupational structure of the stock of unemployed. While there has been a considerable growth of higher-skilled workers within the unemployment stock, the overall unemployment rate, consisting largely of relatively long duration spells of unemployment, is dominated by unskilled and relatively young persons in several major countries.

10.3(b) Partial Early Retirement

Notwithstanding the foregoing comments, it may well be preferable for the individual to experience retirement somewhat gradually rather than by a sudden once-for-all change in the work–leisure pattern. The subject of early partial retirement has been given relatively little attention in the retirement literature and this has not been helped, in a European context, by the seeming failure of government efforts to promote 'job splitting' between older workers and young recruits from the unemployment pool (for references, see Section 2.4). Attention will be restricted here to this aspect of partial retirement (for a fuller discussion in a US context, see Gustman and Steinmeier, 1984).

Given the encouraging European response to (full-time) early retirement programmes, the lack of success with partial early retirement is somewhat puzzling. This is all the more so given that there are indications that there is a large potential interest within households. For example, Drèze (1985) quotes results from a large German survey of workers in 1979 in which 70 per cent of respondents were in favour of 'progressive retirement'.

One possible reason for the failure of such schemes is that the type of worker that would be most suited to partake from the firm's viewpoint would be an older worker who could transfer on-the-job skills to a part-time new recruit. This has potentially much to offer since it might be imagined that on-the-job training may be achieved at lower cost to the firm than investing in specialized training facilities. Three offsetting problems occur, however. In the first place, under the agency hypothesis, it is this type of older worker who is the least likely to want to retire early given a more favourable lifetime earnings profile in later years relative to other types of workers; thus, the inducement of such schemes may simply not be large enough. The second problem is one of matching skills. If it is the case that, in general, there is a relative scarcity of skilled, or potentially trainable, persons on the unemployment register then mandatory replacement provisions in this context may impose a particularly severe constraint. Thirdly, if relatively highly skilled workers' wage earnings per period exceed payroll tax ceilings, then job splitting may involve net increases in social security contributions to the firm.

In order to illustrate some of these cost implications, we extend the approach of Bell (1982) (see also Meltz *et al.*, 1981). For convenience, the notation of Chapter 7 is adopted: the use of small and capital letters refers to part-time (PT) and full-time (FT) workers, respectively. Further, to simplify matters, we take the case of a *single* FT employee and we hold labour costs constant.

Let H_c be 'ceiling hours' or the number of required per-period paid-for hours, at a given hourly wage rate, for wage earnings to coincide with the social security wage ceiling as defined in Section 9.3.

In the first example, suppose that standard hours, H_s, of the FT worker are such that $H_s > H_c$. Now, the worker's cost function, C_L, is in three parts, each dependent on the relation of actual paid-for hours, H, to H_c and H_s. In terms of (7.1) and (7.2) (holding $K = 1$), the cost function may be written

$$C_L = \begin{cases} Z+W_s HP & \text{if } H < H_c \\ Z+W_s H_c \hat{P}+W_s H & \text{if } H_c < H < H_s \\ Z+W_s H_c \hat{P}+W_s H_s +W(H-H_s) & \text{if } H > H_c \end{cases} (10.1)$$

where $P = 1+\hat{P}$ and $W = aW_s$ $(a > 1)$. The function in (10.1) is illustrated in Figure 10.1.

The cost schedule in Figure 10.1 displays kinks at H_c and H_s. Between H_c and H_s, the schedule flattens since the payroll tax $\hat{P}$ does not operate in this region. If the employee works $H > H_c$ then the tax constitutes the fixed labour cost $W_s H_c \hat{P}$. Beyond H_s, the schedule rises more steeply since hours $H > H_s$ are compensated at the premium wage aW_s.

Suppose that the FT employee works $H = H_s$ hours and it is contemplated that the job is to be split into two equal-length PT jobs of $H_s/2$ hours. As in Figure 10.1, we assume $H_s/2 < H_c$. Assume, initially, that for each PT job $w = W$, $\hat{p}$

$= \hat{P}$ and $z = Z$. The cost of the existing FT job is

$$C_L = Z + W_s H_c \hat{P} + W_s H_s$$

and the cost of each PT job given the above assumptions is

$$c_L = Z + W_s(H_s/2)P.$$

Therefore, the change in costs due to job sharing is

$$\Delta C_L = 2c_L - C_L = Z + W_s(H_s - H_c)\hat{P} > 0 \qquad (10.2)$$

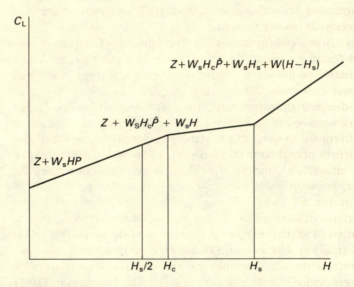

Figure 10.1 Job splitting with $H_s > H_c$.

Costs have increased by the additional fixed cost Z and the payroll tax contribution eligible on the wage gap $W_s(H_s - H_c)$.

Since, in general, $\hat{p} = \hat{P}$ would be expected to hold, four main possibilities would serve to *reduce* the size of the cost increase in (10.2). These are:

(1) $z < Z$. In the absence of government intervention, this direction of inequality is *unlikely* on the average. Specific per-period hiring and training costs associated with PT

workers would be expected, *a priori*, to exceed those of comparable FT workers. By definition, human capital investments in the former involve significantly shorter discount periods than those in the latter. Added to this, the recent increased protective legislation for PT workers in Europe has probably served to increase the differential. Unfortunately, direct evidence on relative fixed costs, at least in Europe, would appear to be rather scant (Robinson, 1979). When compared with employees nearing retirement who have had long tenure in a firm then the per-period fixed cost differentials of new PT recruits may be particularly pronounced. A number of factors may serve to offset this tendency, however.

First, for a proportion of FT workers approaching retirement (or, for example, married women with children), the alternative to job sharing may be *complete exit* from the firm. In these cases, any anticipated increases in discounted per-period specific investments associated with younger PT recruits must be weighed against an implicit higher per-period return to specific investments due to continued activity in the firm of experienced workers who would otherwise have quit altogether. In their demand-side UK questionnaire study, Bosworth and Dawkins (1982) find that an important reason for PT demand was in order for firms to retain experienced workers. Secondly, job splitting between newly qualified apprentices/trainees from government (or even firm) training schemes and older workers may well increase the return on the training investments for those younger workers who would otherwise experience a spell of unemployment: Casey (1984) pursues this argument with respect to the experience in West Germany. Thirdly, as mentioned above, on-the-job training of younger workers by experienced workers sharing the same jobs may be expected to reduce training costs compared to the provision of special training facilities.

(2) $w < W$. There is quite strong evidence (for example, Robinson, 1979) that hourly wage earnings (excluding overtime) of PT workers are less on the average than those of comparable FT occupational groups. Given sharing between young PT workers and older FT workers then the

Lazear-type arguments would tend to reinforce the expected differential in the case of job sharing combined with early retirement. On the other hand, trade unions do attempt to ensure that full wage compensation equivalence between PT and FT jobs is attained under job splitting arrangements.

(3) $H > H_s$ *for the initial FT job.* If the older FT employee normally works overtime then the cost increase of job sharing would be *reduced* by the amount $W_s(a-1)(H-H_s)$.

(4) $H_c < H_s/2$. This would also reduce the cost increase since a proportion of each PT wage compensation would be zero payroll tax rated. Under present ceiling limits operating in most countries, this is a highly unlikely eventuality, however.

As a second example, suppose that $H_s < H_c$. The new cost function, equivalent to (10.1), is given by

$$C_L = \begin{cases} Z+W_sHP & \text{if } H < H_s \\ Z+[W_sH_s+aW_s(H-H_s)]P & \text{if } H_s < H < H_c \\ Z+[W_sH_s+aW_s(H_c-H_s)]P+aW_s(H-H_c) & \\ & \text{if } H > H_c \end{cases} \quad (10.3)$$

and illustrated in Figure 10.2.

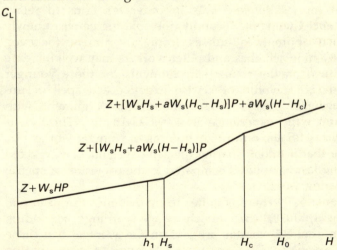

Figure 10.2 Job splitting with $H_s < H_c$.

244

The kinks, at H_s and H_c, now represent different types of slope change. Between H_s and H_c, the schedule steepens as the overtime premium, a, applies to both W_s and $\hat{P}$. Beyond H_c, the schedule flattens since no tax is incurred for $H > H_c$. The tax payment on this third segment constitutes a fixed labour cost of amount $[W_s H_s + aW_s(H_c-H_s)]\hat{P}$.

With respect to Figure 10.2, consider the case of an FT employee with hours $H_0 > H_c$ whose job may be split into two PT jobs of equal length. Each PT job length is $h_1 < H_s$ with $2 \cdot h_1 = H_0$. The cost of the initial FT job is

$$C_L = Z + W_s H_s P + aW_s(H_c-H_s)P + aW_s(H_0-H_c).$$

If c_L is the cost of each PT job, then their combined cost, again assuming $w = W$, $\hat{p} = \hat{P}$ and $z = Z$, is given by

$$2 \cdot c_L = 2Z + W_s H_s P + W_s(H_c-H_s)P + W_s(H_0-H_c)P$$

and the change in cost through job sharing becomes

$$\begin{aligned}\Delta C_L &= 2 \cdot c_L - C_L \\ &= Z+(1-a)W_s(H_c-H_s)P + [W_s(H_0-H_c)](P-a) \gtreqless 0.\end{aligned}$$
$$(10.4)$$

The cost change in (10.4) is in three parts. The first, Z, is the increase in fixed costs given $z = Z$. The second, $(1-a)W_s(H_c-H_s)P$, represents a cost reduction, given $a > 1$, since the firm avoids overtime premium payments between H_s and H_c. The third, $[W_s(H_0-H_c)](P-a)$, is sign indeterminate depending on $P(= 1+\hat{P}) \gtreqless a$; while the firm avoids premium wage payments on hours $H > H_c$, it incurs the payroll tax for the equivalent gap since $h_1 < H_c$.

Note that if initial FT hours were such that $H_s < H < H_c$ then the last term in (10.4) would disappear and the cost of job sharing would rise if $Z > (1-a)W_s(H_c-H_s)P$.

In general, therefore, the change in labour costs due to job sharing is much more ambiguous for $H_s < H_c$.

From the cost-change expressions (10.2) and (10.4), it would appear that increases in quasi-fixed costs provide *the* largest potential barrier to the adoption of partial retirement schemes from the perspective of the firm. On the supply-side, the European take-up of (full-time) early retirement opportunities seems to have been favourable, even with mandatory replacement. From the government's viewpoint, the exchequer costs of such early retirement seem to have been reasonably modest. Also, there appears to be a potentially large demand among workers for partial retirement.

Therefore, the main reason for a differential take-up of full- and partial-early retirement may lie with the attitudes of firms themselves. When an early retiree leaves the job completely, the quasi-fixed costs of the replacement can be discounted over full-time hours of work; this is not the case under 'job splitting' combined with partial retirement. Added to this, the payroll tax ceiling and working hours configurations may be such that the latter retirement strategy involves increased social security contributions.

10.4 Assessment

Policies designed to reduce the average age of retirement in order to stimulate employment would appear, *a priori*, to face considerable risks. Consider, for example, the imposition of greater financial penalties on older workers who wish to remain in employment. These may involve improved social security provisions that are conditional on retirement at the mandatory (or pre-mandatory) age and/or more progressive earnings tests. On the supply-side, the work of Burkhauser and Turner and others suggests that this form of discrimination may not lead to improved employment prospects among unemployed persons but, rather, to greater work intensity (that is, longer hours) among existing workers. On the demand-side, increased social security contributions in order to finance improved benefit may produce adverse employment effects through negative scale impacts and capital–labour substitution. Moreover, these tendencies may be particularly pronounced given that, in many countries, they coincide with demographic trends that are themselves exerting increasing pressures on social security financing.

Further, the extent to which the agency approach of Lazear 'explains' variations in the age of mandatory retirement also limits the prospects of earlier mandatory retirement serving to stimulate employment. Again, the prediction is that labour costs would increase, this time in the form of higher real wages.

Yet, in Europe at least, government attempts to promote early retirement with high job replacement have been relatively successful. To some extent, this may be explained by ill health, or fears of ill health, among older workers. Also, a high proportion of early retirees are probably not the type of skilled worker that best fits the Lazear-type model. The fall in labour force activity rates among older age-groups (see Table 2.7) is undoubtedly due in part to a lack of demand for their labour services rather than to supply decisions. The mystery is why there has been a general reluctance by firms and employees to participate in partial retirement schemes despite evidence of worker support for such initiatives. It is suggested in Section 10.3(b) that one explanation may lie in the fact that fixed employment costs, with respect both to specific investments and social security contributions, are likely to be higher under partial-early retirement with part-time job replacement rather than full-early retirement with full-time job replacement. Marginal employment subsidies to the fixed costs may prove to be a particularly effective means of improving the take-up of such schemes.

CHAPTER ELEVEN

Collective Bargaining Constraints

11.1 Introduction

As stated at the outset, the main purpose of this book is to study economic relationships between working time and employment without imposing collective bargaining constraints on these and their related factor price variables. This has enabled us to deal with a number of quite fundamental and general labour market relationships without being sidetracked by the particular attitudes of given governments, employers and trade unions. Of course, in reality, changes in working time are usually conditioned, to a greater or lesser extent, by interaction among these three groups. In this chapter, the discussion is broadened in order to represent some of the implications to the foregoing developments of these types of consideration.

Large aggregate changes in the standard workweek or part-time working or shiftworking practices are to some degree dependent on mutual agreement among the three main collective bargaining parties; that is, government, employers and trade unions. Agreed solutions depend on a complexity of aims and objectives that are usually not, at least at the commencement of bargaining, mutually consistent. The central problem is that the economic and political constraints under which each party operates may be substantially different from one another.

As a simple example, consider a collective bargaining

policy discussion concerning potential cuts in the standard workweek. The primary objective of the government over this issue would almost certainly be that of reducing unemployment. As is mentioned in Chapter 1, working time reductions may appear to be particularly attractive at a time when monetary and fiscal initiatives are deemed to be inadequate devices for tackling the problem of persistent unemployment. The government would be loath to initiate major cuts, however, if it considered that this might lead to significant increases in wages and prices. It is unlikely, on the other hand, that employers would give much consideration to standard hours reductions as a means of increasing their stock of employees. In the absence of fiscal incentives, they might be expected to contemplate independently the possibility of hours reductions if and only if they perceive concomitant improvements in labour productivity and work organization that more than offset the increased labour costs. As with the government, trade unions may embrace the aim of unemployment falls as an objective for pursuing reductions in the length of the workweek. From the available evidence, however, this would only be a part of their full objectives. They would also be expected to view hours reductions as a way of improving the general conditions of their members since, almost invariably, they insist that reductions should be accompanied by full (or significant partial) wage compensation.

It may not be surprising if these differing objectives and constraints result in no mutually consistent outcome and, therefore, produce little tendency to change. Governments may not view their efforts to curb inflation as being consistent with attempts by unions to maintain real living standards of their members. Further, union efforts to achieve wage compensation for the loss in hours are unlikely to tie in with employers' efforts to minimize labour cost reactions. As we have seen in a large number of models, both governments' and unions' attempts to increase employment/reduce unemployment through reductions in working time may well be inconsistent with firms' optimizing objectives.

It has to be acknowledged at the outset that it is almost an impossible task to summarize collective bargaining attitudes to working time changes within a relatively short space since, unlike much of the foregoing text, this necessitates a factual coverage of the three parties' attitudes to working time across a diverse range of economies and industries. Of necessity, therefore, the discussion here is both fairly aggregate and quite partial. It is based, in large part, on the earlier work in Hart (1984c) where collective bargaining aspects of working time are discussed within a fairly wide OECD perspective. There are many exceptions to the examples singled out for discussion although, hopefully, the experiences and attitudes summarized are quite broadly representative.

The following three sections deal, respectively, with trade union, employer and government attitudes to change in the main working time variables. In the brief final section, 11.5, the working time areas over which there appears to be most mutual agreement are pinpointed.

11.2 Trade Union Attitudes

As indicated in Chapter 2, collective bargaining interest in reductions in the length of the standard workweek is largely a European (and Australasian) phenomenon. Without any doubt, the overwhelming view at 'official' national union level in this group of OECD countries is that substantial reductions in the workweek form an essential strategy for creating new jobs. Moreover, it is almost universally argued that working time reductions should take place *without* proportionate losses in weekly earnings. In other words, it is considered that standard hourly rates of pay should rise in order to compensate for the per-period loss of earnings. Although there are many individual union statements on these issues, the position is best summarized by the European Trade Union Confederation's (ETUC) call for a 10 per cent reduction in working time without loss of pay at the 1979 Munich Congress; this resolution was subsequently reaffirmed at the Hague Congress in 1982. Since then there has been very little backsliding from this position. Indeed, the ETUC's stated objectives in the late 1970s/early 1980s have been followed up by several European union organizations in the form of actual claims for substantial hours reductions. The most vigorous of these was undertaken in the FRG by the important union, IG METALL and resulted in a highly costly strike within the German metalworking industries in 1984. It also achieved an average reduction in the standard workweek of 1½ hours from a goal of 5 hours and the indications are that the union will continue to pursue its initial objectives.

Typically, unions express the view that the cost of workweek reductions are likely to be rather modest since they will be offset by large gains in labour productivity. Several unions' arguments along these lines are brought together by the European Trade Union Institute (1979). A number of channels for such productivity gains are suggested. First, shorter working hours should improve workers' work rhythms. Secondly, they should also reduce the rate of absenteeism. Thirdly, they should help to eliminate 'hidden pockets of unemployment' that are unproductively included within the firm's payroll. Taken together, European unions commonly quote a figure, although usually without substantial quantitative evidence, of a 50 per cent productivity offset to a reduction in the standard workweek.

Such union claims for beneficial productivity offsets are not made simply to support the case of hours reduction *per se*, but *also* as an argument in support of wage compensation for loss of earnings. In some countries, such as Belgium and the Netherlands, trade unions have shown a willingness to accept less-than-full compensation in the event of hours reductions whereas, in others, full compensation is seen as a prime objective (see van Ginneken, 1984).

Theoretical work has been reviewed, in Section 5.6, which incorporates the extreme assumption of monopoly union wage setting. On the basis of this type of model, there is little reason to anticipate positive employment responses given exogenous hours reduction accompanied by some degree of wage compensation. Even in the more optimistic world of the large-scale econometric models (see Section

6.6), the predicted positive employment effects of hours reductions are usually significantly reduced if the constraint of full wage compensation is imposed. (See van Ginneken, 1984, for a review: he claims that where models predict *no* employment differences between no-compensation and full-compensation simulations – particularly in the case of French models – the predictions appear to deviate substantially from *actual* experience with hours reductions.) In the type of micro approaches generally favoured in this book, there is little doubt that imposing wage compensation would lead to (or reinforce) *negative* employment responses to hours reductions. In Section 6.4(a), we quote results of a simulation from such a model by Brunstad and Holm (1984) into the effects on Norwegian employment given a workweek reduction of 6.25 per cent. Each simulation was carried out under the assumption that productivity decreased, remained the same or rose. The comparable employment effects were in the range of 'extremely modest' to 'reasonably significant'. It should be added that these results are very high in the 'optimistic region' of the range of outcomes arising from the various micro models. When the authors rework their simulations under the assumption that full wage compensation is given for the hours reduction then they arrive at the conclusion that the simulations 'end up with heavy job losses in all cases'.

In Section 5.2 and elsewhere particular attention is given to a model that allows for overtime offsets given standard hours decreases. The established union position in Europe may serve to modify the outcome here. National-level unions are strongly opposed to significant levels of overtime working and, at the Munich Congress, delegates called for both a restriction on existing overtime working and compensatory time-off when overtime is worked. Crude limits to the amount of per-period overtime that can be worked have the likely effect of increasing labour costs relatively more than would have been the case if overtime were free to vary. In this case, longer-term capital–labour substitution and negative scale effects may be expected to be more significant. It should be added that this may not be such an acute problem if existing overtime compensation rates rise steeply with hours. Demanding compensating free time for overtime working is another way of increasing overtime premium payments and this *may* have the benefit of increasing the price at the intensive relative to the extensive margin thereby reducing the relative advantage of overtime given standard hours reductions. (See Ehrenberg and Schumann, 1982, for a US demand study of the employment effects of raising overtime premium payments by direct legislation.) Again, however, it is important to be extremely wary of both the capital and scale impacts of increased labour costs.

While the above conclusions with respect to union attitudes are rather bleak, it is not at all clear to what extent the national-level union views are representative of those of firm- or establishment-level union leaders and members.

One of the most thorough European investigations into union attitudes at a more micro level was carried out by the National Board for Prices and Incomes (NBPI) in the UK in 1970. A sample of 2,000 establishments was investigated with a particularly detailed survey of 60 establishments engaged in a wide range of manufacturing and service activities. Over 1,000 manual workers, and in many cases also their wives, were questioned individually and, at the other end of the spectrum, the views of national-level trade union and employers' organizations were also solicited. In line with the position of the ETUC a decade later, the inquiry showed that national union bodies consistently argued for standard workweek reductions. The report was undertaken during a somewhat different economic climate than that of the late 1970s and, not surprisingly, one of the main reasons given for such reductions was to achieve greater leisure for union members. The most revealing point, however, is that the study found a systematically different attitude at individual member level. Thus, it is reported,

on the evidence of actual hours worked, workers them-selves have, on the whole, been inclined to take a different view (*from the 'official' union position*) of the relative attractions of added leisure and added income. Their actual weekly hours in October 1969, at 46.5, were in fact longer than they were 22 years previously in April

1947, when they were 46.3. At the earlier date, with overtime averaging one hour per man, overtime pay represented an insignificant part of the pay package. By September 1968 . . . average weekly overtime pay of all male manual workers amounted to . . . 16% of their total pay.

(NBPI, 1970, p. 22)

Under more recent economic conditions, there is little evidence of a substantial desire by workers to enjoy more leisure at the margin, even with some wage compensation. In a Finnish survey (Gröhn, 1979), 5,700 persons between the ages of 15 and 69 were asked by a postal questionnaire: 'If you had the opportunity to choose between high wages and a reduction in daily hours, would you choose: (1) current working hours and high wages, or (2) shorter working hours than at present with the same wages, or (3) even shorter working hours than the second alternative and slightly lower wages, or (4) some other alternative (what?).' More than two-thirds of respondents preferred the first alternative and less than one-third chose shorter working hours with the same wages. Only 2 per cent of respondents valued leisure to the extent that they were willing to give up their present wage level in order to have substantially greater leisure time. Somewhat surprisingly, the views of the respondents varied little in relation to whether or not they were employed or unemployed.

More recent evidence of conflicting interests with regard to overtime working is also available. In a study on overtime working in Ireland (University College, Galway, 1980), a detailed sample survey of 150 firms in the production and service sectors was undertaken. An interesting dichotomy is drawn between the official union position and management's perception of that position. In the former case, the Irish Congress of Trade Unions (ICTU) argues that

legislative measures and action by trade unions and employers should eliminate the working of excessive overtime as a regular feature of employment.

(p. 57).

When management were asked for their perception of union attitudes towards overtime, the study found that:

> the vast majority of firms reported a trade union attitude to be one of acceptance or indifference. However, within the production sector, 14.1% of firms reported the attitude to be one of encouragement. Less than 3% of the firms perceived the trade union attitude as one of opposition. Opposition where it is perceived, is more likely in the more highly unionized firms.
>
> (p. 97)

As for individual worker attitudes, the report goes on:

> the majority of firms report employees eager or willing to work overtime with only 10% in the service sector reporting employees reluctant to work overtime, and almost 8% in the production sector reporting employees reluctant to work overtime or opposed to overtime working.
>
> (p. 97)

It is reported further that 60 per cent of firms in the production sector and almost 50 per cent in the service sector stated that the conditions under which overtime is worked were laid down in labour–management agreements. Moreover, it was found that firms with no trade union membership among employees in the various occupational groups were *less* likely to have overtime working. For all occupational groups in the production and service sectors there exist a statistically significant relationship between the practice of overtime and the level of trade union membership. In other words, it would appear that explicit contracts between labour and management for significant overtime scheduling exist and, moreover, that worksharing possibilities are not a primary objective at establishment level within many sectors of this particular economy.

It might be added that if the above evidence is consistent with wider experience, then a serious question mark is introduced over the (convenient) assumption in the trade union wage bargaining models (see Section 5.6) that no overtime is worked in unionized firms.

In Chapter 7, we consider some possible relationships between part-time employment and reductions in working time. European trade union attitudes to the use of part-time employment tend to be somewhat hostile. A likely general explanation of this is provided by treating unions as essentially political organizations in the sense of Medoff (1979). The 'median voter' is almost invariably a full-time employee who will not regard efforts to foster part-time employment as being in her/his self-interest. The overwhelming majority of part-time workers are women who are either not represented or weakly represented by a union. Further, most part-time jobs tend to cluster in industries, such as distributive and retail trades, where the degree of unionization is relatively low and/or weak.

A particular reason for unions' opposition to part-time employment is directly related to the issue of working time. As documented in Robinson (1984), European unions regard their goal of achieving workweek reductions as being effectively undermined by an increasing use of part-time work. This issue relates quite closely to the earlier analysis of part-time work in Chapter 7. From the demand-side model in Section 7.2, a reduction in standard hours is predicted to lead to an increase in the proportion of part-time to full-time workers. On the supply-side (Section 7.3), the reduction may induce full-time family members to work longer hours. The joint effect may be an increase in part-time employment with each part-time worker working longer hours. A potentially anomalous position arises for union employment and working time strategies following this sort of analysis: union success in effecting standard hours reductions may itself promote greater pressure for the creation of more part-time jobs on the supply-side and greater acquiescence to such pressure on the demand-side.

It should also be added (see Hart, 1984c, and Robinson, 1984) that unions sometimes recognize cases where part-time employment might be advantageous to their members. Where part-time employment is recognized, then most union attention in this area is directed towards achieving employment contracts that include employment protection clauses on a par with equivalent full-time jobs.

An interesting divergence does seem to have emerged, at least at 'official' union level, between European and US union attitudes to worksharing. The stated goal of European union leaders is to negotiate shorter working hours as a means of alleviating high rates of unemployment. In the USA, as reported in Chapter 8, there is some evidence (Medoff, 1979) of a long-term change in emphasis from shorter average hours to more temporary layoffs as a means of adjusting to cyclical changes in demand. Typical explanations of this trend are as follows. The growing power of unions has enabled their membership to achieve compensation above market rates combined with improved seniority privileges (see Medoff and Abraham, 1980) as well as special firm-related pension and other fringe benefit provisions. These latter payments involve high proportions of deferred compensation. Such firm-related advantages help to increase the employer's expectation that a union member would return after a period of temporary layoff. Union members themselves can often negotiate contracts stipulating that an employment offer would first be made to them and so, on the supply-side, they too may be confident concerning re-hire. Moreover, senior workers who do experience layoff do not tend to lose seniority rights and privileges. As alluded to in Chapter 8, however, it is difficult to imagine that, on aggregate, such explanations are less apparent on the European scene where far higher proportions of workers are unionized and reasonably similar compensation packages exist.

One reason for the apparent difference, as alluded to in the discussion above, is that the US union leaders may represent the views of the median employee somewhat more directly than their European counterparts. Unions in Europe have rather strong political links (for example with the SPD Party in the FRG and the Labour Party in the UK) and union statements at national – or industry – level may in part reflect party political objectives. More detailed plant-level bargaining, on the other hand, may involve somewhat different points of emphasis.

Finally, it will suffice to report briefly on two issues of earlier concern over which there appears to be reasonable unanimity between unions and their membership. First, as summarized by the European Trade Union Institute (1979), European unions are generally opposed to major extensions to the practice of shiftworking. The main reasons given relate to possible deleterious effects on workers' health as well as problems arising from working non-social hours. Secondly, the same report documents wide union support throughout Europe for flexible and voluntary flexible early retirement arrangements *but* displays a much greater reluctance to countenance a once-for-all reduction in the age of mandatory retirement (see ETUI, 1979, pp. 38–41).

11.3 Employers' Attitudes

It is probably reasonable to claim that employers are almost universally hostile towards proposals for major and systematic reductions of the workweek. In two recent attempts to reduce the workweek by 5 hours, in Australia and the FRG (see next section), employers exhibited widespread, strong and sustained resistance. Hart (1984c) summarizes the views of an international group of management experts at an OECD meeting on working time. The delegates at this meeting regarded normal hours reductions as perhaps the most costly and least desirable of all possible working time changes; they were deemed to increase the marginal cost of labour and lead to rises in the price of final goods and services thereby potentially damaging firms' domestic and international competitive positions. One of the main problems raised was that employers treat standard workweek reductions as *irreversible* decisions. General collective bargaining constraints were such that it was regarded as being virtually impossible to reverse decisions to shorten standard hours once reductions had taken place. On the other hand, in the cases of overtime schedules and part-time working it was thought, at least, that potential existed for future reversals of trends. There was also a general scepticism concerning the employment creating impact of reductions in the workweek since, it was felt, that the substitution of better technology, know-how and work organization was a likely long-term reaction.

Overtime, where practised, is typically argued by employers to be employed for sound economic reasons. It provides flexibility in production scheduling, it can help to meet rush orders and unexpected changes in demand and it serves as a way of circumventing the legislative cost of hiring and dismissing workers. (See both the earlier referenced NBPI and Irish reports for detailed examinations of the overtime decision.) As noted in Section 5.3, it would appear (see, especially, the Irish study) that overtime is not only used to meet fluctuations in demand and rush orders but also for reasons connected with maintaining normal production scheduling. These latter include making up shortages of skilled workers, meeting employee gaps due to absenteeism and sickness and set-up activity for production runs during standard working hours.

Perhaps of somewhat more interest are employers' attitudes to part-time working. (For a useful general discussion of arguments for and against part-time employment from the employer's viewpoint, see Commission of the European Communities, 1982.) Bosworth and Dawkins (1982) summarize the findings of a survey of management attitudes to part-time working based on over 750 interviews at establishment level in UK manufacturing and non-manufacturing industries. The most significant reason given for employing part-time workers was that certain jobs did not require full-time cover. This was especially true in firms that needed extra workers for 'busy periods' that occurred during relatively brief periods of the working day. Distributional trades and finance are two major industries that had this type of requirement. Another important reason for employing part-time work was that recruitment was easier than that of equivalent full-time workers. Of all industries and services, 9 per cent reported that part-time work was employed to suit the needs of existing workers or to keep experienced workers or to obtain experienced workers.

As discussed in Chapter 7, one of the economic reasons against part-time employment, especially in relatively skilled occupations, is that the returns to specific investments are discounted over relatively shorter time spans than in equivalent full-time jobs. In a lifetime context, as discussed in Chapter 10, this argument holds far less weight. If a firm trains a worker who then works for a given period of years it might be the case that the only way to retain the worker during future periods is to grant part-time work schedules. An obvious example here is that of a highly skilled married woman who in the early years of raising a family can only offer less than full-time hours.

More detailed evidence on the dichotomy between the working year and working lifetime with respect to part-time working is found in results of a survey of firms in the Hamburg area of the FRG (Hoff, 1981). The firms experienced a reasonably constant demand from *existing* full-time workers to switch into part-time occupations. In general, firms responded favourably to such requests and it was found that, excluding the 'housewives' shift', about 60 per cent of part-time slots were occupied by former full-time employees of the same firm. Typically, such a part-time worker was an older, female white-collar worker who had considerable experience within the firm and displayed a good working record at a non-managerial level. As far as productivity was concerned, the firms clearly benefited from this arrangement as relatively little job reorganization was needed. Indeed, it appeared that, in several cases, the part-time employees managed to undertake roughly the same workload as in their previous full-time capacity. By contrast, the same firms were generally reluctant to create new part-time jobs on their own initiative. Moreover, when existing part-time jobs became vacant, there was a tendency to replace them by full-time employees. No detailed explanation is offered for this hiring policy although it would seem to reinforce aspects of the earlier discussion of partial early retirement in Section 10.3(b). If the loss in labour services from older workers is less than proportional to a reduction in their hours due to a change from full-time to part-time employment, there may be little incentive for the firm to 're-create' the former full-time job slot through job splitting. When the older workers eventually leave the firm completely, their skill levels and know-how are perhaps regained most cost-effectively by discounting hiring, training and other fixed costs of their job replacement over full-time hours.

One reason for employers' reluctance to increase part-time employment, as highlighted by the Netherlands Council of Employers Federations (1981), concerns social security funding. The problem relates closely to the discussion in Section 10.3(b). Where existing employees receive compensation that lies beyond payroll tax ceilings then splitting such jobs into two or more part-time job equivalents can produce a net increase in social security contributions. Further, government and trade union efforts to protect the rights of part-time workers, by attempting to achieve job protection on a par with full-time employees, may well be seen by employers as increasing the fixed costs of employing part-time workers relative to full-timers and thereby acting as a disincentive (for analysis, see Chapter 7).

As far as employers' attitudes towards shiftworking are concerned, the issues seem to be more clear-cut. Given the use of certain types of technology and/or the existence of relatively high capital–labour ratios, there is often a clear advantage in maximizing the return on capital by ensuring a high degree of capital utilization. Returning to the NBPI study, it is reported that the growth of shiftworking throughout the 1950s and 1960s in the UK has been linked primarily to changes in the scale of production and the degree of technological innovations. This finding is largely corroborated in a survey undertaken by the Institute of Economic Research (IFO) at the request of the Confederation of German Employers' Association during 1979. The survey was based on two questionnaires sent to a representative sample of 1,300 industrial undertakings. Within the sample, 870 plants employed night shifts. It was found that 20 per cent of production workers were regularly assigned to night shifts, although with very wide variations according to industrial activity. A close association was found between the size of undertaking and the amount of shiftwork, an indication that scale factors were important in the decision to use shifts. The percentage of undertakings that employed night shifts was also found to be very stable through time; in the years previous to the study very few plants had ceased to use night shifts and even fewer contemplated introducing night shifts in the future. As high as 60 per cent of the enterprises gave a 'technical reason' to explain their use of shifts while 40 per cent gave an 'economic reason' although, of course, these two categories are clearly interdependent. The majority of undertakings that regularly used night shifts argued that it was impossible to stop this practice because of severe constraints imposed by the type of technology incorporated, often requiring continuous production processing. It is also clearly stated that, in many cases, shiftwork was necessary to ensure a rapid amortization of capital investments given fast rates of technical obsolescence.

In relation to the discussion in Section 5.4, there is some evidence that employers and unions perceive a direct link between standard workweek reductions and the introduction of shiftwork. Where a given firm has the possibility of extending shiftworking arrangements – or perhaps even introducing shiftwork for the first time – then one form of employer reaction to pressure for shorter workweeks is to substitute ordinary day-time jobs for more shiftworking in order to achieve a higher utilization of the capital stock. The ETUI report (1979) cites a number of cases of unions reporting this type of strategy by employers in the face of actual or potential workweek reductions.

11.4   The Role of Government

Where there exists an identifiable government attitude to changes in working time, it is often exemplified by the position that, while a broad range of working time initiatives may be worthwhile exploring in order to improve the employment/unemployment position, they should be undertaken firmly within the constraints of minimizing their impact on production costs in particular and on aggregate inflationary responses in general. This type of outlook has led, in general, to government support for relatively modest interventions – such as in the areas of early retirement, youth training and marginal employment subsidies – while displaying considerable reluctance to pursue somewhat bolder initiatives.

Although there are some exceptional instances, governments have tended to oppose strongly union claims for significant once-for-all reductions in the standard workweek. A good example of this is provided by the Australian Federal Government's attitude towards a 1980 campaign for a 35-hour workweek. The campaign was launched by the Amalgamated Metal Workers' and Shipwrights' Union (AMWSU), claiming that the reduction would create a quarter of a million new jobs. Their employers argued that the hours reduction would increase hourly costs by 14 per cent and by as much as 21 per cent if the proposed reduction of 5 standard hours was completely replaced by increased overtime working; in this latter event, it was argued that 70,000 existing jobs would be threatened. The Federal Government took a more macro-oriented approach. At that time, inflation in Australia was over 10 per cent and the government believed that an hours reduction would trigger further price rises for Australian finished goods and services. The potential costs of increased inflation were seen to be considerably greater than the potential short-term employment advantage and so the government vigorously campaigned against the working time reduction and urged companies not to enter into collective agreements over such large reductions in hours. The ultimate compromise was a 38-hour week. A very similar government stance took place in the FRG in 1984 in the case of the dispute between the German Metal Workers Union (IG METALL) and the relevant employers. Again, the union put forward similar employment-creation arguments while the government stressed offsetting inflation and terms-of-trade reactions. The compromise solution turned out to be very similar to the earlier Australian position.

Governments in Europe have been particularly concerned about the high growth of unit labour costs relative to the USA and the Pacific Basin region. Strong union demands for workweek reductions accompanied by full wage compensation are seen as the antithesis of attempts to achieve reduced cost differentials. In times of deep recession, labour market policies in West Germany, the UK and (more recently) France have been geared far more towards holding down public sector wage increases and attempting to encourage similar wage settlements in the private sector.

In the relatively few cases of government-led initiatives over hours reductions, these have usually taken the form of inducements to a cut in the standard workweek through subsidies contingent on net employment increases. In Section 9.2, a number of analytical reasons are outlined as to why such labour market intervention is almost certainly open to severe problems. Hart (1984c) documents the failure of this type of attempt instigated by the French government under the so-called 'solidarity contracts'. (Later attempts by the French government to introduce *general* as opposed to *marginal employment* subsidies also met with extremely poor employment response rates.) Further, Drèze (1985) reports on an attempt by the Belgian government in 1979 to introduce marginal employment subsidies following a standard workweek reduction from 40 to 38 hours. The subsidy was contingent on new hirings that correspond to 3 per cent of the existing employment. The idea was rejected by employers *and* some unions.

Governments have been prepared to introduce legislation that imposes minimum premium rates for overtime hours or, occasionally, per-period limits to the amount of overtime working. This is most apparent in the USA where minimum rates of premium payments are statutorily imposed, although in some European countries – for example Belgium, France, the FRG and Greece – there is some limited control of minimum overtime premium payments. It would appear that significant efforts to increase the costs of overtime are likely to lead to rather limited employment creation (see Ehrenberg, 1971; Ehrenberg and Schumann, 1982). More direct limits to the amount of overtime working are likely to lead to particularly strong resistance given the important role of overtime in the optimizing strategy of the firm. For example, the Danish government attempted to introduce a Bill in 1981 that would have limited overtime working to 100 hours a year for any individual employee. In addition to this limit, it would have been required that employers grant 'time off in lieu' to match any overtime work by their employees. The Bill enabled employers and unions, however, to set aside these conditions if, through collective bargaining agreements, they could arrive at mutually acceptable special arrangements. This proposed measure received particularly strong opposition from employers' associations and the Bill was not enacted.

As far as part-time employment is concerned, European governments have shown some interest in two principal areas. These are:

(1) increased protective legislation for part-time workers (for a useful Europe-wide summary see Robinson, 1984, and for a very detailed UK assessment see Disney and Szyszczak, 1984);
(2) subsidies to encourage partial-early retirement combined with part-time employment of previously unemployed younger persons (see Section 2.4 and 10.3(b)).

Without doubt, the most significant past and likely future efforts are with respect to (1). The greatest benefits accrue to female, largely non-unionized, labour supply and the greatest (fixed) costs to firms with large proportions of part-time workers.

Finally, in the case of retirement, governments have generally been quite reluctant, as with workweek reductions, to support large, once-for-all downward adjustments in the retirement age. Where major intervention has been undertaken or envisaged, it is usually with respect to retirement adjustment in the opposite direction. The best example is the case of Japan where, as outlined in Section 2.4, the rapid ageing of the Japanese workforce is anticipated to put great strains on non-wage labour costs and, particularly, statutory pension contributions. Currently, there are moves to encourage enterprises to adopt 60 as the usual mandatory retirement age (*Japan Labor Bulletin*, December 1985). These measures are in the realm of combating employment shortfalls and excessive labour cost increases and certainly bear little relation to the retirement issues in most other countries. European governments, by contrast, have adopted the policy of targeting changes in retirement by making it easier for specific groups of workers who wish to retire early. As we have seen in Chapter 10, there is reason to believe that such policies are generally more useful as a means of stimulating employment than attempts at systematic reductions in mandatory retirement ages.

11.5 Where Is There Most Mutual Agreement?

There seems to be only one important working time area in which major new initiatives for change might be expected to encounter relatively little collective bargaining resistance. Policies designed to provide subsidies to encourage *voluntary* early retirement accompanied by mandatory job replacement from the unemployment register appear to enjoy significant pockets of support within each of the main collective bargaining parties. Certainly, recent European experience indicates that where efforts have taken place in this direction they have been relatively successful from both employment and labour cost perspectives. Each party may anticipate some gain from early retirement along these lines. For the government, it provides a relatively effective device for creating new jobs given an offsetting saving of unemployment/social security benefits associated with replacement workers. For both employees and unions, supporting those workers who wish to retire early – on the grounds of ill health, reduced interests in work activity, and so on – may, in many cases, be regarded as being consistent with their own, albeit different, economic and political objectives.

Despite widespread union opposition, part-time employment provides another possible area in which further change might be achieved in the absence of strong collective bargaining frictions. The main reason is simply that most part-time jobs are in non-unionized or weakly unionized firms. For their parts, governments and certain employers have consistently supported some degree of part-time activity. Unfortunately, more encouragement of part-time working along existing lines may only have a limited appeal. There is no question that the most essential new direction on which to concentrate effort is in the growth of part-time activity within male-dominated occupations and industries. For example, this is one of the stated main current objectives of the Commission of the European Community in the area of job creation. Here, however, strong union resistance seems almost inevitable, although legislation to improve the employment status and security of part-time workers may help to alleviate some of the main union concerns.

In other areas, such as large reductions in the length of the workweek or the age of mandatory retirement as well as significant extensions to the incidence and degree of shiftworking, the position is far more gloomy. The collective bargaining constraints are such that only relatively small potential changes seem feasible, at least in the short run, without risking high costs associated with prolonged industrial disputes that end in generally unsatisfactory compromise settlements. As is mentioned in the following chapter, the evidence would seem to point to the conclusion that, at best, small changes in these labour market variables will produce negligible positive employment responses.

CHAPTER TWELVE

More Jobs through Shorter Hours?

The title of this chapter provides the basic question posed in countless articles, from a wide range of sources, on the subject of working time and employment. An attempt has been made in this book to show that, in most specific instances, any headway towards providing realistic answers is dependent on a reasonably precise and careful evaluation of a number of economic relationships among a set of key economic variables. Attention has been focused primarily on the labour market and the discussion has stopped short of an in-depth evaluation of the interconnected role of other markets. Since the issues are fairly complex and the analysis somewhat partial, it is the intention here to restrict comments to an assessment of which avenues appear least and which most promising for further exploration.

In Europe and Australasia, *the* most debated working time change as a means of increasing employment/reducing unemployment is a reduction in the length of the working week and/or working year. As we have seen in Chapter 6, if we were to apportion greatest weight to the predictions of macroeconometric models then there is some reason to suppose that this strategy provides potentially beneficial employment effects. As in many other instances, however, acting on the basis of outcomes of econometric models is a dangerous game to play. In this particular case, one of the serious problems with such models is that they often come nowhere near to modelling adequately the underlying labour market relationships. This may well be a crucial deficiency since, as we have seen in Chapters 4 and 5 and elsewhere, restricting modelling to the immediate labour market produces the overwhelming conclusion that work-week reductions may well lead to *negative* employment responses or, at best, rather weak employment creation.

In Chapter 5, we investigated a wide range of micro-economic models that have been designed to study the employment effects of changes in exogenous per-period hours. Not all the models (see, especially, Section 5.7) are restricted to an examination of the labour market. Their outcomes point strongly towards the need of *either* exercising great caution towards *or* rejecting outright a policy of reducing hours as a means of stimulating employment growth. It might be argued that the models consist primarily of partial equilibrium comparative static exercises and, therefore, provide only a limited insight into general employment repercussions. This would be to miss the essential point concerning the value of this work, however. Limitations in the scope of such models stem, in many instances, from the difficulties that exist in attempting to capture adequately the immediate labour market relation-ships. These types of model should be regarded as providing part of the bedrock for later, more adventurous, developments rather than as providing analytical alterna-tives. Wider-based discussions of the employment effects of hours reductions, be they with respect to econometric models or less quantitative macro analyses, often fail to represent the essential features of the micro studies and, therefore, tend to be built on somewhat shaky foundations.

Irrespective of theoretical findings, it might be argued in the light of collective bargaining constraints (see Chapter 11) that substantial reductions in weekly or annual hours are, in any case, not feasible in the short or medium term. Where compromise solutions are reached they involve, almost inevitably, rather modest reductions in hours. For instance, this has been the outcome of recent attempts in several countries to reduce the standard workweek by 5 hours. Where relatively small changes in working hours are eventually envisaged then, perhaps, the force of some of the more adverse employment outcomes emanating from the micro models is somewhat tempered. It by no means follows, however, that smaller working time changes will produce more favourable employment responses. Firms and enterprises are more likely to be able to accommodate the change, in large part, by reorganizing existing resources. Two recent and important examples would tend to support this conclusion.

In the first case, an INSEE study (see Marchand *et al.*, 1983) examined the effects of a cut in the standard workweek by one hour in France in 1982. It revealed that large enterprises differ from small enterprises in their response. In the former, positive employment repercussions were most likely to be observed in firms that employed shiftworking. On the other hand, it was also found that tighter time management – such as increased work pace, less slack time, seasonal fluctuations of working hours and subcontracting – was an important vehicle of response in such enterprises. Of course, these types of reaction might lead to employment creation both through their direct effects on supplier firms as well as through their indirect demand effects due to decreases in unit costs. Small firms, on the other hand, were found to reduce production capacity rather than increase employment. In general, in the 9-month period following the reduction, there was a general increase in overtime working in the relevant industries and the overall employment response was very modest.

Quite similar conclusions are reached in a study of the effects of a one-hour cut in the standard workweek in the UK engineering and printing industries (White and Ghobadian, 1984). In this case, the loss in working time was met substantially by increases in labour productivity per unit as well as some offsetting reduction in unit wage costs. Further, total hours decreased and overtime increased in the 9 months following the workweek reduction and so there was a net decrease in employment. In the case of productivity, White and Ghobadian draw attention to the fact that shorter working hours may have *signalled* the need for productivity improvements and that, in the event, these were easily achieved.

In summary, there is little reason to doubt that losses in total working hours due to relatively small reductions in the length of the workweek may be offset in large part by work reorganization combined with an increased utilization of existing resources. Moreover, on the basis of direct evidence, as opposed to indirect econometric modelling, it is unlikely that the employment reactions would be other than quite modest or even negative.

It should be stressed that, except under very crude modelling assumptions, the employment responses (positive or negative) to either large or small reductions in standard hours are liable to be rendered worse if full rather than partial wage compensation is achieved by the existing workforce for their loss of earnings.

One explanation of productivity increases advanced in the White and Ghobadian UK study is that the hours reduction led to a greater utilization of slack time. The extent to which overtime hours are also observed to increase limits this sort of argument but, nevertheless, many writers have expressed the view that cuts in the workweek during recessionary periods may lead to relatively large productivity gains due to the fact that a proportion of total hours are hoarded at such times. As mentioned in Chapters 2 and 6, recent work in the USA suggests that hoarding might indeed be a relatively important phenomenon during downturns in aggregate demand. If hoarding is a general phenomenon – and indirect econometric evidence suggests that it probably is – then it would seem that the force of these productivity claims may be quite strong and that positive scale impacts on employment may be expected to result in the longer term.

This type of productivity argument begs a number of fundamental questions concerning the reasons for labour hoarding itself. At a simple level, in the quasi-fixed cost theory of the firm, hoarding is undertaken for optimizing reasons, such as to maximize the joint discounted gains from specific investments. To the extent that this is a prevalent objective, it is not at all clear that reducing labour utilization through cuts in the standard workweek is in the best interest of the firm and its workforce. Recessions may be expected to be relatively short-lived and *once-for-all reductions* in labour utilization due to cuts in the workweek may not be consistent with long-term maximizing objectives. Further ramifications to this sort of argument can be found in relation to the wage setting model outlined in Section 5.5.

Nor is it clear at a macroeconomic level that labour hoarding is necessarily an undesirable phenomenon from a welfare standpoint. In a Keynesian macroeconomic analysis, Odagiri (1986) argues that a general strategy by firms to give more weight to employment stability rather than short-run profits not only stabilizes macro employment, in the sense of less unemployment in cyclical downturns, but also stabilizes national income. Interestingly he finds that in Japan, France and the UK the employment trends in relation to GNP and other measures would seem to indicate that the employment stability strategy dominates short-run optimization while the US data are not consistent with this hypothesis. In many important respects, Odagiri's empirical tests are in line with the international comparison of hours and working time presented in Section 2.2(a).

Notwithstanding these labour hoarding comments, there is a reasonable case for arguing, following several of the foregoing points, that future work should concentrate far more attention on studying the implications of achieving greater pro-cyclical fluctuations in working hours *other than overtime hours*. Perhaps too much of the debate on worksharing, particularly in Europe, has focused on long-term structural changes in working time patterns rather than on more state-contingent contractual agreements. One, relatively minor, exception is provided by the short-time working subsidies provided to employees in the FRG and a few other countries (see Table 2.6 and Section 8.4). The United States is somewhat exceptional in this respect: as discussed in Chapter 8, the main labour market interest in working time and employment has centred on the topic of temporary layoff unemployment and, therefore, concentrates far more on cyclical labour force adjustment. It is not at all clear from the associated implicit contract literature that temporary layoffs alone provide an efficient (second-best) response to uncertainty (see FitzRoy and Hart, 1985) nor that the models themselves provide results consistent with actual fluctuations in workers and hours (see Rosen, 1985, and Section 8.3). Nevertheless, the work goes some way towards rationalizing optimum adjustment to business cycle fluctuations and it certainly points to the possibility that – at least at certain critical times (see the developments in Section 8.3) – greater hours flexibility may provide marked efficiency gains.

From the trends in average annual manufacturing hours in Figure 2.2 (see also Table 2.1), only Japan displays a significant pro-cyclical hours adjustment around the mid-1970s' OPEC supply shock. Such flexibility is enhanced, on the compensation side, by the Japanese profits-related bonus system. It may be that this hours' flexibility provides some of the advantages on the intensive margin that have been claimed for temporary layoffs on the extensive margin in the USA. In Europe, by contrast, the working time debate remains dominated by arguments for systematic reductions in hours accompanied by full – or, at least, partial – wage compensation. Little has been discovered in the analysis contained within this text to recommend the European approach.

Rather than attempting to change the length of working hours, an alternative employment strategy by governments has been to alter the relative prices of hours, workers and capital in order to encourage an increase in the employment stock relative to factor utilization. The developments in Chapter 9 come down firmly in favour of marginal employment subsidies as the policy initiative with most potential. While general subsidies may produce positive scale effects on employment, it is not clear that the workers–hours substitution effects will be in the desired direction. Also, the adverse macroeconomic consequences of general subsidies seem to be greater than equivalent expenditures targeted at net additions to the labour force. Another factor favouring marginal relative to general labour subsidies relates specifically to recessionary periods, and, again, involves the concept of labour hoarding. It is a point stressed by Drèze (1985) using arguments from general implicit contract theory. The idea is perhaps most simply

273

illustrated with regard to quasi-fixed cost theory. Following Oi (1962), suppose the firm sets the wage equal to the value of the marginal product of labour *adjusted for* the discounted per-period user costs (for example, hiring and training) of labour. Although a temporary fall in marginal product would prevent the attainment of this optimum condition, the firm may be disinclined to lay off workers in order to re-establish the equality. User costs are sunk costs in the short term and as long as the wage remains above the value of the marginal product and the periodic rent remains positive, it may pay the firm to 'hoard' labour. A general wage subsidy in this situation is by no means certain to lead to an employment expansion. It may simply help to restore, partially or fully, the firm's expected periodic rent by moving back towards the pre-recessionary equilibrium. In other words, the degree to which firms hoard labour in an economy during a recession serves to blunt the potency of providing general wage/non-wage subsidies. To the extent that subsidies are directed towards firms that are expanding *despite* the prevailing economic conditions then such resource misallocation may be circumvented.

It was emphasized in Chapter 9, however, that marginal subsidy provision should *not* be contingent on workweek reductions. It is probably the case that decreases in employment costs relative to other factor components due to the subsidy would be offset by relative increases in employment costs due to shorter hours. It is not surprising to find that attempts in Europe at such strategies have proved to be particularly unsuccessful.

For reasons closely linked to the above comments on general labour subsidies, it is unlikely that reductions in firms' payroll taxes would provide major incentives to create new jobs (see Section 9.3). Such taxes represent, essentially, *variable* labour costs to the firm and from the underlying theory – supported by empirical evidence for West Germany – it is average hours rather than employment that may rise as a result of cuts in tax rates.

From the information presented in Section 2.3(a), part-time employment constitutes both a major component of total female employment (see Figure 2.5) and, for several countries, an important element in employment growth (see Table 2.5). The main objective in Chapter 7 has been to highlight, on both the demand- and supply-sides of the labour market, the interactions among full- and part-time workers and hours given changes in working time and relative factor prices. If nothing else, the work here points to the fact that attempting to understand the full employment consequences of efforts to stimulate more part-time working involves a complex set of interrelationships. For example, on the demand-side (see Table 7.1), an increase in the quasi-fixed costs of part-time workers, perhaps through legislation to provide more employment protection, may have the effect of increasing average hours of existing part-time workers and/or producing full-time/part-time worker substitution. Where employment decisions involve choice between part- and full-time workers and hours, the *net* employment outcome arising from hours and factor price changes are particularly difficult to calculate.

Attention might be drawn to two policy issues with respect to part-time employment. First, much more investigation is needed on the *demand-side* of the subject. The supply-dominated literature may well be totally out of balance with actual part-time employment experience. During the long periods of recession as recently experienced, a high proportion of employment decisions could well be demand constrained. Secondly, a significant new growth in part-time employment would appear to be dependent, in many countries, on significantly higher proportions of *male workers* taking up part-time jobs. Unfortunately, as mentioned in Chapter 11, there would appear to be rather severe union opposition to such a development.

A reduction in the average age of mandatory retirement is a measure which, like a cut in the standard workweek, may be expected to have significant labour market repercussions. As with standard hours, however, it is by no means clear that employment growth would be included in the list of likely outcomes. While, as with hours changes, enhanced labour productivity might be an advantageous by-product, other features working in the opposite direction would tend to leave great uncertainty over the net employment outcomes. As seen in Chapter 10, these may include (1) adverse employment effects due to increased pension funding, (2) increased worker utilization among the prime-aged working population in the anticipation of shorter working life and lower pension benefits, and (3) reduced private saving due to increased pressures on pay-as-you-go social security systems. In so far as firms and workers plan compensation schedules over expected working lifetimes then reductions in mandatory retirement ages are likely to be detrimental to employment prospects. Indeed, in Japan, with high average specific human capital and adverse demographic trends, the pressure is firmly for increases, not decreases, in the age of mandatory retirement (Hashimoto and Raisian, 1985).

In the case of early retirement, it has been noted that full-time early retirement schemes with mandatory job replacement have been reasonably successful in Europe in contrast to equivalent attempts to encourage partial-early retirement. One reason suggested for this seeming inconsistency – especially given information that workers are generally favourably inclined to partial retirement – is as follows. New recruits can be employed for full-time hours under full-early retirement and so investments in new skills and know-how can be discounted over 'normal' work spells. Where part-timers are employed to work alongside (partial) retirees then investments cannot be amortized as quickly. Perhaps marginal employment subsidies designed to overcome this particular relative disadvantage may realize better employment returns.

The indications are that, both from collective bargaining and economic perspectives, the possibilities of stimulating employment through early retirement and partial-early retirement offer among the most hopeful strategies and further efforts in these areas should be encouraged.

Bibliography

Åberg, Y. (1976), 'Kortare arbeidstid, Nör? Hur?', *Swedish Government Committee Report*, 34, Stockholm.

Akerlof, G. A. (1979), 'The case against conservative macroeconomics: an inaugural lecture', *Economica*, 46, 1–19.

Akerlof, G. A., and Main, B. G. M. (1980), 'Unemployment spells and unemployment experience', *American Economic Review*, 70, 885–93.

Allen, R. (1980), 'The economic effects of a shorter workweek', HM Treasury, Working Paper no. 33 (London).

Arnott, R., Hosios, A. and Stiglitz, J. E. (1983), 'Implicit contracts, labor mobility and unemployment', Princeton University, Discussion Paper 543.

Ashenfelter, O., and Heckman, J. (1974), 'The estimation of income and substitution effects in a model of family labour supply', *Econometrica*, 42, 73–85.

Baily, M. N. (1977), 'On the theory of layoffs and unemployment', *Econometrica*, 45, 1043–64.

Barzel, Y. (1973), 'The determination of daily hours and wages', *Quarterly Journal of Economics*, 87, 220–38.

Bell, D. N. F. (1982), 'Labour utilisation and statutory non-wage costs', *Economica*, 49, 335–43.

Blinder, A. S., Gordon, R. H., and Wise, D. E. (1980), 'Reconsidering the work disincentive effects of social security', *National Tax Journal*, 33, 431–42.

Booth, A., and Schiantarelli, F. (1985), 'The employment effects of a shorter working week', University of Essex, Dept. of Economics, Discussion Paper no. 263.

Bosworth, D., and Dawkins, P. (1982), 'Women and part-time work', *Industrial Relations Journal*, 13, 32–9.

Brechling, F. (1965), 'The relationship between output and employment in British manufacturing industries', *Review of Economic Studies*, 32, 187–216.

Brechling, F. (1977), 'The incentive effects of the US unemployment insurance tax', in *Research in Labor Economics*, vol. 1 (Greenwich, Conn.: JAI Press).

Brechling, F. (1981), 'Layoffs and unemployment insurance' in Sherwin Rosen (ed.), *Studies in Labor Markets*, National Bureau of Economic Research (Chicago: Chicago University Press).

277

Bronfenbrenner, M., and Mossin, J. (1966), 'The shorter work week and the labor supply', *Southern Economic Journal*, 33, 322–31.

Brown, C. V., Levin, E. J., Rosa, J. P., Ruffell, R. J., and Ulph, D. T (1984), 'HM Treasury project, direct taxation and short run labour supply', Working Paper no. 18, University of Stirling.

Brunstad, R. J., Holm, T. (1984), 'Can shorter hours solve the problem of unemployment?', Institute of Economics, University of Bergen, Norway (mimeo).

Burkhauser, R. V., and Turner, J. A. (1978), 'A time-series analysis on social security and its effect on the market work of men at younger ages', *Journal of Political Economy*, 86, 701–15.

Burkhauser, R. V., and Turner, J. A. (1982), 'Social security, preretirement labor supply, and saving: a confirmation and a critique', *Journal of Political Economy*, 90, 643–6.

Calmfors, L. (1985), 'Job sharing, employment and wages', *European Economic Review*, 27, 293–309.

Calmfors, L., and Hoel, M. (1985), 'Work sharing, overtime and shift work', Institute for International Economic Studies, Stockholm (mimeo).

Casey, B. (1984a), 'Recent trends in retirement policy and practice in Europe and the USA', in P. K. Robinson *et al.* (eds), *Aging and Technological Advances* (New York: Plenum Press).

Casey, B. (1984b), 'Teilzeitarbeit nach der Lehre: ein neues Arbeitsphänomen', *Mitteilungen aus der Arbeitsmarkt- und Berufsforschung*, 17, 336–45.

Centraal Plan Bureau (1979), *Centraal economisch plan 1979*, Staatsnitgeverij, The Hague.

Chang, J. (1983), 'An econometric model of the short-run demand for workers and hours in the US auto industry', *Journal of Econometrics*, 22, 301–16.

Chapman, S. J. (1909), 'Hours of labour', *Economic Journal*, 19, 354–79.

Clark, K. B., and Summers, L. M. (1979), 'Labor market dynamics and unemployment: a reconsideration', *Brookings Papers*, vol. 1, 13–61.

Cogan, J. F. (1981), 'Fixed costs and labor supply', *Econometrica*, 49, 945–63.

Coleman, T. (1984), 'Essays on aggregate labor market business cycle fluctuations', unpublished PhD thesis, University of Chicago.

Commission of the European Communities (1982), 'On the redistribution of available work', Working Paper V/2169/82-En, Brussels.

Craine, R. (1973), 'On the service flow from labour', *Review of Economic Studies*, 40, 39–46.

Department of Employment (1978), 'Measures to alleviate unemployment in the medium term: early retirement', *Department of Employment Gazette*, (March) (London: HMSO).

278

Disney, R., and Szyszczak, E. (1984), 'Protective legislation and part-time employment in Britain', *British Journal of Industrial Relations*, 22, 78–100.

Drèze, J. H. (1985), 'Work sharing: why? how? how not . . .', Université Catholique de Louvain, Belgium (mimeo).

Drèze, J. H., and Modigliani, F. (1981), 'The trade-off between real wages and employment in an open economy (Belgium)', *European Economic Review*, 15, 1–40.

Duggan, J. E. (1984), 'The labor-force participation of older workers', *Industrial and Labor Relations Review*, 37, 416–30.

Ehrenberg, R. G. (1971), *Fringe Benefits and Overtime Behavior* (Lexington, Mass.: Heath).

Ehrenberg, R. G. (1979), 'Retirement policies, employment and unemployment', *American Economic Review (Proceedings)*, 69, 131–6.

Ehrenberg, R. G., and Schumann, P. L. (1982), *Longer Hours or More Jobs?* Cornell Studies in Industrial and Labour Relations, no. 22 (Ithaca, NY: Cornell University).

European Trade Union Institute (1979), *Reduction of Working Hours in Western Europe (Parts I and II)* (Brussels: ETUI).

Evans, M. K. (1969), *Macroeconomic Activity* (New York: Harper and Row).

Fair, R. C. (1969), *The Short-run Demand for Workers and Hours*, (Amsterdam: North-Holland).

Fair, R. C. (1984), *Specification, Estimation, and Analysis of Macro-econometric Models* (Cambridge, Mass.: Harvard University Press).

Fair, R. C. (1985), 'Excess labor and the business cycle', *American Economic Review*, 75, 239–45.

Fay, J. A., and Medoff, J. L. (1985), 'Labor and output over the business cycle: some direct evidence', *American Economic Review*, 75, 638–55.

Feldstein, M. S. (1967), 'Specification of the labour input in the aggregate production function', *Review of Economic Studies*, 34, 375–86.

Feldstein, M. S. (1973), 'The economics of the New Unemployment', *Public Interest* (Fall), 3–42.

Feldstein, M. S. (1974), 'Social security, induced retirement and aggregate capital accumulation', *Journal of Political Economy*, 82, 906–26.

Feldstein, M. S. (1975), 'The importance of temporary layoffs: an empirical analysis', *Brookings Papers on Economic Activity*, 3, 725–45.

Feldstein, M. S. (1976), 'Temporary layoffs in the theory of unemployment', *Journal of Political Economy*, 84, 937–57.

Feldstein, M. S. (1977), 'Social security and private savings: international evidence in an extended life-cycle model', in M. S. Feldstein and R. P. Inman (eds), *The Economics of Public Services* (London: Macmillan).

Feldstein, M. S. (1978), 'The effect of unemployment insurance on temporary layoff unemployment', *American Economic Review*, 68, 834–46.

FitzRoy, F. R., and Hart, R. A. (1985), 'Hours, layoffs and unemployment insurance funding: theory and practice in an international perspective', *Economic Journal*, 95, 700–13.

FitzRoy, F. R., and Hart, R. A. (1986), 'Part-time and full-time employment: the demand for workers and hours', International Institute of Management, Wissenschaftszentrum Berlin (mimeo).

Franz, W. (1984), 'Is less more? The current discussion about reduced working time in West Germany: A survey of the debate', *Zeitschrift für die gesamte Staatswissenschaft*, 140, 626–54.

Freeman, R. B. (1981), 'The effect of unionism on fringe benefits,' *Industrial and Labor Relations Review*, 34, 489–504.

Freiburghaus, D. (1978), *Dynamik der Arbeitslosigkeit*, (Meisenheim: Anton Hain).

van Ginneken, W. (1984), 'Employment and the reduction of the work week: a comparison of seven European macro-economic models', *International Labour Review*, 123, 35–52.

Gordon, R. H., and Blinder, A. S. (1980), 'Market wages, reservation wages, and retirement decisions', *Journal of Public Economics*, 14, 277–308.

Gordon, R. J. (1982), 'Why US wage and employment behaviour differs from that in Britain and Japan', *Economic Journal*, 92, 13–44.

Gordon, R. J. (1983), 'A century of evidence on wage and price stickiness in the United States, the United Kingdom and Japan', in James Tobin (ed.) *Macro-Economics, Prices, and Quantities* (Oxford: Basil Blackwell).

Görres, P. A. (1981) 'Will a shorter workweek help to reduce unemployment? A critical assessment of simulations and studies from several OECD countries', University of Munich (mimeo).

Görres, P. A. (1984), *Die Umverteilung der Arbeit. Beschäftigungs-, Wachstums- und Wohlfahrtseffekte einer Arbeitszeitverkürzung*, Frankfurt/M.

Greer, D. F., and Rhoades, S. A. (1977), 'A test of the reserve labour hypothesis', *Economic Journal*, 87, 290–9.

Gröhn, K. (1979), 'Views on shortening daily working hours', Ministry of Social Affairs and Health, Research Department, Helsinki, Julkaisuja Publications, no. 15.

Gustman, A. L., and Steinmeier, T. L. (1984), 'Partial retirement and the analysis of retirement behavior', *Industrial and Labor Relations Review*, 37, 403–15.

Gustman, A. L., and Steinmeier, T. L. (1985), 'The 1983 social security reforms and labor supply adjustments of older individuals in the long run', *Journal of Labor Economics*, 3, 237–53.

Hall, R. E. (1982), 'The importance of lifetime jobs in the US economy', *American Economic Review*, 72, 716–24.

Hall, R. E., and Jorgenson, D. W. (1967), 'Tax policy and investment behavior', *American Economic Review*, 57, 392–414.

Hall, R. E., and Lazear, E. P. (1984), 'The excess sensitivity of layoffs and quits to demand', *Journal of Labor Economics*, 2, 233–57.

Hall, R. E., and Lilien, D. M. (1979), 'Efficient wage bargains under uncertain demand and supply', *American Economic Review*, 69, 868–79.

Hamermesh, D. S. (1976), 'Econometric studies of labor demand and their application to policy analysis', *Journal of Human Resources*, 11, 507–25.

Hamermesh, D. S. (1981), 'Comment on Brechling's paper', in Sherwin Rosen (ed.), *Studies in Labor Markets*, National Bureau of Economic Research (Chicago: Chicago University Press).

Hart, R. A. (1982), 'Unemployment insurance and the firm's employment strategy: a European and United States comparison', *Kyklos*, 35, 648–72.

Hart, R. A. (1983), 'The Phillips curve and cyclical manhour variation', *Oxford Economic Papers*, 35, 186–201.

Hart, R. A. (1984a), *The Economics of Non-wage Labour Costs*, (London: Allen & Unwin).

Hart, R. A. (1984b), 'Worksharing and factor prices', *European Economic Review*, 24, 165–88.

Hart, R. A. (1984c), *Shorter Working Time: A Dilemma for Collective Bargaining* (Paris: OECD).

Hart, R. A. (1986), 'The employment and hours effects of a marginal employment subsidy: a microeconomic approach', Dept. of Economics, University of Stirling Discussion Paper no. 122.

Hart, R. A., and Kawasaki, S. (1986), 'Payroll taxes and factor demand', in *Research in Labor Economics*, (vol. 9 (forthcoming) (Greenwich, Conn.: JAI Press).

Hart, R. A., and McGregor, P. G. (1987), 'The returns to labour services in West German manufacturing industry', *European Economic Review* (forthcoming).

Hart, R. A., and Sharot, T. (1978), 'The short-run demand for workers and hours: a recursive model', *Review of Economic Studies*, 45, 299–309.

Hart, R. A., and Wilson, N. (1986), 'The demand for workers and hours: micro evidence from the UK metal working industry', in Robert A. Hart (ed.), *Employment, Unemployment and Hours of Work* (London: Allen & Unwin) (forthcoming).

Hashimoto, M. (1975), 'Wage reduction, unemployment and specific human capital', *Economic Inquiry*, 13, 485–504.

Hashimoto, M. (1979), 'Bonus payments, on-the-job training, and lifetime employment in Japan', *Journal of Political Economy*, 87, 1086–104.

Hashimoto, M. (1981), 'Firm-specific human capital as a shared

281

investment', *American Economic Review*, 71, 475–82.

Hashimoto, M., and Raisian, J. (1985), 'Employment tenure and earnings profiles in Japan and the United States', *American Economic Review*, 75, 721–35.

Hashimoto, M., and Yu, B. T. (1980), 'Specific capital, employment contracts, and wage rigidity', *The Bell Journal of Economics*, 11, 536–49.

Hausman, J. A. (1980), 'The effect of wages, taxes and fixed costs on women's labour force participation', *Journal of Public Economics*, 14, 161–94.

Heckman, J. J. (1984), 'Comments on the Ashenfelter and Kydland papers', *Carnegie-Rochester Conference Series on Public Policy*, 21, 209–24.

Heckman, J. J., and MaCurdy, T. E. (1980), 'A life cycle model of female labour supply', *Review of Economic Studies*, 47, 47–74.

Helliwell, J. F. (1976), 'Aggregate investment equations: a survey of issues, in J. F. Helliwell (ed.), *Aggregate Investment* (Harmondsworth, Middx.: Penguin Education).

Henize, J. (1980), 'An evaluation of the effects of a reduction in working hours using the German employment policy model', Gesellschaft für Mathematik und Datenverarbeitung, Internal Report: Bonn.

Henize, J. (1981), 'Can a shorter work week reduce unemployment? A German simulation study', *Simulation* (La Jolla, California), 145–56.

Hiraishi, N. (1980), *Social Security*, Japanese Industrial Relations Series (Tokyo: The Japanese Institute of Labour).

Hoel, M. (1983), 'Employment and allocation effects of reducing the length of the workday', Memorandum from the Institute of Economics, University of Oslo.

Hoel, M. (1984), 'Short- and long-run effects of reduced working time in a unionized economy', Department of Economics, University of Oslo, Working Paper no. 10.

Hoel, M. (1986), 'Employment and allocation effects of reducing the length of the workday', *Economica*, 53, 75–85.

Hoel, M., and Vale, B. (1985), 'Effects of reduced working time in an economy where firms set wages', University of Oslo (mimeo).

Hoff, A. (1981), 'The responsiveness of manufacturing firms to employees' and applicants' preferences for part-time work', International Institute of Management, Wissenschaftszentrum Berlin, Labour Market Policy Discussion Paper 10.

Holt, C. C. (1970), 'Job search, Phillips' wage relation, and union influence: theory and evidence', in E. S. Phelps *et al.* (eds), *Microeconomic Foundations of Employment and Inflation Theory* (New York: W. W. Norton).

IFO-Institut für Wirtschaftsforschung (1983), *Gesamtwirtschaftliche Auswirkungen einer Verkürzung der Arbeitszeit*, Ifo-Studien zur Arbeitsmarktforschung no. 3/I, Munich.

Japan Labor Bulletin (1985), '60-yr. retirement age recommended', vol. 24, no. 12, December, Japan Institute of Labor.

Journal of Labor Economics (1985), *Trends in women's work, education, and family building*, vol. 3, no. 1, part 2, University of Chicago Press.

Kaufman, R. T. (1980), 'Patterns of unemployment in North America, West Europe and Japan', in E. Malinvaud and J. E. Fitoussi (eds), *Unemployment in Western Countries* (London: Macmillan).

Killingsworth, M. (1983), *Labor Supply* (Cambridge: Cambridge University Press).

Klein, L. R., and Preston, R. S. (1967), 'Some new results in the measurement of capacity utilization', *American Economic Review*, 57, 34–58.

Kmenta, J. (1971) *Elements of Econometrics* (New York: Macmillan).

Kreps, J. M. (1977), 'Age, work, and income', *Southern Economic Journal*, 43, 1423–37.

Layard, R., and Nickell, S. J. (1980), 'The case for subsidising extra jobs', *Economic Journal*, 90, 51–73.

Layard, R., Barton, M., and Zabalza, A. (1980), 'Married women's participation and hours', *Economica*, 47, 51–72.

Lazear, E. P. (1979), 'Why is there mandatory retirement?', *Journal of Political Economy*, 87, 1261–84.

Lazear, E. P. (1981), 'Agency, earnings profiles, productivity, and hours restrictions', *American Economic Review*, 71, 606–20.

Leslie, D., and Wise, J. (1980), 'The productivity of working hours in UK manufacturing and production industries', *Economic Journal*, 90, 74–84.

Lilien, D. (1980), 'The cyclical importance of temporary layoffs', *Review of Economics and Statistics*, 62, 24–31.

McKee, M., and West, E. G. (1984), 'Minimum wage effects on part-time employment', *Economic Inquiry*, 22, 421–8.

Macrae, C. D., and Yezev, A. M. J. (1976), 'The personal income tax and family labor supply', *Southern Economic Journal*, 43, 783–92.

Main, B. G. M. (1981), 'The length of employment and unemployment in Great Britain', *Scottish Journal of Political Economy*, 28, 146–64.

Marchand, O., Rault, D., and Turpin, E. (1983) 'Des 40 heures aux 39 heures: processus et réactions des entreprises', *Economie et Statistique*, Apr., 3–15.

Medoff, J. L. (1979), 'Layoffs and alternatives under trade unions in US manufacturing', *American Economic Review*, 69, 380–95.

Medoff, J. L., and Abraham, K. G. (1980), 'Experience, performance, and earnings', *Quarterly Journal of Economics*, 95, 703–36.

Meltz, N. M., Reid, F., and Schwartz, G. S. (1981), *Sharing the Work* (Toronto: University of Toronto Press).

Metcalf, D. (1985), 'Shrinking work time and unemployment',

Centre for Labour Economics, London School of Economics, Working Paper 708.

Miller, R. L. R. (1971), 'The reserve labour hypothesis: some tests of its implications', *Economic Journal*, 81, 17–35.

Mincer, J. (1985), 'Intercountry comparisons of labor force trends and of related developments: an overview', *Journal of Labor Economics*, vol. 3, no. 1, part 2.

Mitchell, O. S., and Fields, G. S. (1984), 'The economics of retirement behavior', *Journal of Labor Economics*, 2, 84–105.

Modigliani, F., and Sterling, A. (1983), 'Determinants of private saving with special reference to the role of social security: cross-country tests', in F. Modigliani and R. Hemming (eds), *The Determinants of National Savings and Wealth* (London: Macmillan).

Moy, J. and Sorrentino, C. (1981), 'Unemployment and layoff practices in 10 countries', *Monthly Labor Review*, vol. 104, no. 12, 3–13.

Nadiri, M. I., and Rosen, S. (1969), 'Interrelated factor demand functions', *American Economic Review*, 59, 457–71.

Nadiri, M. I., and Rosen, S. (1973), *A Disequilibrium Model of the Demand for Factors of Production* (New York: National Bureau of Economic Research).

National Board for Prices and Incomes (1970), *Hours of Work, Overtime and Shiftworking*, Report no. 161 (London: HMSO).

Neale, A. J., and Wilson, R. A. (1985), 'Average weekly hours of work in the UK 1948–80: a disaggregated analysis', University of Warwick (mimeo).

The Netherlands Council of Employers Federations (1981), *Towards individualization of the working time*, Discussion Paper.

Nickell, S. J. (1978), 'Fixed costs, employment and labour demand over the cycle', *Economica*, 45, 329–45.

Nickell, S. J. (1979), 'Unemployment and the structure of labour costs', *Journal of Monetary Economics Supplement*, Carnegie-Rochester Public Policy Conference, no. 11, 187–222.

Nickell, S. J. (1984), 'Dynamic models of labour demand', L.S.E, Discussion Paper no. 197.

Odagiri, H. (1986), 'Firm employment policy and macroeconomic stability: theory and international comparison', Discussion Paper no. 292, University of Tsukuba, Japan.

Oi, W. (1962), 'Labor as a quasi-fixed factor', *Journal of Political Economy*, 70, 538–55.

Okun, A. M. (1981), *Prices and Quantities* (Oxford: Basil Blackwell).

Oswald, A. J. (1982), 'The microeconomic theory of the trade union', *Economic Journal*, 92, 576–95.

Oudiz, G., Raoul, E., and Sterdyniak, H. (1979), 'Reduire la durée du travail, quelles conséquences?' *Economie et Statistique*, May, 3–17.

Owen, J. D. (1979), *Working Hours* (Lexington, Mass.: Lexington Books).

Raisian, J. T. (1978), 'Cyclical variations in hours, weeks and wages', PhD dissertation, University of California, Los Angeles, University Micro-films International, Ann Arbor, Mich.

de Regt, E. E. (1984), 'Shorter working time in a model of the firm – theory and estimation', Institute for Economic Research, Erasmus University, Rotterdam (mimeo).

Rehyer, L., Bach, H.-U., Kohler, H., and Teriet, B. (1983), 'Arbeitszeit and Arbeitsmarkt', in T. Kutsch and F. Vilmar (eds), *Arbeitszeitverkürzung. Ein Weg zur Vollbeschäftigung?* (Opladen).

Robinson, O. (1979), 'Part-time employment in the European Community', *International Labour Review*, 118, 299–314.

Robinson, O. (1984), 'Part-time employment and industrial relations developments in the EEC', *Industrial Relations Journal*, 15, 58–67.

Rosen, S. (1968), 'Short-run employment variations on Class-I railroads in the US, 1947–1963', *Econometrica*, 36, 511–29.

Rosen, S. (1978), 'The supply of work schedules and employment', in *Work Time and Employment* (Washington, DC: National Commission for Manpower Policy), Special Report no. 28.

Rosen, S. (1985), 'Implicit contracts: a survey', *Journal of Economic Literature*, 23, 1144–75.

Rossana, R. J. (1983), 'Some empirical estimates of the demand for hours in US manufacturing industries,' *Review of Economics and Statistics*, 65, 560–9.

Rossana, R. J. (1985), 'Buffer stocks and labor demand: further evidence', *Review of Economics and Statistics*, 67, 16–26.

Salop, S. C. (1973), 'Wage differentials in a dynamic theory of the firm', *Journal of Economic Theory*, 6, 321–44.

Salop, S. C. (1979), 'A model of the natural rate of unemployment', *American Economic Review*, 69, 117–25.

Sampson, A. A. (1983), 'Employment policy in a model with a rational trade union', *Economic Journal*, 93, 297–311.

Santamäki, T. (1983), 'The overtime pay premium, hours of work, and employment', Helsinki School of Economics Working Paper, F-75.

Santamäki, T. (1984), 'Employment and hours decision, and the willingness to work overtime hours', Helsinki School of Economics Working Paper, F-86.

Santamäki-Vuori, T. (1986), *Cyclical Adjustment of Hours and Employment* (Helsinki: Helsinki School of Economics).

Schlicht, E. (1978), 'Labour turnover, wage structure and natural unemployment', *Zeitschrift für die gesamte Staatswissenschaft*, 134, 337–46.

Sheldon, G. (1986), 'Beschäftigungswirkung der Regelung der Kurzarbeitsentschädigung', in H. Schelbert, N. Blattner, P. Halbherr, and N. Harabi (eds), *Mikroökonomik des Artritsmarktes* (Bern: Paul Haupt).

Shimada, H. (1980), *The Japanese Employment System*, Japanese

Industrial Relations Series (Tokyo, The Japanese Institute of Labour).

Smith, J. P. (1975), 'On the labour-supply effects of age-related income maintenance programs', *Journal of Human Resources*, 10, 25–43.

Stiglitz, J. E. (1984), 'Theories of wage rigidity', National Bureau of Economic Research, Working Paper 1442.

Strøm, S. (1983), 'Is a reduction in the length of the work day an answer to unemployment?', Institute of Economics, University of Oslo (mimeo).

Tegle, S. (1985), *Part-time employment*, Lund Economic Studies no. 35, Lund, Sweden.

Topel, R. H. (1982), 'Inventories, layoffs and the short-run demand for labor', *American Economic Review*, 72, 769–87.

Topel, R. H., and Welch, F. (1980), 'Unemployment insurance: survey and extensions', *Economica*, 47, 301–22.

Tsujimura, K. (1970), 'Working hours and productivity' (in Japanese), Japan Ministry of Labour (mimeo).

University College, Galway (1980), *A Study of Overtime Working in Ireland*, Report in 2 volumes.

Wachter, M. (1977), 'Intermediate swings in labor force participation', *Brookings Papers on Economic Activity*, 2, 545–74.

White, M. (1983), 'Shorter hours through national agreements', *Employment Gazette*, 91, 432–6.

White, M., and Ghobadian, A. (1984), *Shorter Working Hours in Practice*, London: Policy Studies Institute no. 631.

Whitley, J. D., and Wilson, R. A. (1983), 'The macroeconomic merits of a marginal employment subsidy', *Economic Journal*, 93, 862–80.

Whitley, J. D., and Wilson, R. A. (1986), 'The impact on employment of a reduction in the length of the working week', *Cambridge Journal of Economics*, 10, 43–59.

Wilson, N. (1985), 'Work organisation, employees' involvement and economic performance: a survey of the UK metal working industry', Management Centre, University of Bradford (mimeo).

Woodbury, S. A. (1983), 'Substitution between wage and nonwage benefits', *American Economic Review*, 73, 166–82.

Zabalza, A., Pissarides, C., and Barton, M. (1980), 'Social security and the choice between full-time work, part-time work and retirement', *Journal of Public Economics*, 14, 245–76.

Zeitzer, I. (1983), 'Social security trends and developments in industrialized countries', *Social Security Bulletin*, 46, 52–62.

Index

absenteeism 103, 135, 141, 251, 259
Age Discrimination in Employment
    Act 232
agency hypothesis 237–40, 247
aggregate demand 71, 154, 217
Amalgamated Metal Workers' and
    Shipwrights' Union (AMWSU)
    263
Australasia 1, 11, 250, 268
Australia 258, 263

balance of payments 6, 123–5, 127,
    154, 157, 217
Belgium 37, 154, 210, 251, 264
benefits 21, 45, 50, 89, 136, 158, 183, 257
bonuses 18, 60–1, 72, 204
budgets 154, 177, 218

Cambridge Growth Project 219
Canada 34, 171
capacity utilization 59–60, 81–5, 87,
    108–11, 142, 148–50, 152, 154–5,
    160, 261
capital 11, 18, 20, 56–7, 60, 63,
    79–81, 83–5, 108–11, 142, 151–2,
    168, 187, 237, 262
  costs 60, 84, 155, 158, 167–8
  services 59, 81, 83, 85, 87, 108,
    110, 142
  stock 20, 42, 46, 56–7, 59–60, 62–3,
    65, 70, 81–7, 93–4, 108, 119–21,
    126–7, 130, 140, 142, 148–9, 152,
    167–8, 225, 236
  substitution 54, 56, 80, 236, 246
  utilization 60, 82–6, 108–11, 148–9,
    156, 170, 262
Cobb–Douglas production function
    84, 109–10, 147, 167
collective bargaining 5, 8, 11, 18, 21,
    45, 55, 60–1, 64, 66, 103, 128,
    145, 197, 200, 248–67, 269

comparative
  cost structure 86
  static analysis 10, 169
  static model 70, 85, 173, 218
  static theory 79, 132–3, 159
compensation 25, 61, 104, 110, 116,
    136, 205, 216, 237, 252–3, 257,
    261, 265
  see also wage compensation
Confederation of German
    Employers' Association 261
construction industry 143
contract
  models 186–94, 197–201, 203, 207
  theory 1, 3, 32, 186–7, 193–4, 196,
    200, 207, 273
contracts 7, 19, 71, 140, 185–208,
    210, 217, 255, 257
cost
  minimization 70, 78, 84, 93–102,
    104–5, 109, 126, 128, 133, 137,
    142, 148, 216–17
  minimizing model 51, 71, 75,
    94–7, 110, 226, 228
costs
  fixed 60, 72, 116, 136, 141, 158,
    165, 170, 175, 178, 183, 200–1,
    217, 220–1, 243, 261, 265
  marginal 51, 75, 95–6, 105, 111
  non-wage 39, 45, 60, 72, 145, 158,
    199, 265
  opportunity 72, 88
  part-time variable 174
  quasi-fixed 45, 50, 60, 64, 114,
    167, 199, 215, 222, 229, 246
  set-up 60, 71, 77, 97
  training 72, 112, 115–16, 215, 240,
    242–3, 261, 274
  user 60, 228, 274
  wage 72, 150, 270
  see also labour costs

INDEX

demand 24, 27, 47, 49, 62–3, 80, 88, 164–84, 207
models 90, 166, 181, 256
theory 139
demographic
factors 35, 39, 236–7
trends 5, 246, 276
depreciation 57, 60, 81, 83–4
dishoarding labour 57, 70, 85, 153
dismissal 191, 197–8, 259
dynamic factor adjustment 133

early retirement 4, 8, 33, 37, 39, 58, 253, 238–47, 258, 262, 266, 276
cost of 238–9, 246
full-time 8, 238–40, 246, 276
partial 8, 39, 240–7, 260, 265, 276
earnings 176, 178, 182–3
/ceilings ratios 236
loss of 206, 250
tests 236, 246
see also wages
econometric models 6, 142, 154–9, 251
EEC 183, 259, 267
efficiency 6, 47, 62, 76, 103, 131, 136, 273
elasticity 53, 70, 74, 79–80, 84, 103–4, 109, 134, 139, 145–51, 155, 157–8, 202–3, 217, 234
employers 8, 248, 250, 258–62
associations 61, 104, 209, 253, 265
employment 1, 20, 55, 88, 101, 111, 139, 185, 187, 202, 209, 237, 272
contracts 232, 257
elasticity 147-8, 155, 157–8, 202–3
expansion 210, 228–9, 238, 274
increased 100, 124, 269–70
mandatory retirement age and 233, 246–7, 275
protection 173, 183, 257
reduction 100, 111, 119, 122
stock 13, 17, 19–21, 39, 43, 45–6, 236
subsidies 209–10, 213–19
general 218, 228, 264
marginal 211–19, 228–9, 262, 264, 273, 276
workweek reductions and 91–163
see also full-time, part-time
engineering industry 143, 270
Europe 1–2, 4, 6, 11–12, 27–8, 32, 35, 37, 39, 134, 175, 187, 196–8,

201, 203–4, 206–7, 232–3, 238–40, 243, 246–7, 250–3, 256–8, 263–4, 266, 268, 272–3, 276
European Trade Union Confederation (ETUC) 250–3
European Trade Union Institute 232, 251, 258, 262
exchange rates 41, 124–5, 157
extensive margin 7, 49, 51, 54, 62, 75, 95–6, 107, 200, 204, 206–9, 230, 235, 253

factor demand
analyses 19, 70, 85, 90, 149
model 20, 150, 226
factor inputs 20, 42, 59, 62–3, 80, 82, 85–8, 149
Finland 254
firm size 136–7, 139, 168, 270
France 13–15, 17, 37, 154–6, 210, 217, 252, 264, 270, 272
FRG 12–15, 17–19, 25–6, 28, 33–4, 37, 39, 131, 133–9, 142, 148, 152, 154–6, 159, 161–2, 175, 197–8, 226–7, 243, 251, 257–8, 260, 263–4, 274
fringe benefits 21, 50, 136, 158, 183, 257
full-time
employment 3, 12, 27–8, 58, 170, 177, 180, 182–3, 257
/part-time worker substitution 275
workers 7, 165–73, 176, 178, 181, 241, 243, 256, 260–1, 275

general implicit contract theory 273
generalized linear regression (GLS) model 138, 145
German Metal Workers Union (IG METALL) 251, 263
government 2, 8, 24–5, 28, 35, 39, 45, 104, 156–7, 240, 243, 248–50, 261–6, 273
intervention 51, 56, 125–6, 209–11, 218, 220, 228–30, 242
Greece 264

Hessian matrix 128
hiring 21, 49–50, 60, 86, 158, 172, 191, 206, 257, 259
costs 72, 183, 242, 261, 274

hoarding 47, 70, 192, 206, 271
  see also labour hoarding
hours
  effective 61, 108, 116
  elasticity 147–8, 150–1
  – employment substitution effects
    100, 107
  fixed 189
  measured 61, 70
  normal 60, 134, 140
  optimal 202
  paid for 42, 46–7, 61, 70–1, 83, 87,
    140, 148, 153, 160
  part-time 3, 27, 62, 90, 164, 170,
    174, 176, 182–3
  per worker 13–17, 20–1, 24, 46,
    59–60, 89, 186
  premium 102, 152
  reductions 6–7, 62, 78–81, 132,
    142, 144, 252, 269, 273
  returns to 148–51, 154
  scheduled 132–3, 139, 145
  total 13–17, 19, 76, 131–2, 139,
    146
  weekly 12, 17, 21, 47, 59–60, 80,
    141, 155, 234, 269
  worked, actual 47, 148, 152
  – worker substitution 220, 228–9
  working 1, 6, 9, 12–13, 17, 19–21,
    24, 39, 59–60, 71–3, 80, 83, 85–6,
    89, 104, 131, 145, 151, 176,
    269–70
    effective 5, 42, 46–7, 61, 66–71,
      82–3, 85, 87, 160, 206, 225,
      229
    length of 60, 150, 273
    paid-for 5, 66–70, 229
    reduction 1–3, 6–7, 12, 32, 62,
      78–9, 91, 100, 106, 111,
      113–18, 125, 132, 142, 144,
      251–2, 256, 269, 271, 273
  see also manhours
human capital investments 72, 92,
  150, 172, 190, 205, 243

IFO-Institut für
  Wirtschaftsforschung
  (IFO-Institut) 156, 261
implicit contract theory 1, 3, 32, 89,
  186, 193–4, 196, 207
implicit contracts 7, 71, 185–208
incentive schemes 145
incomes policies 56, 210

inflation 2, 6, 41, 93, 123–5, 154,
  187, 249, 263
insurance 55, 187, 190, 197, 199,
  201, 220, 226
intensive margin 7, 13, 24, 49, 51,
  62, 75, 85, 95–6, 107, 112, 116,
  158, 204, 206, 208–9, 230, 235,
  253, 273
interest 2, 57, 156–7
international trade 93, 217
interrelated factor demand
  models 149, 170
  system 139, 192
inventory accumulation 192
inventory holdings 56, 60, 70
investment 60, 63, 83, 154, 156, 172,
  243
  capital 18, 262
  labour 72, 83, 92, 193, 196, 205,
    243
  specific 68, 76, 183
Ireland 4, 104, 254, 259
Irish Congress of Trade Unions
  (ICTU) 254
Italy 4

Japan 4, 11, 13, 15, 17–19, 25–8,
  33–5, 37, 39, 151, 159, 196, 201,
  207, 265, 272–3
  mandatory retirement age 232–3, 276
  profits-related bonus scheme 273
job
  creation 1–2, 8, 39, 156, 209, 250,
    266–7
  losses 53, 112, 252
  opportunities 4, 43, 54
  protection 207, 261
  sharing 33, 39, 58, 243–7, 276
  splitting 240–5

labour 63, 79, 142, 151–2
  costs 24, 39, 41, 52–4, 57, 60, 72,
    74, 89, 95, 97, 113, 123, 144–5,
    158, 164, 190, 199, 210–12, 224,
    227–9, 249, 252–3, 263, 265–6
    changes 93–101, 238
    fixed 72, 116, 141, 158, 170, 175,
      178, 200, 217, 220–1
    of job sharing 245–6, 276
    non-wage 39, 72, 145, 158, 199,
      265
    quasi-fixed 21, 97, 134, 158, 166,
      245

reductions 56, 216, 228–9
variable 72, 97, 134, 141, 158, 166, 170, 200–1
demand 9, 47, 62, 70–80, 97, 131–43, 145, 153, 164–84, 193
function 7, 119–20, 133, 147–51, 169
models 6, 62, 93–101, 131–2, 159, 165, 186, 211
dishoarding 57, 70, 85, 153
hoarding 42, 50, 55, 67–71, 83, 85, 87, 132, 142, 153–4, 160, 229, 271–4
input 42, 70–1, 83, 92, 113–15, 131, 142, 149, 153, 165–8, 189, 209, 211, 219–20, 228
investments 72, 92, 205, 243
market 1, 5, 9–10, 13, 41–58, 86, 88, 115, 122–3, 127, 133, 158, 174, 180–1, 185, 189, 196, 207, 210, 217, 264, 267–9, 272, 275
female 3, 7, 25, 27–8, 90, 124
productivity 5, 7, 62, 78–81, 143, 147, 234, 249, 251, 270, 275
services 59–60, 71–4, 79, 81–2, 87–8, 139, 142, 153
function 94, 98, 101–3, 105–6, 113, 123–5, 128–30, 213
subsidies 1, 7, 56, 204, 209–30, 274
supply 9, 176, 178
turnover 136
utilization 21, 46–52, 71, 82, 86, 149, 170, 187, 209, 219–20, 227–8, 236, 271–2, 276
Labour Party 257
Lagrangian constraint 95
large firms 136–7, 139, 270
layoffs 3, 7, 18, 24, 33, 43, 53, 55, 88–9, 112, 185–208, 274
temporary 1, 3, 5, 7, 12, 24–5, 28, 32–3, 39, 186–7, 190–8, 204, 207, 257, 272–3
legislation 3, 60–1, 103, 166, 171–3, 183, 198, 243, 253–4, 264–5, 267, 275
leisure 88, 119, 187–8, 240, 253–4
lifetime
compensation schedule 237
earnings profile 240
productivity profile 237–9
wage profile 237–9
working 11–12, 33–9, 231

maintenance 43, 77–8, 81, 103
mandatory
age of retirement 4, 8, 11, 33, 35, 37, 39, 45, 232–3, 238, 246–7, 265–7, 275–6
job replacement 238–9, 276
manhours 43, 45–7, 49–52, 57, 63–5, 70, 82, 87, 215, 224
manufacturing industries 133–9, 141, 152–3, 161–2, 190–3, 226–7, 259, 273
maximizing models 94, 110, 124, 201, 216, 226
metalworking industry 144–6, 251
monetary policy 123, 125, 154, 157
moral hazard 185, 191, 206
multisectoral dynamic model 219

National Board for Prices and Incomes (NBPI) 253–4, 259, 261
National Institute of Statistics and Economic Studies (INSEE) 156
Netherlands 154–5, 157, 251, 261
Norway 150–1, 252

OECD 4–5, 11, 13, 19, 21, 25, 27, 34–5, 37, 39, 92, 133, 187, 194, 196, 208, 211, 220, 227, 232–3, 236–7, 250, 258
OPEC 1–2, 15, 17, 273
optimization 70, 74, 77, 89, 91, 187, 199
output 80, 82–4, 87, 101, 137, 237
elasticity 70, 74, 84, 149
overemployment 179–80, 182
overtime 2, 6, 12, 22, 24, 36–7, 41–2, 46–7, 49–51, 57, 61, 64–5, 75–6, 78–9, 82, 86, 88, 94–7, 99–100, 103–4, 108, 111–12, 115–16, 126, 131, 134–5, 139–41, 144–7, 151–2, 155–7, 159–60, 166, 170, 178, 181, 185, 204, 209, 243–5, 252–6, 258–9, 263–4, 270, 272
hours 22, 61, 77–8, 81, 92, 102–6, 114, 127, 132, 135–7, 140, 144–6, 151–2, 159–60, 166, 264, 271
pay 51, 76, 106–7, 254
premiums 12, 82, 88, 93, 96, 101, 106–8, 171, 253, 264

part-time
employment 1, 4, 7, 12, 21, 25–8, 33, 57–8, 71, 90, 164–84, 238,

245, 256, 261, 265–6, 274–5
/full-time demand model 176
hours 3, 27, 62, 90, 164, 170, 174, 176, 182–3
jobs 27, 39, 156, 247, 256, 266
protection legislation 172, 183, 243, 265, 275
work 3, 5, 24, 39, 47, 79, 166, 180, 248, 258–60
workers 3, 7, 14, 17, 46, 90, 158, 165, 167–73, 175–6, 178, 181–3, 241–4, 256, 259, 265, 275
payroll tax 7, 72, 108, 165, 167, 174–5, 198, 201, 217, 220–8, 232, 236, 241–2, 244, 246, 261
cuts 227–9, 274
pensions 37, 39, 45, 191, 220, 226, 234–6, 238, 257
contributions 37, 39, 199, 234, 265
financing 4, 39, 236, 276
personnel records 145
pharmaceutical industry 143
Phillips curve 122–5, 127
premium payments 88–9, 147, 185, 264
prices 52, 56–7, 60, 71, 79–80, 83, 124, 167, 177–8, 210–11, 217, 219, 249, 263
elasticity 80, 150, 217, 234
printing industry 143, 270
product
demand 18–19, 21, 24, 46, 64, 79–83, 86, 185–6, 188, 193
elasticity 104
of capital 79, 151
of demand 53, 79, 151, 234
of hours 79, 103
production 7, 20, 87, 103, 145, 147–53, 155, 157, 262–70
functions 82, 102–6, 110, 132, 142, 147–53, 158, 160, 167–8, 188
productivity 53, 55, 70, 76, 79–81, 104, 113, 128, 144, 150–3, 155–6, 160, 237–9, 252, 260, 270–1, 275
hourly 70, 104, 131–2, 144, 147–53, 160, 234
marginal 73, 106, 234
of older workers 11, 33, 35, 37, 231, 233–4, 239
see also labour
profit
maximization 62, 71, 89, 97–101, 113, 124–6, 133, 137, 166, 168, 199

maximizing model 94, 110, 216, 226
pseudo tax transfer 179–80

quasi-fixed
cost theory 1, 21, 187, 204, 271, 274
costs 45, 50, 60, 64, 114, 167, 199, 215, 222, 229, 246
labour costs 21, 97, 134, 158, 166, 245
quit rate 54, 72, 76–7, 112–13, 134, 136, 141
quits 43, 45, 49, 53–4, 88, 91, 111, 115–16, 135, 139, 191, 197, 205–6, 243

recession 2, 9, 142, 158, 192, 263, 271–5
redundancy payments 64, 69
reflation 218–19
relative factor prices 6–7, 42, 50, 72, 77, 85, 131, 142, 158, 165, 170
relocation grants 45
retirement 1, 4, 8, 12, 231–47, 265–6, 275
age 4, 8, 11–12, 33, 35, 37, 39, 45–6, 232–3, 238, 246–7, 265–7, 275–6
early 4, 8, 33, 37, 39, 58, 184, 235, 238–47, 258, 260, 262, 265–6, 276
see also early retirement
full- 8, 232
men 232
partial early 8, 33, 39, 184, 232, 240–7, 260, 265, 276
progressive 240
social security 232, 236, 246
women 232–3
revenue maximization 187

seniority-based payment structure 116
shiftwork 21, 47, 57–8, 61, 82, 93, 110–11, 127, 155, 157–8, 258, 261–2, 267, 270
premiums 88–9, 185
productivity 111
practices 85, 108, 110, 148, 248
sickness 61, 103, 134, 139, 259
leave 66, 134–5, 141

single-shift system 43, 79
slack times 42, 61, 63, 66, 270–1
small firms 270
Social Democratic Party (SDP) 198, 257
social security 39, 89, 187, 197, 211,
    217, 226, 232, 234–7, 241, 246
  benefits 235, 266
  contributions 33, 39, 58, 158,
    172–3, 199–200, 220–1, 226,
    236–7, 241, 246
  funding 11, 194, 209–30, 261
solidarity contracts, French 210, 217
spot value of marginal product
    237–9
standard hours 6–7, 21–2, 41, 43, 47,
    60, 76–9, 81, 93–106, 112, 114,
    133–4, 139–41, 143, 147, 150–1,
    166–7
  changes in 11–12, 24, 42, 50–2, 54,
    93–102, 112, 123, 126–7, 131,
    140–2, 152, 159, 178, 182, 209,
    211, 249, 253, 256, 271, 275
  productivity of 104
standard wage 28, 51, 60–1, 106, 116
standard workweek 43, 47, 63, 81,
    151–2
  reductions 11–12, 24, 39, 41–2,
    45–7, 51, 80, 143, 156, 215, 249,
    251, 253, 262, 264, 269–71
stock
  of capital 20, 42, 46, 56–7, 59–60,
    62–3, 65, 70, 81–7, 93–4, 108,
    119–21, 126–7, 130, 140, 142,
    148–9, 152, 167–8, 225, 236
  of employment 13, 17, 19–21, 39,
    43, 45–6, 236
  of labour 71, 149, 192
  of manhours 50
  of unemployment 45–6, 239
  of vacancies 47, 49
stoppages 65–7
subsidies 1, 7, 25, 28, 32, 39, 56, 60,
    128, 186–7, 190, 194, 204, 206–7,
    209–30, 264, 273–4, 276
  early retirement 39, 238, 247, 265
  employment 209–10, 211–19,
    228–9, 262, 264, 273, 276
  short-time working 204, 206–7,
    272
  unemployment 187–94, 196–7, 207
  wage 28, 45, 229, 274
substitution 51, 54, 56, 71, 80, 110,
    220, 228–9, 236, 246, 275

supply
  constraints 22, 70, 88
  models 165, 181
  -side 10, 24, 27, 62, 88–90, 164,
    174, 176, 182, 207, 256–7
Sweden 4, 12, 25–6, 28, 176

tax 60, 83, 156, 165, 177, 189–90,
    200, 210
  ceilings 217, 225–6, 228, 236, 241
  cuts 218, 227–8
  rates 217, 225
  revenues 41, 218
  shifting 220, 224, 236
  see also payroll tax
technological change 145, 148, 259,
    261–2
tenure 18, 136
time off 252–3, 265
TOBIT estimator 146
trade unions 8, 54–5, 57, 61, 91, 104,
    117–22, 127, 191–2, 198, 232,
    244, 248–54, 256–8, 261–6
  attitudes 250–8, 267, 275
  members 191, 253, 257
  utility function 90, 119–20, 122
  wage bargaining models 6, 62,
    131, 256
  wage setting and 91–3, 251
  working time and 54–5
training 10, 21, 33, 43, 45, 50, 52, 60,
    86, 88, 113–14, 145, 158, 172,
    183, 231, 262
  costs 72, 112, 115–16, 215, 240,
    242–3, 261, 274
Treasury model (UK) 155, 157
turnover 91–2, 145

UK 9, 12–15, 18–19, 25–6, 33–5, 37,
    39, 96, 104, 133, 139–41, 143–6,
    150, 154–5, 159–60, 173, 183,
    257, 261, 264–5, 270–2
underemployment 179
unemployment 2, 3, 9, 12, 32–3, 43,
    45, 47, 49, 51, 54, 111, 114–15,
    119, 122–7, 158, 186–7, 193–6,
    204, 232–3, 238, 240, 249, 251,
    257, 262, 266, 272–3
  benefits 187–8, 190, 194, 197–201,
    203, 206–7
  expenditure 218
  insurance 12, 189, 190, 193, 197,
    199, 201, 206, 220, 226

long-term 2, 33, 164, 193, 239
    short-term 32–3, 186, 207
    subsidies 187–94, 196–7, 207
    voluntary 3, 32
unionization 89, 145, 192, 256
unionized firms 54, 89, 191, 196,
    255–6
unions, see trade unions
USA 1–3, 7, 11–15, 18–20, 25, 27–8,
    32–5, 37, 39, 141, 153, 159–60,
    171, 186–7, 189–98, 201–5, 207,
    232–3, 235–6, 240, 253, 257,
    263–4, 271–3
utility 89, 118–19, 124
utilization
    of capital 60, 82–6, 108–11, 148–9,
        156, 170, 262
    of existing workers 50, 158
    see also labour utilization

vacancies 43, 47, 111, 183
vacations 61, 66, 134
variable labour cost 72, 97, 134, 141,
    158, 166, 170, 200–1
Vintaf model 155

wage
    ceilings 165, 174, 176, 220–8, 241
    compensation 54, 92, 104, 150,
        155–7, 209, 244, 249, 251–2, 254,
        263, 271, 273
    distributions 221, 225–6
    increases 264
    premium 76, 96
    profile 234, 237–9
    protection 207
    public sector increases 264
    rates 54, 72, 76, 80, 114, 125, 167,
        174, 177, 179, 198, 204, 250
    real 88, 179, 182, 191, 197
    reductions 56, 88, 204–5
    schedule 76, 94, 182
    setting 55, 91, 93, 272
        by firms 111–16, 127
        by unions 117–22, 127, 251
    subsidies 28, 45, 229, 274
wages 6, 17–18, 60, 72, 75–6, 96,
    102, 109, 114, 124, 144–5, 157,
    165, 167, 171, 188, 191, 203, 205,

    207, 210–11, 240, 249–50, 254
welfare 195, 207
women
    economically active 24, 164
    labour market 3, 7, 25–8, 90, 124
    workers 3, 134–5, 139, 176, 265
    working hours 7, 12, 28, 90, 274
work
    intensity 46–7, 83, 148
    – leisure pattern 240
    organization 63, 65, 155, 158, 249,
        259, 271
worker substitution 71, 110, 236, 275
workers
    demand for 5, 227
    female 3, 134–5, 139, 176, 265
    hire of 21, 49–50, 60, 86, 172, 259
        costs 72, 183, 242, 261, 274
    – hours combination 65
    – hours substitution 97, 126, 224,
        273
    non-union 62, 191, 265–6
    number of 14–17, 43, 59–60, 72,
        86, 89, 152, 158
    senior 116, 257
    supply of 124, 164
    utility 187–8, 198, 201
workforce 11, 35, 62, 114, 145, 211
    changes 56, 64, 95, 97, 106, 218
    size of 50, 86–7
working
    short-time 5, 7, 12, 24–5, 28, 32,
        46–7, 49–50, 57, 103, 134, 139,
        178, 187, 197–8, 203–7
    time, changes 12, 32, 52, 54–5,
        91, 100, 111, 113, 116–18, 256,
        270
        employers' attitudes to 250,
            258–62
        governments and 250, 262–6
worksharing 2–4, 7, 25, 55, 78, 89,
    184, 186–7, 189, 191, 203–5, 207,
    228, 255, 257, 272
workweek 33, 42–3, 47, 81, 140
    reductions 1, 53, 56–7, 70, 91–163,
        166, 178, 182, 209–19, 229, 252,
        256, 259, 263, 265, 268–9, 271,
        274
world market 123–4, 125